Not Half No End

The Frontiers of Theory

Series Editor: Martin McQuillan

The Poetics of Singularity: The Counter-Culturalist Turn in Heidegger, Derrida, Blanchot and the later Gadamer
Timothy Clark

Dream I Tell You
Hélène Cixous

Scandalous Knowledge: Science, Truth, and the Human
Barbara Herrnstein Smith

Geneses, Genealogies, Genres and Genius
Jacques Derrida

Insister of Jacques Derrida
Hélène Cixous

Not Half No End: Militantly Melancholic Essays in Memory of Jacques Derrida
Geoffrey Bennington

The Book I Do Not Write
Hélène Cixous

Reading and Responsibility
Derek Attridge

Not Half No End

Militantly Melancholic Essays in Memory of Jacques Derrida

Geoffrey Bennington

Edinburgh University Press

Edinburgh University Press Ltd
22 George Square, Edinburgh

www.euppublishing.com

First published in hardback by Edinburgh University Press in 2010

Typeset in Adobe Sabon
by Servis Filmsetting Ltd, Stockport, Cheshire, and
printed and bound in the United States of America

A CIP record for this book is available from the British Library

ISBN 978 0 7486 3985 4 (hardback)
ISBN 978 0 7486 4316 5 (paperback)

'For those wanting to discover or rediscover Jacques Derrida still alive and thinking after life, Geoffrey Bennington is the exemplary guide, scholarly and acrobatic, grave and droll. Let's follow him. Along the way with fear and trembling he reminds us that reading lives between the possibilities and impossibilities of an opening onto no end. Combining the strength of a rigorous pedagogy with the creative and extravagant powers of the poet-philosopher, GB is a bookworm of genius, actively inhabiting the entire Derridian archive. He has read everything, he hears and understands everything. Working from a double experience (his own and Derrida's), he reconstitutes the philosophical hero's adventure, from the age of 22 until his final days. Bennington, who knows Derrida's script by heart, becomes Derrida's actor: played by Bennington, Derrida becomes the hero of a devastating philosophical epic. This admirable book which claims to be melancholic is also a triumph of freedom in fidelity, not half.'

Hélène Cixous, Director of the Centre d'Études Féminines,
Université Paris VIII, Emerita

'Geoffrey Bennington was Derrida's close friend, and is his distinguished translator, his collaborator (in their *Jacques Derrida*), and one of Derrida's most profound readers. He has an exemplary knowledge of all Derrida's work. One distinctive value and originality of the essays in this book is the way they show in detail how Derrida's "early work" foreshadows the later books and essays, down to the final seminars. A necessary book for all those interested in Derrida's writing.'

J. Hillis Miller, UCI Distinguished Research Professor of
Comparative Literature and English, The University of California
at Irvine

Contents

Series Editor's Preface

Since its inception Theory has been concerned with its own limits, ends and after-life. It would be an illusion to imagine that the academy is no longer resistant to Theory but a significant consensus has been established and it can be said that Theory has now entered the mainstream of the humanities. Reaction against Theory is now a minority view and new generations of scholars have grown up with Theory. This leaves so-called Theory in an interesting position which its own procedures of auto-critique need to consider: what is the nature of this mainstream Theory and what is the relation of Theory to philosophy and the other disciplines which inform it? What is the history of its construction and what processes of amnesia and the repression of difference have taken place to establish this thing called Theory? Is Theory still the site of a more-than-critical affirmation of a negotiation with thought, which thinks thought's own limits?

'Theory' is a name that traps by an aberrant nomial effect the transformative critique which seeks to reinscribe the conditions of thought in an inaugural founding gesture that is without ground or precedent: as a 'name', a word and a concept, Theory arrests or misprisons such thinking. To imagine the frontiers of Theory is not to dismiss or to abandon Theory (on the contrary one must always insist on the it-is-necessary of Theory even if one has given up belief in theories of all kinds). Rather, this series is concerned with the presentation of work which challenges complacency and continues the transformative work of critical thinking. It seeks to offer the very best of contemporary theoretical practice in the humanities, work which continues to push ever further the frontiers of what is accepted, including the name of Theory. In particular, it is interested in that work which involves the necessary endeavour of crossing disciplinary frontiers without dissolving the specificity of disciplines. Published by Edinburgh University Press, in the city of Enlightenment, this series promotes a certain closeness to that spirit: the continued exercise of critical thought as an attitude of inquiry which counters modes of closed or conservative opinion. In this respect the series aims to make thinking think at the frontiers of theory.

Martin McQuillan

nec me meminisse pigebit Elissae,
dum memor ipse mei, dum spiritus hos regit artus.

Introduction

> I speak of mourning as the attempt, always doomed to failure – a constitutive failure, precisely – to incorporate, interiorize, introject, subjectivize the other in me. Even before the death of the other, the inscription of that other's mortality constitutes me. I am in mourning therefore I am – dead with the other's death, my relation to myself is primarily one of mourning, a mourning that is moreover impossible. This is also what I call ex-appropriation, appropriation caught in a double bind: I must and must not take the other into me; mourning is an unfaithful fidelity if it succeeds in interiorizing the other ideally in me, i.e. if it fails to respect the other's infinite exteriority.[1]

This volume gathers a number of pieces about Jacques Derrida which, with the exception of the first, were all written since his death in October 2004. Some of them explicitly attempt to address that death and its impact (at least its impact on the author), but all, in spite of their differences of occasion and audience, of tone and style, whether directed to a more or less 'professional' deconstructive audience ('That's Life, Death' or 'Handshake') or one presumed to be less familiar with Derrida's work ('Foundations' or 'The Limits of My Language') are profoundly marked by Derrida's death, and are often struggling to go on thinking in its wake. Several of these pieces invoke Derrida's own reflections on mourning and melancholia, and more especially on what he sometimes calls half-mourning or *demi-deuil*, a kind of suspended or interrupted state of the 'normal' work of mourning as famously described by Freud in *Mourning and Melancholia*.[2] If this 'normal' mourning works in view of a recovery of the self from the loss of the other through a withdrawal of cathexes from that other back into the ego, then *demi-deuil*, insofar as it implies incomplete mourning, clearly has affinities with mourning's doublet, melancholia. But this melancholia is no longer seen as a pathological condition, and rather as a kind of ethics of death, whereby the other's loss is *not* lost in the interests of the self, as is the case in 'normal' mourning, but is in a certain sense maintained *as* loss, and therefore mourned in a process that is structurally non-teleological and always incomplete. 'Normal' mourning *gets over it* and gets to the end of itself in the more or less triumphant reaffirmation of the subject and its constitutive narcissism: *demi-deuil*, in Derrida's use of the term if not in its traditional specification, is a kind of structural state of not getting over it, and therefore remaining permanently somewhat short of *recovery*, surviving with a 'slash-scar, or narcissistic disfiguration'.[3]

Demi-deuil, half-mourning, is not *simply* an espousal of melancholia, however, in spite of the impression one or two of these pieces might give, written as they were from a distress that often seemed on the point of compromising any further ability to work at all. Part of that distress as it bore specifically on these pieces was the thought that, whatever happened, Jacques Derrida would never read them. For although I did not systematically send him everything I wrote, even about him, he was in a certain sense the implied reader of everything I had ever written. The intrinsically unpredictable and slightly crazy structure of reading, which he had helped me think about,[4] and that is explored again here in more than one chapter, was now cut through by a cold certainty of a different order: whatever else happens, Jacques will not have read this.

And yet if, as he suggests more than once, all work is work of mourning, then there is clearly mourning as well as melancholia in these still quite industrious pieces, and in the volume they are now brought together to constitute, and some appeal still to reading across and through the interruption of death. Indeed, *demi-deuil* in Derrida's construal is, according to a pattern familiar from elsewhere in his thinking, not really *opposed* to mourning, nor is it even an etiolated form of mourning, but, affirmatively and even militantly, *the only possible mourning*, even as it marks mourning with a kind of impossibility. (For the possible in general to be really possible, radically possible, and not just the unfolding of a pro-gramme, it must always in a certain sense be impossible.[5]) Half-mourning, we might suspect, *just is life itself* as the state of survival or living on we might also venture to call half-life: *life is always half-life*. And again, as 'That's Life, Death' and 'Half-Life' here suggest, half-life is not a restricted or second-rate life, but life itself, as alive as can be, as good as it gets.

Demi-deuil, half-mourning, then, might be re-formulated as *not half mourning*, if I can exploit the ambiguity (in colloquial British English at least) whereby 'not half' can function, as it were, *either side of half*, moving undecidably in either direction from the halfway line: 'it's not half bad' means it's less than half bad, and therefore not so very bad, really quite good: but the rejoinder 'Not half!' (or perhaps more often glottally stopped as 'No?'alf!') usually functions antiphrastically as an intensifier, so that in the exchange 'Was it good?'; 'No?'alf!' the response means that it was *really* good, much *more* than (merely) half good. 'Are you in mourning?'; 'No?'alf!'[6]

In a short piece written as a very free translation of an earlier French text, and delivered in London on what turned out to be the last occasion I saw Jacques Derrida, in July 2004, I related this idiomatic use of 'not half' to another English idiom – 'no end'.[7] 'I had no end of trouble writing this piece', or 'writing this piece troubled me no end'.[8] There is no end of mourning in these essays: they are not half melancholic. The apparent restraint of 'not half', with its internal antiphrastic double, and the apparent limitlessness of 'no end' in fact work together to describe what elsewhere and more technically I have tried to describe as 'interrupted teleology', and which I believe to be a specific but generalisable structure within the absolute generality of what Derrida himself most often calls *différance*.[9] In the present case, this underlying thought of interrupted teleology shows up especially in relation to a perception about the structure of Derrida's work itself, as its 'progress' always involves a kind of looping back or rereading of its own earlier moments, so that (and exemplarily here in the case of the concepts of mourning and life) apparently unobtrusive or perhaps simply ill-read moments in 'early' Derrida can be shown, but only retroactively, *nachträglich*, to open up, through rereading, more obviously thematised later occurrences. The life of Derrida's work (for example on the concept of life, but also all the other concepts) is itself bound up in this half-mournful reading relation to itself (for example in relation to the concept of mourning, but also all the other concepts). 'Not half', then, affects half-mourning, making it always less than half and more than half; and by the same token makes it endless, so there's no end of (not-half) mourning. And this 'no end' also responds to Derrida's own contention, in a number of late texts recalled more than once in this volume, that death is always a *fin du monde*, an end of the world; not the end of this or that world, but each time uniquely the end of the one and only world. For if this were simply or literally true there would be no mourning at all, and no survival or living on (and thus no reading) either: so the end of the world must be also, simultaneously, *no end of the world*, and one of the most immediate and most intolerable experiences of the death of the loved other is just this fact that *the world does not end when it ends*, that it simply carries on after its end, has no end, that the end of the world is not the end of the world, that its end in death is also the perspective of an endlessness, an *ad infinitum* that opens onto just the not-half-mourning I have been describing, which is also the not-half melancholia of this very situation in which I continue to read.

Not half (life mourning death) no end.

New York, May 2009

Notes

1. Jacques Derrida, *Points de suspension* (Paris: Galilée, 1992), p. 331. Although I have on occasion benefited from consulting published translations, all translations from the French in this book are my own.
2. To my knowledge, Derrida first invokes the concept of *demi-deuil* in the interview 'Ja ou le faux-bond' (October 1975), reprinted in *Points de suspension* (Paris: Galilée, 1992), p. 54), where it seems to be assimilated to a process of 'mourning (for) mourning', *faire son deuil du deuil*. *Demi-deuil* subsequently appears in *La Carte postale* (Paris : Aubier-Flammarion, 1979), pp. 355–6; *Parages* (Paris: Galilée, 1986), p. 161, and 'Circonfession' (in Bennington and Derrida, *Jacques Derrida* (Paris: Seuil, 1991)), period 31.
3. *La Carte postale*, p. 361. *Demi-deuil* is what also troubles the psychoanalytic distinction between introjection and incorporation. See 'Fors', Derrida's introduction to Abraham and Torok's book *Le verbier de l'homme aux loups* (Paris: Aubier-Flammarion, 1976).
4. See especially my *Dudding: des noms de Rousseau* (Paris: Galilée, 1991), *Other Analyses: Reading Philosophy* and *Open Book/Livre ouvert* (both 2005, from bennington.zsoft.co.uk).
5. See, for example, Derrida's improvised comments in Simon Glendinning (ed.), *Arguing with Derrida* (Oxford: Blackwell, 2001), p. 55.
6. **3. *not half***: a long way from the due amount; to a very slight extent; in mod. *slang* and *colloq.* use = not at all, the reverse of, as 'not half bad' = not at all bad, rather good; 'not half a bad fellow' = a good fellow; 'not half long enough' = not nearly long enough; also (*slang*), extremely, violently, as 'he didn't half swear' (*OED*).
7. 'Not half: no end', delivered to a seminar at Queen Mary, London, July 2004, to mark Jacques Derrida's Honorary Doctorate there. Published along with the French text 'De mon mieux . . .', of which it is a sort of translation, in *Deconstruction is Not What You Think* (e-book, 2005). I had first proposed 'not half' and 'no end' as semi-serious candidates to translate Derrida's use of the French idiom 'plus d'un', meaning both 'more than one' and 'no more (only) one' in my translation of Derrida's 'Et Cetera . . .', in N. Royle (ed.), *Deconstructions: A User's Guide* (Basingstoke and New York: Palgrave, 2000), p. 304, n. 27.
8. **21. *no end***: (*colloq.*) a vast quantity or number (*of*). Also (*mod. slang*) as adv., = 'immensely', 'to any extent'; and (with *of*) qualifying a predicate (*OED*).
9. See especially my *Frontières kantiennes* (Paris: Galilée, 2000) and 'Almost the End', in *Interrupting Derrida* (London: Routledge, 2000), pp. 141–52. See too my translation of part of *Frontières kantiennes* as 'The End in Here', *Tekhnema*, 6 (2001), 34–50.

Auto-

(Little polyparergonal frame for three 'photographs with automobile' that were never taken.)[1]

-affections

'*Auto*-affection constitutes the self-same by dividing it.'[2]

'Before all else one must affect oneself with one's own death (and the self does not exist before all else, before this movement of auto-affection), make death be auto-affection of life or life auto-affection of death. The whole of *différance* is lodged in the desire (desire is only this) of this auto-tely.'[3]

According to the analyses of the *Grammatology*, there is no auto-affection without hetero-affection, without *exposure*, without a vulnerable surface and a relation with a certain *outside*.[4] I affect myself – always with the other. I am – I live – as *revenant*: returning to myself from this outside. Vital and mortal exposure, skin deep. Narcissistic *revenant* that keeps exposing its vulnerability. No inner sense without this relation to the outer, no time without this space. Whence, among other things, a certain return of 'experience', after the warnings in the *Grammatology*:[5] experience would be nothing without peril, without perishing – all experience would be in some sense *traumatic*.[6] There are a thousand figures of this configuration: 'l'Un se garde de l'autre'; 'l'Un se fait violence'.[7]

No exposure without protection, however. What exposes me protects me: what protects me exposes me. In Freud, this would be the fable in the *Project* as well as in *Beyond the Pleasure Principle*:

> Let us picture a living organism in its most simplified possible form as an undifferentiated vesicle of a substance that is susceptible to stimulation. Then the surface turned towards the external world will from its very situation be differentiated and will serve as an organ for receiving stimuli. Indeed embryology,

> in its capacity as a recapitulation of developmental history, actually shows us that the central nervous system originates from the ectoderm; the grey matter of the cortex remains a derivative of the primitive superficial layer of the organism and may have inherited some of its essential properties. It would be easy to suppose, then, that as a result of the ceaseless impact of external stimuli on the surface of the vesicle, its substance to a certain depth may have become permanently modified, so that excitatory processes run a different course in it from what they run in the deeper layers. A crust would thus be formed which would at last have been so thoroughly 'baked through' by stimulation that it would present the most favourable possible conditions for the reception of stimuli and become incapable of any further modification.[8]

I am – done. It's a fable, though, fabulous because of the origin thus dreamed: in fact everything has to begin double already, the undifferentiated must be *already* differentiated – in the beginning was the membrane, already, then, difference.[9] Around me the limit closes, and therefore opens on its other side: for every interior there is an external surface that can never quite be internalised. This protection exposes me, protects me as it exposes me. Franz Kafka's *Burrow* or Todd Haynes's film *Safe*. This is life itself, as 'economy of death', because total exposure would be instant death (looking straight at the sun), just as total protection would be asphyxia. Auto-hetero-thanato-bio-. (Perhaps, as in cybernetics: even so-called 'closed' systems are a little open; even 'open' systems are a little closed.) And -graphy: according to 'Freud and the Scene of Writing': 'there is no writing that does not constitute itself as protection, *protection against itself*, against the writing whereby the "subject" is itself threatened in letting itself be written, *exposing itself*.'[10]

-mobile I

Just about our first meeting. Oxford, November or December 1979. A colleague who is a bad driver is taking us in her car from the station to the room where the seminar will take place. Filthy weather, very 'English', grey wet streets. JD, sitting in front, imperturbable in spite of several very near misses, turns round and says calmly to me, sitting in the back, in a tone of polite conversation, knowing that the driver does not speak French: 'Je vois la mort à chaque tournant [I'm seeing death at every turn].'

-immunities

Auto-immunity figures for the first time in *Specters of Marx* and *Politics of Friendship*, but gets its first real development in *Faith and*

Knowledge.[11] Religion and reason (philo-techno-scientific reason) have the same source: 'Religion and reason develop together, from this common resource: the testimonial gage of any performative, which engages one to answer just as well *before* the other as answer *for* the high-performing performativity of technoscience.' (*Foi et savoir*, p. 46) A single source but immediately double, the mechanical duplicity of which does not immediately call up the more organic figure that will follow: 'The same single source divides mechanically, automatically, and opposes itself reactively to itself: whence the two sources in one. This reactivity is a process of *sacrificial* indemnisation, it attempts to restore the unscathed (*heilig*) that it threatens itself' (ibid.). To be formalised twenty pages later: 'This same movement that renders indissociable religion and tele-technoscientific reason in its most critical aspect inevitably reacts *to itself*. It secretes its own antidote but also its own power of autoimmunity. We are here in a space where all self-protection of the unscathed, of the safe and sound [*du sain[t] et sauf*], of the sacred (*heilig*, *holy*) must protect itself against its own protection, its own police, its own power to reject, its ownness in a word, i.e. its immunity. It is this terrifying but fatal logic of the *auto-immunity of the unscathed** that will always associate Science and Religion' (ibid., p. 67).[12] The logic of auto-immunity (which will always subsequently be a *double* logic of immunity/auto-immunity) will thus attempt to describe a situation in which, to protect oneself, one also protects oneself against *what protects*, attacks one's own protection for protection. So religion is hand in glove with technoscience, but 'it wages a terrible war against what protects it only by threatening it' (ibid., p. 71). Which gives rise to a new, still more complex formulation, which will open onto political perspectives that interest us more especially: 'auto-immunity haunts community and its immunitary survival system like the hyperbole of its own possibility. Nothing *common*, nothing immune, safe and sound, *heilig* and *holy*, nothing unscathed in the most autonomous living present without a risk of auto-immunity' (ibid.).

-mobile II

End of the 1980s. When we leave the restaurant after a debate at the *Collège international de philosophie*, the car is boxed in on the Place du Panthéon: impossible to open the doors because of other cars parked too close. JD, a bit roguishly, cigar clamped between his teeth, gets in through the back hatch and makes it to the wheel by crawling over the seatbacks.

-craties

As is always the case in deconstruction, then, what a 'metaphysical' thinking would like to separate from the essence (according to the logic of immunity, precisely), is reintegrated into the heart of the essence as the necessary (essential, automatic, mechanical) possibility of its destruction as well as of its 'life'. *That's life.* What makes possible will also make necessary the becoming-impossible of what is thus made possible. Here, explicitly, community: 'Community as com-mon auto-immunity [*commune auto-immunité*] there is no community that does not maintain its own auto-immunity, a principle of sacrificial self-destruction ruining the principle of self-protection (of the maintenance of the intact integrity of the self) . . . This self-contestatory attestation keeps the auto-immune community alive, i.e. open to something other and more than itself: the other, the future, death, freedom, the coming or the love of the other . . .' (ibid., p. 79). To what happens in general, as it happens, for better and for worse, as it were, *at the same time.*

'Auto-immunity' itself will return, dozens of times this time, in *Voyous*,[13] quoting *Foi et savoir*, and sketching the relation that this figure might entertain with others (namely *double bind* and aporias (*Voyous*, p. 60): I would say many others too, starting with *différance* itself: that there be such a dispersion of terms is evidently to be thought as an 'effect' of auto-immunity). Opening what always also tends to close itself again to the necessary possibility of the event of the other, auto-immunity cannot fail to open too a 'political' dimension. Whence 'democracy (to come)', because, from the 'inside' of politics, 'democracy' would name the reason why politics does not simply have an inside. And this is why, in *Politiques de l'amitié*, and precisely in the context of a discussion of the name 'democracy', one finds this bringing together of democracy and deconstruction:

> In saying that the maintenance of the Greek word 'democracy' is a matter of context, rhetoric or strategy, of polemics even, in reaffirming that this name will last the time it must but scarcely more, in saying that things are accelerating curiously these days, one is not necessarily giving in to the opportunism or the cynicism of the antidemocrat concealing his hand. Quite to the contrary: one is keeping one's indefinite right to question, critique, deconstruction (rights which are in principle guaranteed by every democracy: no deconstruction without democracy, no democracy without deconstruction). One keeps this right in order to mark strategically what is no longer a matter of strategy: the limit between the conditional (the borders of the context and the concept that enclose the real practice of democracy and feed it with earth and blood) and the unconditional that, from the beginning, will have inscribed an auto-deconstructive force in the very motif of democracy, the possibility and the

> duty of democracy to de-limit itself. Democracy is the *autos* of deconstructive auto-delimitation. (*Politiques de l'amitié*, pp. 128–9)

Autos. Let us also understand this: democracy de-limits itself also by limiting and holding itself back. If democracy can, in principle, interrupt itself to protect itself against the democratic arrival of the anti-democrat (the example of the 1992 Algerian elections, evoked in *Voyous*, pp. 53ff.), this is because democracy can always also interrupt itself to protect itself against itself, and *this is all that it does*. Auto-immunity and auto-delimitation do not supervene on an otherwise 'normal' democracy: rather they constitute it as 'default of proper and same' (*Voyous*, p. 61). No auto. Democracy is made only of this self-interrupting 'process', that alone prevents democracy from being fully 'itself', which would be the end (the death) of the political, pure auto-maticity that would put an end to every decision and every event. Democracy works only unhinged, limping, out of joint, heterocracy.

Auto- without *auto-*, then. The auto comes to a halt. The 'auto-deconstructive force' of democracy is a force that auto-deconstructs, of course, but in so doing also deconstructs the *auto-*. And so never deconstructs *itself* all by itself. The other deconstructs. The other – who is not another self, or who is another self only insofar as the self is itself already, if not exactly tainted, then at least altered, othered. I am – the other other. The other deconstructs and is deconstructed. The other auto: the *autro*. Democratic authrority: autronomy.

JD: the authror of everything he writes, autrobiographical animal.

-mobile III

Suburb of Paris, beginning of the 1990s. Deserted streets. JD slows down and stops, good as gold, at a red light. M., feigning incredulity at such good behaviour, points at the traffic light: 'But . . . it's *red!*'

Notes

1. This short piece was originally written in French, on the invitation of René Major, for a projected volume to celebrate Jacques Derrida's 75th birthday, which would have fallen in July 2005. The book was subsequently published as *Jacques Derrida pour les temps à venir* (Paris: Stock, 2007), pp. 480–9: the French version of this text is also published in my book *Deconstruction Is Not What You Think* (from bennington.zsoft.co.uk), pp. 125–37. The motif of 'photograph with automobile' refers to a series of pictures of Jacques Derrida reproduced in Bennington and Derrida, *Jacques Derrida* (Paris: Seuil, 1991).

2. *De la grammatologie* (Paris: Minuit, 1967), p. 237.
3. *La Carte postale* (Paris: Aubier-Flammarion, 1980), p. 382.
4. Among others: 'By affecting oneself with another presence, one *adulterates* oneself [*on* s'altère *soi-même*]. Now Rousseau neither wants to nor can think that this adulteration does not supervene on the self, that it is its very origin' (*De la grammatologie*, p. 221; cf. too pp. 263–5). We should also have to read here *Le Toucher, Jean-Luc Nancy*: see, for example, p. 206: 'must we not rather distinguish between several types of auto-hetero-affection without any pure, purely proper, immediate, intuitive living and psychic auto-affection?' There are no doubt 'effects' of auto-affection but the analysis of them cannot, or so we believe, skirt the hetero-affection that makes them possible and continues to haunt them even where that hetero-affection *in general* (coming from the transcendent thing or the other living being) seems to be effaced, returning irresistibly to impose itself in the analysis and the exposition of its results.
5. Ibid., p. 89: 'As for the concept of experience, it is here extremely awkward. Like all the notions we are using here, it belongs to the history of metaphysics and we can use it only under erasure. "Experience" has always designated the relation to a presence, whether or not this relation has the form of consciousness. However we must, according to this contortion or contention that the discourse cannot avoid here, exhaust the resources of the concept of experience before we can, and in order to, get at it, through deconstruction, in its final depth.' See too pp. 400–1.
6. 'Experience' returns from the 1980s onward, no doubt in part because of its reinscription by Jean-Luc Nancy in *L'Expérience de la liberté* (Paris: Galilée, 1988) (although Derrida is critical of other aspects of that book in *Voyous* (Paris: Galilée, 2003)). 'Experience' comes apparently to name the opening (without horizon of expectation) to the other in general, and thereby to the event which by definition interrupts 'traumatically' the ordinary course of experience in the sense deconstructed in the *Grammatology*. See *Papier machine* (Paris, Galilée, 2001), pp. 114 and 146. This traumatic aspect is already recognised in 'Freud et la scène de l'écriture', in *L'écriture et la différence* (Paris: Seuil, 1967), especially pp. 300–1. More generally, the description of deconstruction as an 'experience of the impossible' often imposes itself: see *Sauf le nom* (Paris: Galilée, 1993), p. 32 ('the very experience of the (impossible) possibility of the impossible'), which also refers to 'Psyché: invention de l'autre', in *Psyché: inventions de l'autre* (Paris: Galilée, 1987), p. 59.
7. See *Mal d'archive: une impression freudienne* (Paris: Galilée, 1995), pp. 124–5: 'The One both keeps some other and keeps itself from the other; the One does violence to itself and itself turns violent, becomes violence.'
8. *The Standard Edition of the Complete Psychological Works of Sigmund Freud*, 24 vols (London: Hogarth Press, 1966–74), Vol. XVIII, p. 26.
9. See my 'Membranes: a reading of Freud's metapsychology', *Journal of the Institute of Romance Studies*, 3 (1994–5), 369–82, reprinted in *Other Analyses: Reading Philosophy* (e-book available from bennington.zsoft.co.uk), pp. 97–123.
10. Jacques Derrida, *L'Écriture et la différence* (Paris: Seuil, 1967), p. 331.
11. See *Spectres de Marx* (Paris: Galilée, 1993), p. 224; *Politiques de l'amitié*

(Paris: Galilée, 1994), p. 94, where it is already about an 'auto-immunity from which would be exempt no region of being, *physis* or history'. *Foi et savoir* is a text that is more complex than others as to its dates: it does revolve around a specific meeting (at Capri, 28 February 1994 (as recalled in §3, p. 11)), but without simply being reducible to that meeting: 'At the beginning of a preliminary exchange, Gianni Vattimo suggests that I improvise some suggestions. Let me recall them here, in italics, in a sort of schematic and telegraphic foreword. Propositions that were different, no doubt, were sketched out in a text of a different character I wrote after the fact, restricted by merciless limits of time and space. A quite different story, perhaps, but it is the memory of what I ventured at the beginning, that day, that will continue to dictate more or less closely what I write' (*Foi et savoir* (Paris: Seuil, 2001), pp. 11–12). The thought of auto-immunity is developed only in the second (non-italic) part of the text.

12. It is in the note that Derrida explicitly defines immunity and auto-immunity: 'The immune reaction protects the *indemnity* of the body proper by producing antibodies against foreign antigens. As for the process of auto-immunisation . . . it consists for a living organism . . . in protecting itself basically against its self-protection by destroying its own immune defences.' Given this figure's political developments to come, note that the general explanation given by the *National Institutes of Health* website metaphorises the process in terms of 'friendly fire': the body fires on its own cells as though they were 'enemies'. That these 'enemy' cells be precisely those charged with normal immune protection (rather than just any cells) seems to take auto-immunitary logic to the point of a certain crisis of the *autos* itself. Auto-immunity: autro-immunity.
13. *Voyous*, for example pp. 43, 57–60, 64–6, 70–1, 74, 80, 83, 95, 120, 126, 128, 130, 143–4, 154–5, 160, 173, 175–6, 178, 198, 208, 210–11, 214–15.

Jacques Derrida: . . . A Life

Here's my story.[1] The story of my life. Jacques Derrida taught me everything, but he couldn't, and didn't, prepare me for this. I was not ready, I am not ready. Nowhere near ready, still, one year on. I am still speechless. I really have nothing to say. Nothing. Anything I said would already be too much: I need and want to spend my time here saying nothing. Nothing, nothing, maybe seven times nothing. Nothing about Jacques Derrida's life, or his death. As Jacques himself was saying, increasingly towards the end, towards death, death is each time the end of the world,[2] not of this or that world, but of the one and only world, the world itself, leaving only a world after the end of the world, as he says in *Béliers*, written in homage to Hans-Georg Gadamer, and goes on:

> For each time, and each time singularly, each time irreplaceably, each time infinitely, death is no less than the end of *the* world. Not *merely one* end among others, the end of someone or something *in the world*, the end of a life or a living being. Death does not put an end to someone in the world, nor to *one* world among others, it marks each time, each time in defiance of arithmetic the absolute end of the single and same world, of what each one opens as a single and same world, the end of the one and only world, the end of the totality of what is or what can present itself as the origin of the world for such and such a unique living being, human or not.[3]

So the world ended. Leaving nothing. It's nothing. I'll get over it. I'm surviving. Melancholically – for this *is* melancholy, almost militant melancholy, a melancholy that Derrida says later in *Béliers* is a condition of ethics in its very protest against so-called 'normal' mourning – melancholically saying nothing about Jacques Derrida's life, but wondering, having seen and heard some of the more or less ridiculous and offensive things that have been said since he died, what will get said about that life. We might imagine that sooner or later some form of 'biography' might get written, and it would seem difficult in this case to imagine a biography that managed to take into account what the subject of that biography thought and wrote. What would a biography of Jacques Derrida have to look like to be a Derridean biography? I have tried to argue elsewhere that biography is itself a fundamentally philosophical concept, so that a biography of a philosopher is in some senses the most biographical biography imaginable. It is easy to show, on the basis, say, of Plato's *Phaedo*, that the character we call 'the philosopher' is in part defined by leading a life that will have been philosophical enough to warrant a biography, and that life is philosophical enough insofar as it is oriented towards death, a preparation for or pedagogy of death. The philosopher becomes the philosopher he was going to be in death, and his 'life' can then be written as sealed by that death. Philosophy needs philosophers, and it needs them to live and die philosophically. In this regard, among others, Jacques Derrida was not simply a philosopher, famously refusing this schema:

> . . . no, I've never learned-(how)-to-live. Not one bit! Learning how to live ought to mean learning how to die . . . Since Plato, this is the old philosophical injunction: to philosophise is to learn how to die.[4]

* * *

Jacques Derrida taught me everything. Here's one thing he taught me. Life is an economy of death. This seems to mean something like this. If life were simply life, purely life or merely life, it would be death. Life may seem as though it would tend teleologically toward a fullness of itself, its own plenitude, life itself, transcendental life, but such life is, or would be, death.

This is true in Freud as much as in Descartes or Husserl. The latter, call it transcendental, version works broadly (a little caricaturally) as follows: I think, and my thinking bears witness to my being an essentially immortal thinking substance. From the height of this essential immortality, my death looks like a mere empirical accident, a contingency that can be essentially discounted. Look at that contingency down there: it's nothing. But, says Derrida, the transcendental position was only achieved in the first place on the back of the relation to death. My death is a condition of possibility of the transcendental position itself, a sort of perverse transcendental of the transcendental. Transcendental life is the life of death, life after death. And this is the pattern against which Derrida protests near the end, whereby philosophy would be to do with learning how to die. From Socrates onwards, philosophers, apparently, cannot wait to die, to piggy-back out of contingency into the death-free (because already dead) realm of the concept.

The Freudian version goes something like this: life is ruled by the so-called pleasure principle, the model for which is the discharge of energy stored in the living system. But a system that simply obeyed this principle without further ado would die immediately, as Freud admits breezily enough (it is this admission that opens up the realm of what Freud also rather breezily calls a 'theoretical fiction'). As we could confirm in a slightly different way in Bataille, a purely living life, a sovereign life, would be instant, if glorious, death, a flash and then the night. As Derrida lays out in both 'Freud et la scène de l'écriture' and 'Spéculer – sur Freud',[5] the result is that life is itself, is life, is alive, only to the extent that it compromises its life with a principle of reserve (in Freud, that it maintains a non-zero inner level of energy even though that in principle entails unpleasure), a principle of reserve that is also already a principle of death. In order to live at all without simply going up and out with a bang, life must die a little: life is life only to the extent that it is not purely or merely life; life inhibits itself as life, inoculates itself with death in order to be life at all. To anticipate on some later Derrida formulations, a life *worthy of its name*, *digne de son nom*, must fall short of itself, not quite be itself, hold itself back, be a little less than itself, *in order to be itself*. The life most worthy of the name 'life' is a life that's a little less than full or pure life: life must *re*serve itself in order to *pre*serve itself, inhibit or restrain itself, and that inhibition, restraint or falling short involves already a relation to death. Life is, then, life-death, or else survival, living on. As Derrida says again in the interview to *Le monde*, this concept of survival or living on is *originary*, it does not derive from life (or death, for that matter), and it is originary with respect to Derrida's own conceptuality: 'All the concepts that have helped me to work, especially the concept of the trace or the spectral, were related to "living on" as a structural dimension'. At the origin, then, there is a life that is not pure or mere life, but life-death, or life as the economy of death. Whence too what Derrida calls 'originary mourning' that must inhabit life from the start.[6]

This then, is my story, the story of my life. Naturally I have no intention of telling you the story of *my* life. In fact, in saying 'my story' or 'the story of my life', I was quoting Jacques Derrida, who was himself quoting Diderot at the beginning of *Apories*, Diderot reacting by saying 'c'est mon histoire' to Seneca's text *De Brevitate Vitae*, and more especially to Chapter 3 of that text, although Derrida also says that Diderot 'is right to recommend reading [Seneca's text], from the first word to the last, in spite of this brevity of life which in any case will have been so short' (p. 16). In fact Derrida says that 'c'est mon histoire' is 'what always has to be understood when someone talks about someone else, cites or praises him' (p. 17), in fact my story, the story of my life, is not just the story of *my* life, as we might also have confirmed by reading the rather extraordinary reflections on autobiography to be found throughout Derrida's work, but more especially at the beginning of *Papier machine*, where he is wondering about the possibility and necessity of thinking together 'event' (as unprogrammable and unforeseeable singularity) and 'machine' (as principle of repetition or repeatability), whereby even the story of my life, with all its singular events, would be marked by a *mekhanè*.[7] The story of my life is in a complex relation of repetition, almost of quotation, to many other lives and their stories.

Let's take a moment to re-establish the context of Diderot's comment, the 'c'est mon histoire', which Derrida is quoting from the *Essai sur la vie de Sénèque le philosophe*. Derrida is picking up on Diderot's on the one hand criticising, or appearing to criticise, Seneca for 'going beyond the limits of truth' in *De Brevitate Vitae*, but then on the other accusing himself of wasting his *own* life, thus confirming Seneca's main point. And it is in glossing this part of Diderot's commentary that Derrida suggests 'One might translate into the future perfect the tense of this murmur: "Ah! How short life will have been!" [*Que la vie aura été courte!*]' (*Aporias*, p. 17).

Diderot criticises Seneca for going beyond the limits of the truth, but then recommends that everyone read the treatise on the brevity of life, and more especially everyone who works in the arts (the precise point at which Diderot thinks Seneca goes beyond the limits of truth is to do with his apparent condemnation of involvement in public affairs); and Derrida too recommends that we read the treatise from start to finish. And if, in spite of the brevity of life, which Derrida asserts at least five times, like a mantra, in *Aporias*,[8] we find or make the time to follow Derrida's recommendation and read Seneca's text, the first thing we will find, surprisingly enough, already in Chapter 1 of *De Brevitate Vitae*, is that *life is not really short at all* ('Life is long enough . . . the life we receive is not short . . . our life is amply long' says Seneca in that first chapter). Life, says Seneca, is not *really* so short, life, at least life as given by nature, is long enough, *if it is well invested*; the life we receive is not short, *but we make it so, nor do we have any lack of it, but are wasteful of it;* our life is amply long *for him who orders it properly*.' And again, at the opening of Chapter 2, 'Life, if you know how to use it, is long'.[9]

Seneca's persistent and apparently familiar analogy in his text is between time and money, or at least between time and wealth. Life is short only if time is squandered or scattered (more literally 'dissipated'):

life is long if time is *invested*. But life is not *simply* time, or a matter of time. Already in Chapter 2 of his treatise, Seneca, quoting with approval 'that utterance which the greatest of poets delivered with all the seeming of an oracle: "The part of life we really live is small"', goes on to say that 'all the rest of existence is not life, but merely time [*Ceterum quidem omne spatium non vita sed tempus est*]'. Life is short if time is squandered, and squandered time, we might be tempted to say, is just time, or merely time: whereas time not squandered or dissipated, but capitalised and invested, is life, and life is intrinsically not short at all.

Life, as non-squandered time, comes into its own when not devoted to others (this is the point of Diderot's complaint about the limits of truth). Derrida, in the context of the Cerisy conference on *Le passage des frontières* in 1992 to which his text was first presented, emphasises Seneca's analogy of one's paradoxical tendency to defend one's property and wealth against the least incursion across its borders, as opposed to one's readiness to distribute one's life or spread one's time about with abandon.

Pursuing Seneca's text a little beyond this preliminary use Derrida makes of it, we can see that the potential tension between life and time (or life and mere being or existence, as Seneca sometimes says [Chapter VII, *non ille diu uixit, sed diu fuit*]) develops into a number of paradoxical consequences. These are, I think, entirely consistent with what Derrida goes on to develop so spectacularly in *Aporias* around Heidegger and the death-analysis in *Being and Time*, but perhaps sit curiously with the repeated insistence on the future-perfect-brevity-of-life. Let's pursue a little the logic of Seneca's text: business (busy-ness) is the enemy of the relation to time that Seneca calls life or living. In Chapter VII he says: 'There is nothing the busy man is less busied with than living: there is nothing that is harder to learn', and immediately goes on to make the familiar link between living and dying, learning (how) to live and learning (how) to die:

> There is nothing the busy man is less busied with than living: there is nothing that is harder to learn. Of the other arts there are many teachers everywhere; some of them we have seen that mere boys have mastered so thoroughly that they could even play the master. It takes the whole of life to learn how to live, and – what will perhaps make you wonder more – it takes the whole of life to learn how to die. Many very great men, having laid aside all their encumbrances, having renounced riches, business, and pleasures, have made it their one aim up to the very end of life to know how to live; yet the greater number of them have departed from life confessing that they did not yet know – still less do those others know. [So even given control of one's own time, learning how to live, as learning how to die, is not straightforward: taking control of one's own time may be a necessary condition for that learning, but appears

> far from sufficient. However the principle whereby it might at least be possible to learn how to live and die seems clear enough – not allowing others to take one's time away.] Believe me, it takes a great man and one who has risen far above human weaknesses not to allow any of his time to be filched from him, and it follows that the life of such a man is very long because he has devoted wholly to himself whatever time he has had. None of it lay neglected and idle; none of it was under the control of another, for, guarding it most grudgingly, he found nothing that was worthy to be taken in exchange for his time. And so that man had time enough, but those who have been robbed of much of their life by the public, have necessarily had too little of it.

What kind of great man might fulfil these conditions? Well, unsurprisingly enough, perhaps, the philosopher seems to be a promising candidate, and this is in part because the philosopher has a particular relationship to time. Time, remember, is not life, but life, the life one can learn how to live by learning how to die, is lived on the basis of a certain way of comprehending or managing time. This comprehension is based on the fundamental trope we have seen, and that Derrida stresses, of a kind of jealous guarding of one's time by analogy with a jealous guarding of one's money or wealth.

The slightly tortuous argumentative sequence in Seneca that culminates with the philosopher begins with a consideration of the future: there is no better way to squander time than to subordinate the present to the future, says Seneca. This is one of the many figures of busy-ness that pervade the text:

> Can anything be sillier than the point of view of certain people – I mean those who boast of their foresight? They keep themselves very busily engaged in order that they may be able to live better; they spend life in making ready to live! They form their purposes with a view to the distant future; yet postponement is the greatest waste of life; it deprives them of each day as it comes, it snatches from them the present by promising something hereafter. The greatest hindrance to living is expectancy, which depends upon the morrow and wastes today. (Chapter IX)

This does not, however, lead to the perhaps expected conclusion that life would involve a straightforward inhabiting of the present. In spite of certain appearances, living in the present is *not* quite the way to live, insofar as living in the present takes the essential form of being 'engrossed' (*occupatus*).[10] Even if I do not mortgage the present to the future, the attempt to seize the present *as* present fails, and this seems to be true even without the further problem of *dissipation* or *distraction*, that now appears to be rather tacked on to the more essential problem of engrossment, to do with the nature of the present itself. Seneca presents it as follows:

> Present time is very brief, so brief, indeed, that to some there seems to be none; for it is always in motion, it ever flows and hurries on; it ceases to be before it has come, and can no more brook delay than the firmament or the stars, whose ever unresting movement never lets them abide in the same track. The engrossed, therefore, are concerned with present time alone, and it is so brief that it cannot be grasped, and even this is filched away from them, distracted as they are among many things. (Chapter X)

It follows that 'living', the kind of living that has to be learned and that is bound up with dying, with learning how to die, will rely essentially on a relation to neither the future nor the present, but to the past. The point about not being distracted or, more fundamentally, engrossed in the present, and more generally the point about jealously keeping one's time to and for oneself, is that only thus does one have time, in the present, to inhabit the past. Living, truly living, involves using the present time to live in the past, and the reason for this is that, in contradistinction to the fleeting present and the contingent future, the past is, as Seneca puts it, *certain.* Fortune or chance as a general figure of uncertainty has no more control over the past, 'the part of our time that is sacred and set apart [*pars temporis nostri sacra ac dedicate:* sacrosanct or immune, we might be tempted to say in the light of Derrida's late work], put beyond the reach of all human mishaps, and removed from the dominion of Fortune, the part which is disquieted by no want, by no fear, by no attacks of disease; this can neither be troubled nor be snatched away – it is an everlasting and unanxious possession [*omnis humanos casus supergressa, extra regnum fortunae subducta, quam non inopia, non metus, non morborum incursus exagitet; haec nec turbari nec eripi potest; perpetua eius et intrepida possessio est*]' (Chapter X). The leisure and tranquillity that is a condition of learning how to live is the leisure to allow the present (no longer occupied by engrossment, busy-ness or distraction) to be taken over by the past. And this is why life is not *intrinsically* short, however short it in fact is – for those who live the past in the present, time is always 'ample' [*spatiosa*]:

> None of it is assigned to another, none of it is scattered in this direction and that, none of it is committed to Fortune, none of it perishes from neglect, none is subtracted by wasteful giving, none of it is unused; the whole of it, so to speak, yields income. And so, however small the amount of it, it is abundantly sufficient, and therefore, whenever his last day shall come, the wise man will not hesitate to go to meet death with steady step. (Chapter XI)

After a long catalogue of different forms of being engrossed (including, incidentally, 'spending one's time on useless literary problems' and thereby seeming 'more of a bore than a scholar' (Chapter XIII)), Seneca finally comes, as I was saying, to the philosopher. The philosopher is (as philosophers often claim) the one who *really* knows how to live (and therefore how to die), and this true knowledge extends or supplements the kind of freeing up of the present for the past that had been proposed thus far. This extension or supplement seems to involve a transgression of the individual propriety or even jealousy that has marked the argument thus far, and that Derrida comments on at the beginning of *Aporias*. Taking time now for the past is one thing: but *really* living, really overcoming the brevity of life, involves not being content merely with one's *own* past and the time it capitalises:

> Of all men they alone are at leisure who take time for philosophy, *they alone really live* [my emphasis]; for they are not content to be good guardians of their own lifetime only. They annex every age to their own; all the years that have gone before them are an addition to their store. Unless we are most ungrateful, all those men, glorious fashioners of holy thoughts, were born for us; for us they have prepared a way of life. By other men's labours we are led to the sight of things most beautiful that have been wrested from darkness and brought into light; from no age are we shut out, we have access to all ages, and if it is our wish, by greatness of mind, to pass beyond the narrow limits of human weakness, there is a great stretch of time through which we may roam. We may argue with Socrates, we may doubt with Carneades, find peace with Epicurus, overcome human nature with the Stoics, exceed it with the Cynics. Since Nature allows us to enter into fellowship with every age, why should we not turn from this paltry and fleeting span of time and surrender ourselves with all our soul to the past, which is boundless, which is eternal, which we share with our betters? (Chapter XIV)

The past is 'certain', we have seen, as opposed to the contingent future and the fleeting present: now it is also boundless (so that our jealous guarding of the bounds of our time, that marked the beginning of Seneca's argument and that Derrida insisted on, here opens up differently to an outside) – boundless, and endlessly and perpetually available: a little later in the same chapter, Seneca adds Zeno, Pythagoras, Democritus, Aristotle and Theophrastus to the list of names, and says that 'all mortals can meet with them by night or by day'.

Philosophy, then, reconciles life and time, and confirms that life is not short, need not be short: the philosophers whose company I keep, says Seneca, teach me how to die (Chapter XV) without forcing me to die. The point here for Seneca seems less the positive lesson I might draw from one or other of these philosophers, and more something to do with philosophy itself. In philosophy, I know how to die without really dying, and that's really knowing how to live. Philosophy, moreover, *allows me to choose my fathers*, says Seneca strikingly in Chapter XV, and to inherit their name and property which I will no longer have to guard jealously (whence the boundlessness mentioned earlier): and by this fact, philosophy of itself opens onto immortality: just because philosophical works cannot be harmed by time, the life of the philosopher,

> The life of the philosopher . . . has wide range, and he is not confined by the same bounds that shut others in. He alone is freed from the limitations of the human race; all ages serve him as if a god. Has some time passed by? This he embraces by recollection. Is time present? This he uses. Is it still to come? This he anticipates. He makes his life long by combining all times into one. (Chapter XV)

We might wonder what such a life would look like. In order to free himself from the brevity of life, the philosopher needs leisure, and that leisure is not devoted to a still engrossing and anxiety-producing pursuit of pleasure (which, in an important development, Seneca says makes the time *seem* long but thereby in fact only accentuates the brevity of life), but to a practice of philosophy itself as frequentation of the philosophy of the past. The philosopher 'makes his life long by combining all times into one', but that operation depends on a rigorous subordination of present and future to the past.

All of which is, of course, very edifying: the very basis of all that is edifying. Worse still, it is clearly mortiferous. Imagine for a moment the 'life' here described. The fleeting present is filled with the solid past, which suffices to predict and therefore disallow the future. The life recommended by Seneca has no future: it is a kind of living death. We are, naturally enough, inclined to say to Seneca, 'get a life!' In so doing, we are not necessarily endorsing Diderot's actual complaint or accusation,[11] nor in general preferring the so-called active life over the so-called contemplative life. The life it would be a matter of 'getting' could still be figured (broadly speaking) on the side of what might normally be thought of as the contemplative life: where Diderot complains and needs *his* philosopher to be more estimable in the Senate than at school, in the law court than in the library, we might reasonably suggest that the essential problem with Seneca's argument is that it closes off anything like 'life' *even in the library*. And this may be why there was no explicit mention made of *reading* in Seneca's description of the philosopher defined by his dealings with other philosophers – Seneca in fact always evokes one's commerce with the philosophers of the past in terms of frequentation and conversation. If we take reading seriously (and this really is what Jacques Derrida taught me, this really *is* my story and my history), then we have to factor into it a relation that short-circuits the temporality as described by Seneca and allows the possibility of *events* of reading in the very time that Seneca has designed to foreclose any events at all. That opening up of reading will unsettle any opposition between the active and the contemplative life. Worse, it will also mean that the remedy for the perceived shortness of life is illusory: Seneca says life is not short so long as we are philosophers in the way he describes. The life that is devoted to learning how to live by learning how to die (or by having already learned how to die) is always plenty long enough, says Seneca (and we might be tempted to say that it is both interminable and deathly, however short): but once we register the irreducible trace of reading in that life, then it will again have been too short, always too short, but only that essential brevity gives it whatever length it will have had. And perhaps, in the end, that's not exactly nothing, that's life, that's survival, *c'est mon histoire.*

Notes

1. This previously unpublished paper was originally written for the April 2005 Georgetown University conference 'Jacques Derrida: Cosa Mentale': this revised version was read to a special Derrida memorial session of the October 2005 meeting of the Society for Phenomenology and Existential Philosophy in Salt Lake City.
2. Already in fact in *Apories* (Paris: Galilée, 1992), p. 131: 'nothing less than the end of the world with each death'.
3. *Béliers, le dialogue interrompu: entre deux infinis, le poème* (Paris: Galilée, 2003), p. 23.
4. *Apprendre à vivre enfin* (Paris: Galilée, 2004), p. 24.
5. 'Freud et la scène de l'écriture', in *L'Écriture et la différence* (Paris: Seuil, 1967), pp. 293–340; 'Spéculer – sur "Freud"', in *La Carte postale de Socrate à Freud et au-delà* (Paris: Aubier-Flammarion, 1980), pp. 277–437.
6. *Apories* (Paris: Galilée, 1996), p. 133.
7. *Papier machine* (Paris: Galilée, 2001), pp. 33–6. Is it by chance that the type of event brought out here as in some way exemplary should be that of a theft?
8. *Apories*, pp. 16, 55, 91–2, 123, 136.
9. I quote Seneca's essay in John Basore's translation, from the Loeb classical library edition of Seneca's *Moral Essays*, Vol. II (Cambridge, MA and London: Harvard University Press, 1932).
10. This would be one essential difference between Seneca's text and its often literal *reprise* in Rousseau's *Emile*: see, for example, the opening of Book IV.
11. 'I would have no difficulty finding in Seneca more than one place where he complains about the quantity of business affairs and the rapidity of the hours. The animal knows when it is born everything it needs to know; man dies when his education has scarcely begun. [. . .] *Pace* Seneca, when one has compared the difficulty of perfecting a science, of perfecting oneself, with the rapidity of our days, one finds that the man who has managed his moments with the greatest economy, who has let none of them be stolen

from him out of facility, who has lost nothing of his hours to illness, laziness or negligence, and who has reached extreme old age, has nonetheless lived very little. [. . .] Your doctrine tends to give pride to the lazy and the mad, and to disgust good princes, good magistrates, truly essential citizens. If Paulinus does his duty badly, Rome will be in turmoil. If Paulinus does his duty badly, Seneca will be short of bread. The philosopher is a man who is estimable everywhere, but more so in the Senate than in school; more so in the law-court than in a Library; and the sort of occupations that you disdain are really those that I honour; they require labour, precision and probity; and the men who are endowed with these qualities seem common to you! When I see those who have made a name for themselves in the magistracy, at the bar, far from thinking that they have lost their years so that only one of those years should bear their name, I shall be in despair not to be able to count such a fine year in my whole life. How many must one have consumed in study, and stolen from pleasures, passions and sleep, to obtain that one! Wise is he who ceaselessly meditates on the epitaph that the finger of justice will engrave upon his tomb. [. . .] It is such a general fault, to allow oneself to be carried away beyond the limits of truth, out of interest for the cause one is defending, that one must sometimes forgive Seneca for it. [. . .] I was unable to read Chapter 3 without blushing: it is my story. Happy the man who will not emerge from it convinced he has lived only a very small part of his life! This treatise is very fine: I recommend that all men read it; but especially those who are drawn to perfection in the fine arts. They will learn from it how little they have worked, and that it is as often to wasting time as to lack of talent that one must attribute the mediocrity of artistic productions of all sorts' (Denis Diderot, *Essai sur les regnes de Claude et de Néron et sur les mœurs et les écrits de Sénèque*, ed. Roger Lewinter, 2 vols (Paris: Union Générale d'Édition, 1972), vol. 2, pp. 172–9).

Foundations

Since Jacques Derrida died in October 2004, during what for me has been a nameless process of mourning, or rather of melancholia, 'militant melancholia' as I first called it, of half-mourning or *demi-deuil* as he often said[1] (that *demi-deuil* that would traditionally begin one year after the loss, that one year being the period of *grand deuil*) – since that day in 2004, I have found myself thrown back to something like my own 'childhood memories' of Jacques, and more especially of my 'early' reading of what one might call his 'early' work.[2] Not for the first time, I have been tempted (tempted perhaps almost in a religious sense), tempted by the thought that somewhere, if I looked and worked hard enough, I would find the starting point or the origin of his thought. In the curious kind of coherence that marks Jacques Derrida's thinking, for which there is no doubt as yet no good working model, no satisfactory representation, it is as though I were searching for an origin-point, a point of founding or grounding, a moment of originary insight in which Derrida would have seen, if only perhaps in some embryonic or otherwise undeveloped form, what was to come, a moment that would provide the foundation for an edifice of thought, or perhaps be the first call for that 'institution of reading' called for, according to Jacques Derrida, by every text,[3] and be simultaneously the beginning of the structure of legacy and inheritance that he taught us (especially in *Spectres de Marx*) is just part of being, and that has come more starkly into view since his death.

Such a (more or less lucidly desperate) search for an origin rapidly finds of course that Derrida's 'originary' insight, if there were such a thing, would be something like that there is no origin (and therefore, perhaps, no founding insight). Put more correctly, Derrida says that there is *complexity* at the origin. From his very early Master's thesis on Husserl, in which he writes of an 'originary dialectic' and an 'originary synthesis', it seems that his thinking turns around the thought that *the origin is not simple*, and that a non-simple origin has immeasurable consequences for thought. One of the many ways in which these consequences appear throughout his work is in a thinking about institutions, and more especially about the founding gesture of institutions, the very instituting or the *institution* of institutions.

* * *

Let me first briefly establish the argument about complex origins. This argument is, as they say, 'well-known', but it is nonetheless often misrepresented, as for example a proposal or project or programme. Derrida's most general argument is that what he calls the attempts of 'metaphysics' to derive complexity from simplicity, and more especially from an origin which always comes down to some form of *presence*. Even if we *now* find ourselves in a situation of complexity, and even of negativity and evil, that situation has arisen (so metaphysics says) on the basis of a presence that (perhaps only ideally, in some sense of 'ideal') came before it as its origin. Very different stories can then be told about how the original presence or plenitude came to fail, or fall, or be lost, but they all share a common structure. And this 'archaeological' dimension to metaphysics is often (probably always) mirrored by a 'teleological' dimension in which current complexity can be (perhaps only ideally again, in some sense of 'ideal') directed towards some final, perhaps redemptive, state of presence. This archaeo-teleological schema is in fact definitive of what Derrida means in general by 'metaphysics'.

Derrida wants to argue that any such 'presence' is not really originary at all, but at best a *secondary* effect that must emerge from an 'earlier' state that he famously calls (among other names) *différance*. Simple, present origins are always in fact projected (or, rather, retro-jected) on the basis of a situation in which they are already lost: retro-jecting them *as* origins is an attempt to overlook or avoid the fact that they never really come first, but are only said to come first from a situation that precedes that retro-jective saying or naming of that origin. The supposedly simple and present origin itself has an origin in something else, and that something else, the origin's origin, is not an origin in the normal sense at all, because it cannot be simple or simply present. For many of us, the most perspicuous way to think about this 'earlier' moment, what precedes the origin, is in terms of the *trace*, which Derrida most clearly develops in his reading of Saussure, but which he famously says in the *Grammatology* combines in one and the same possibility, 'and without it being possible to separate them other than by abstraction, the structure of the relation to the other, the movement of temporalisation, and language as writing'.[4] Broadly speaking, what Derrida is able to show is that Saussure's insight concerning language as a 'system of differences without positive terms' entails a thinking of identity in which any element in a plurality is identifiable as the element that it is only insofar as it in some way bears the 'trace' of all the elements that it is not. This 'trace-structure' means that apparently 'present' elements are never *simply* present (because to be what they are they are necessarily bearing the trace of all the 'absent' elements that they are not) and that the apparently 'absent' elements cannot be *simply* absent, in that their 'absence' is somehow *present* (but present *as* absence, as a *trace* of absence, precisely) as a condition of the apparently 'present' element's being 'present' at all. This complication of presence and absence, derived here from a description of language, but rapidly proposed by Derrida as a matrix for thinking about effects of identity *in general*, is what justifies Derrida's claim that *différance* precedes even what Heidegger calls the ontico-ontological difference, and indeed Being more generally, and is what will give rise in his later work to the thematics of ghosts and haunting, and the more sweeping proposal, in *Specters of Marx,* to rethink ontology as *hauntology*.

The trace, which allows things to emerge as apparently 'present' while being itself never simply present, is in this sense *more originary* that anything one might have wanted to think was at the origin, and is thus the origin and possibility of the origin itself. The trace is the origin of the origin. Derrida is quick to point out, however, that 'trace' cannot in fact be thought of in traditional terms as an origin, just because 'origin' has traditionally entailed precisely the value of presence that we have just seen 'trace' disrupt. The trace is 'originary' in such a radical sense that it disrupts the very concept of an origin. At the origin of the origin is something non-originary, what Derrida sometimes refers to as a kind of radical or absolute past that was never present. This radical or absolute past is 'past' in a sense that the normal sense of 'past' (as past *present*) cannot capture, and so is arguably in excess of the very concept of time itself, at least insofar as time is thought by metaphysics, or insofar as time itself is (as Derrida at least once famously suggests) an irremediably metaphysical concept.[5] And a similar (though not entirely symmetrical) argument can be developed around the future, so that just as the thought of the trace gives rise to an 'absolute past', it also secretes a kind of 'absolute future' (what Derrida sometimes, often in political contexts, calls an *à-venir,* literally a to-come, rather than an *avenir*) which never will be present. I shall return to this strange kind of futurity a little later.

These points are now no doubt somewhat familiar, even if 'familiarity' is just what they most obviously and immediately unsettle. The trace can never really be familiar, whence the importance of rehearsing these points, each time. It is, however, striking in our context here that in the course of the very dense and difficult pages from *Of Grammatology* in which he lays out the thought of the trace, Derrida already has recourse to the concept of institution. This is perhaps not so very surprising, in that Saussure, who is of course Derrida's main reference in this discussion, already has some quite complicated and interesting things to say about language as an institution, and even as a 'pure' institution, by which he seems to mean that language is, precisely, an originary institution that makes all others possible, the institution to begin and end all institutions, the institution without which there could be no other institutions. (This is what separates Saussure's view of language from the kind of traditional conventionalism with which it is sometimes confused.) Once language is up and running, as it were, other institutions can come into being by conventional or contractual means: but the institution of language itself is radical, and 'pure' in Saussure's sense, in that it cannot have come about this way – the traditional conventionalist account of the origin of language (according to which people at some point agree on what words to use for what things or what ideas) must in fact presuppose a language already in existence, a problem which Saussure recognises when he says that I do not consent to the language-system within which I speak, but receive it like the law.[6]

Saussure's own remarks about the institutionality of language are complex and, not unusually, a little inconsistent. Let me cite a few of these comments, not only to show Saussure struggling to isolate the specificity of language in this respect, but also because his reflections have recourse to a political and juridical language that will be of interest to us in a moment. For example (all emphasis mine):

> . . . for Whitney, who assimilates language to a social institution just like any other, it is by chance, for simple reasons of convenience, that we use the vocal apparatus as the instrument of language: men might just as well have chosen gesture and employ visual instead of acoustic images. No doubt this thesis is too absolute; *language is not a social institution in all points like others*; what is more, Whitney goes too far when he says that our choice fell by chance on the vocal organs; they really were in some ways imposed on us by nature. But on the essential point the American linguist seems to us to be right: *language is a convention*, and the nature of the sign agreed upon is indifferent. The question of the vocal apparatus is thus secondary in the problem of language.[7]

> [The language system] is the social part of language, external to the individual, who alone can neither create it nor modify it; it exists only in virtue of *a kind of contract passed between the members of the community.*[8]

> With respect to the linguistic community which uses it, [the signifier] is not free, it is imposed . . . the mass itself cannot exercise its sovereignty [note this reference to sovereignty, which will return as a problem] on a single word; it is bound to the language system as it is.[9]

> *Language can therefore no longer be assimilated to a contract pure and simple*, and it is precisely from this angle that the linguistic sign is particularly interesting to study; for if one wants to show that the law admitted in a collectivity is something one suffers and not a rule freely consented to, it is indeed language that offers the most striking proof of that.[10]

> Language . . . is at every moment everybody's business; dispersed in a mass and handled by that mass, it is something that all individuals use all day. On this point, *one can establish no comparison between language and other institutions*. The prescriptions of a code, the rituals of a religion, maritime signals, etc., only ever occupy a certain number of individuals at once and for a limited period; in language, on the contrary, everyone participates at every moment, and this is why it ceaselessly undergoes the influence of all. This capital fact suffices to show the impossibility of a revolution. Language of all social institutions is the one that offers the least purchase for initiatives.[11]

> The other human institutions – customs, laws, etc. – are all founded, to diverse degrees, on the natural relations of things; there is in them a necessary fit between the means employed and the ends pursued. [. . .] Language, on the contrary, is in no way limited in the choice of its means, for one cannot see what would prevent any given idea being associated with any given sequence of sounds.

> To bring out clearly that *language is a pure institution*, Whitney quite rightly insisted on the arbitrary character of signs, and in so doing has placed linguistics on its true axis. But he did not go far enough and did not see that *this arbitrary character radically separates language from all other institutions*.[12]

In Derrida's terms, this 'pure' institutionality of language shows up in the thought that language, which we have already seen to entail the trace, consists in *instituted* traces. As instituted trace, language will, in due course, be better described, says Derrida, as writing, in part just because of this institutional character: 'If "writing" signifies inscription and primarily durable institution of a sign (and this is the only irreducible nucleus of the concept of writing), then writing in general covers the whole field of linguistic signs.'[13]

* * *

It is no doubt this radically inaugural or 'pure' sense of institution that leads to Derrida's later, more thematised reflections on institutions and their institutionality. For example, in '*Mochlos* or the Conflict of the Faculties', commenting more especially on the institution of the University:

> The question of the right of right, of the founding or foundation of right is not a juridical question. And the reply to it can be neither simply legal nor simply illegal, neither simply theoretical or constative nor simply practical or performative. It can take place neither inside nor outside the University that the tradition has bequeathed to us. This response and this responsibility as to the basis [*fondement*] can only take place in terms of foundation. Now the foundation of a right is not more juridical or legitimate than the foundation of a University is a university or intra-university event. If there can be no pure concept of the University, if there can be within the University no pure and purely rational concept of the University, this is quite simply, to say it a little elliptically [. . .] because the University is *founded.* An event of foundation cannot simply be understood in the logic of what it founds. The foundation of a right is not a juridical event. The origin of the principle of reason, which is also implied at the origin of the University, is not rational, the foundation of a university institution is not a university event. The anniversary of a foundation might be, but not the foundation itself. Although it is not simply illegal, such a foundation does not yet come under the internal legality it institutes. Although nothing appears more philosophical than the foundation of a philosophical institution – be it the University, or a school or department of philosophy – the fondation of the philosophical institution as such cannot be *already strictly* philosophical.[14]

Or again, in *Force de loi:*

> The origin of authority, the foundation or grounding [*fondement*], the positing of the law being unable by definition to lean finally on anything but themselves, they are themselves a groundless violence. Which does not mean that they are unjust in themselves, in the sense of being 'illegal' or 'illegitimate'. They are neither legal nor illegal in their foundational moment. They exceed the opposition of the founded and the unfounded, as of any foundationalism or anti-foundationalism. Even if the success of performatives that found a right (for example and it is more than an example, of a State guaranteeing a right) – even if that success presupposes prior conditions and conventions (for example in the national or international space), the same 'mystical' limit will reemerge at the supposed origin of those conditions, rules or conventions – and of their dominant interpretation.[15]

This paradox of the foundation, whereby the act of foundation (the act of instituting the institution, the institution of the institution) cannot ever quite be understood within the logic of what is founded by the act of foundation, opens the institution from the start to an ongoing relation to the violence in and against which the foundation took place, so that in a Hobbesian, Rousseauian or even Kantian view of politics, the founding contract that is supposed to get us out of the intolerable violence of the state of nature would, on this reading, remain marked or haunted by the violence of the context from which it supposedly emerged. The pre-legal – a-legal if not yet strictly illegal – violence of the founding act, whereby the institution comes to be, persists as something like the 'essence' of the political as such, or at least as something without which there would be no politics or institution, but only nature. The full measure of this paradox[16] can be gauged from the thought that the founding act *itself* is neither legal nor illegal, just because it precedes the institutional law to which it gives rise, but the *repetition* of that act (which no institution can do without, if only because of the analytic relation between law and repetition[17]), just because it takes place *within* the institution thus violently and pre-legally founded, is *both* legal *and yet* illegal, confirming the legality of the institution, the legitimacy of its institution, just as it shows up its illegitimacy. Whence the fact that institutions indeed *are* institutions (and not just nature), and whence too the fact that institutions are constantly subject to contestation, modification and overthrow, or to the very violence against which they were instituted in the first place, i.e. what we usually call 'nature' (but that in the tradition has other names too, such as 'civil war' in Hobbes). Institutions by definition mark a break with nature, yet insofar as their founding moment can never be fully integrated and institutionalised, but remains as a kind of traumatic memory of their non-legal foundation, they remain *haunted* by a nature they have never quite left behind (I want to say – I'm not sure if Derrida would agree – that *that's just what nature is*),[18] and which can always re-emerge to destroy them (this is a constant theme in Rousseau's political thought, for example, where the very fragile cohesion of the State is always on the verge of breaking and dispersing back into nature). Institutions thus 'live' in a kind of constitutive dissension or even permanent revolution that affects every institutional act or event imaginable, and explains their constitutive shiftiness and inevitable tendency to corruption. Institutions, we might say, are 'corrupted' and made fragile from the start by the violence of their institution, of their foundation, which is also however the only measure of their legitimacy.

This is why, among other things, it is possible for language to change and new things to get said, even though the institution of language tends also to secrete sub-institutions (academies, dictionaries, etc. . . .) the job of which is to attempt to prevent, or at least to restrain, change. Just as every act or event that takes place within an institutional framework both confirms the institution within which it takes place and simultaneously opens up the perspective of that institution's demise (just because it *is* an act or event, and as such not quite totally within the grasp of the institution that nonetheless made it possible), so every act of *parole* (in Saussure's sense) both confirms the *langue* which makes it possible (so that everything I say here in English cannot fail to confirm the English language in its Englishness, so to speak) and, insofar as it is an event at all, makes something new happen, and however minutely changes the very *langue* it also confirms.

* * *

This disconcerting logic opens up a strange diremption within institutions between what it is tempting to call a transcendental dimension (the apparently immutable practices of the institution itself, its capacity to repeat itself or reproduce itself as itself, its tendency to acquire a kind of timeless or immemorial quality, whereby things are done a certain way just because that is the way they have 'always' been done, and nobody can do anything about it), and what it is tempting (but certainly inadequate) to call an empirical dimension, whereby the transcendental is both confirmed *and* challenged by the events that come about, always with a measure of contingency, and without which the institution (which insofar as it is not natural in the usual sense, is always, *ex hypothesi*, historical) would not exist. This 'empirical' or contingent dimension is then what Derrida would call the *chance* of the institution, and simultaneously the constant threat to its survival, the permanent possibility of its ruin.

I think I can show this in political thinking by again taking the example of Rousseau. According to Rousseau's theory of the social contract, the 'sovereign' produced by the founding contract itself is necessarily perfect: 'The Sovereign, by the very fact of being, is always all it should be',[19] but in fact the social body as merely or purely sovereign is also atemporal and powerless, living in an atomistic succession of pure present moments, unable to establish any temporal link to past or future because in so doing it would compromise its sovereignty. (This is, incidentally, the point at which what Rousseau calls 'sovereignty' looks surprisingly similar to what Bataille calls 'sovereignty'.) The purity of the institution is its sovereignty, but that sovereignty is *nothing* (least of all an institution) unless it finds a way to exist and maintain itself in time. In Rousseau's terms, this means that it must give itself a government in order to *be* sovereign, but as Rousseau shows remorselessly and rigorously, the government, which cannot simply coincide with the Sovereign in some kind of radical democracy (a people of gods, says Rousseau, would govern itself democratically, but that would be a 'government without government' and the same as no politics at all)[20] – the government cannot fail to usurp the sovereignty of the sovereign and lead to the eventual ruin of the social body itself. The institution can interpose between itself and this inevitable ruin any number of intermediate bodies, but the most that can be hoped is that they can delay what is an absolutely inevitable process. The outcome of that process is a return to a ('natural') violence that the social body was formed to guard against. Rousseau says this, in what I'm tempted to describe as a 'fabulous' account of the demise of the institution:

> The Sovereign People wills by itself, and by itself it does what it wants. Soon the inconvenience of this concourse of all in everything forces the Sovereign People to charge some of its members with the execution of its wishes. After having fulfilled their charge and reported on it, these Officers return to the common equality. Soon these charges become frequent, and eventually permanent. Insensibly a body is formed that acts always. A body that acts always cannot report on every act: it only reports on the principal ones; soon it gets to the point of reporting on none. The more active the acting principle, the more it enervates the willing principle. Yesterday's will is assumed to be today's; whereas yesterday's act does not dispense one from acting today. Finally the inaction of the willing power subjects it to the executive power; the latter gradually renders its actions independent, and soon its will: instead of acting for the power that wills, it acts on it. There then remains in the State only an acting power, the executive. The executive power is mere force, and where mere force reigns the State is dissolved.[21]

Of course we are not obliged to accept the narrative-historical account that Rousseau gives of this process on its own terms: rather the point would be to recognise that it is a *structural* description in which the aspects that we have isolated are clearly visible.

Similarly, I have tried elsewhere to show in some detail how a similar problem besets Kant's political theory, even as Kant is arguably more lucid than most about the violent nature of the foundation of the state. In the *Doctrine of Right*, part of the doctrinal text *Metaphysics of Morals*, Kant recognises that the *factual* origin of the state is most probably (almost certainly) a violent one, and to that extent marked with illegitimacy: but *transcendentally* speaking, the state *must* be considered legitimate, just because sovereignty is necessarily *right*, as we saw Rousseau saying. (The form of the argument about sovereignty's necessary rightness is disconcertingly simple: to argue that the sovereign was illegitimate or wrong would imply adopting a position of sovereignty above sovereignty, which is either contradictory (it would mean that there were two sovereigns), or else resolves into the same necessary rightness at the level of the 'new' sovereign. Sovereignty is not so easily escapable, and indeed, as Spinoza points out, it is part of sovereignty to interpret sovereignty and decide what it is.) Kant's solution to the problem is to say that subjects must therefore *not even inquire* as to the origin of the state, in that any investigations they might undertake would tend to undermine the transcendental legitimacy of the sovereign just by insinuating that the sovereignty of the sovereign *might* have been founded on an act of violence (rather than on an act of contractual agreement, which is the *transcendental* truth of the matter). The factual truth of the origin of the state must therefore remain a *secret*, and that secret is always a secret about violence. Kant's idea (which of course he violates in the very fact of formulating it in a published work) is that what we might call the violence of politics (the violence without which there would be no politics at all, what I am here assimilating to the foundation of institutions in general) can be managed only by containing it as a sort of secret enclave or crypt (as Derrida sometimes used to say on the basis of Abraham and Torok) within the state itself. This conversion of founding violence into something secret or unspeakable would then be a fundamental feature of institutions as such.

If we had time, we could pursue this logic in what Derrida says more specifically about the institution of the University. For although the most general level at which the question of foundations can be asked is that of the institution in general (and perhaps especially the so-called 'pure institution' of language, as we suggested), there is a specificity to the institution of the University (and indeed this is already hinted at in the paradoxical fact that Kant, in an essentially 'university' context, as we have just seen, argues for the legitimacy of secrecy in the State in a way that *ipso facto* opens that secret). In *L'Université sans condition*,[22] Derrida argues that the University should be a place of absolute, unconditional resistance, where in a sense *nothing need be secret,* where everything can be said (and, crucially, said *publicly*, published), and that this opens it to a kind of responsibility that is not the same as that of other institutions: *as* an institution, the University must subject the institution in general, the very institutionality of institutions, to a kind of questioning that institutions in general can hardly fail to want to repress according to the kind of logic we just saw in Kant. The University, and more especially, says Derrida, the 'Humanities', have a responsibility to foster *events* of thought that cannot fail to unsettle the University in its Idea of itself. For this to happen, the special institution that the University is must open itself up to the possibility of unpredictable events (events 'worthy of the name', as Derrida often says, being by definition absolutely unpredictable) in a way that always might seem to threaten the very institution that it is. On this account, the University is in principle the institution that 'lives' the precarious chance and ruin of the institution as its very institutionality.

In the last ten years or so of his life, Derrida increasingly turned to a language of immunity and auto-immunity to describe this kind of situation and to pursue the deconstruction of sovereignty. In conclusion, I would like to suggest that this recourse, which can sometimes appear a little puzzling, flows directly from the early questions directed to Saussure, and notably from the complex concept of 'instituted trace' that I mentioned earlier. Derrida himself says several times in that context that a meditation on writing ought to unsettle the opposition between nature and institution, *physis* and *nomos* (*De la Grammatologie*, p. 66) that he suggests is 'everywhere', and particularly in linguistics, used as though it were self-evident.[23] It now seems that the logic of foundation itself entails a troubling of that opposition, given that an institutional foundation must, as we have seen, retain or secrete within it a pre-institutional moment, a moment of 'nature', which then inhabits the institution as the permanent haunting possibility of its violent collapse or overthrow. Something like a nature, then, always to some extent encrypted or secret, secreted within the institution that was erected against it, not only threatens the institution, but gives it a chance of being, as it were, *alive*, in the sense that life entails an openness (a 'hospitality', perhaps, to use another late-Derridean concept) to alterity and event, which is also an openness to the possibility of instant death and destruction (for a life that did not involve this openness would not be a life worthy of the name 'life', at best a kind of suspended animation or living death). As Derrida shows in his repeated use of the concept of auto-immunity – whereby the efforts of an organism (literal or analogical) to secure its own immunity lead it to turn on itself and even destroy itself after the fashion of auto-immune disorders – a measure of auto-immunity is in fact a condition for there to be an event at all. For example, in the second essay collected in the book *Voyous*:

> If an event worthy of the name is to happen, it must, beyond all mastery, affect a passivity. It must touch a vulnerability that is exposed, without absolute immunity, without indemnity, in its finitude and in a non-horizonal fashion, where it is not yet or already no longer possible to face up to, to put up a front, to the unpredictability of the other. In this respect, auto-immunity is not an absolute evil. It allows for exposure to the other, to *what* is coming and to *who* is coming – and must therefore remain incalculable. Without auto-immunity, with absolute immunity, nothing would ever happen again. One would no longer wait, expect, expect oneself and each other, or any event at all.[24]

'Auto-immunity' is the last in the long series of 'quasi-transcendental' terms that Derrida introduced, beginning with trace, archi-writing, *différance*, dissemination, and so on. It attempts, perhaps more clearly than some of those others, to capture a certain undecidability of life and death (including the 'life' and 'death' of institutions), but to do so *on the side of life*, as it were. (The much earlier Derridean development of 'lifedeath' is perhaps more concerned to stress death as a way of questioning the metaphysical concept of life as, essentially, presence.) Deconstruction is, so Derrida often says, essentially an affirmation, and an affirmation of life: whence too his expressions of reserve and even revolt (for example in his last interview with the journalist Jean Birnbaum) against the old philosophical presentation of philosophy as 'learning [how] to die'.[25] All the early work's efforts to find something like death at work 'in' presence, and in naive conceptions of life as essentially presence, lead to the idea that these efforts – deconstruction itself – take place in the interests of a life that would be 'worthy of its name', which is a life that involves death in itself as part of its affirmation. Life, including the life of institutions (but it would probably not be difficult to show that life in this sense always involves a certain institutionality or institutionalisation) affirms itself as life just by affirming its exposure to the absolutely unpredictable event that is, as it were, the life of life, the chance of life, just as it always might end life at any instant. Only thus would life have any future, in the radical sense I mentioned at the beginning, but this is now a future that comes from no 'horizon of expectation', and indeed no horizon at all, and can hardly be thought of within the traditional philosophical terms available for thinking about time.

Here's a passage from the same late text in which these strands come together quite clearly, and indeed explicitly go back to the early work on Husserl:

> It is reason that puts reason into crisis, in an autonomous and quasi autoimmune way. It could be shown that the ultimate 'reason', in the sense of cause or ground, the *raison d'être* of this transcendental phenomenological autoimmunity, is to be found lodged in the very structure of the present and of life, in the temporalisation of what Husserl calls the Living Present (*die lebendige Gegenwart*). The Living Present produces itself only by altering and dissimulating itself. I do not have the *time*, precisely, to go down this route, but I wanted to mark the necessity of it, in the place where the question of becoming and thereby of the time of reason appears indissociable from the immense, ancient and quite new question of life (*bios* or *zoe*), at the heart of the question of being, of presence and the entity, and therefore the question of being and time, of *Sein und Zeit* – a question this time accented on the side of life rather than the side of death, if that still makes – as I am tempted to believe it does – a certain difference.[26]

Derrida increasingly related this thought to his call for an unconditionality *without* sovereignty. We might recast this now by saying that sovereignty (as we saw briefly in Rousseau, but as we could verify in more detail in Bodin, or conversely, from the other direction, as it were, in Bataille or Schmitt) is just the attempt at immunity that would be a kind of death through foreclosure of any possibility of event, the kind of 'living death' we often experience as institutional or political paralysis, the sense that nothing can happen; the unconditionality referred to here involves exposure to the absolutely unexpected event as a condition of anything like 'life'. This is the only chance of institutions, but one against which they also necessarily guard themselves.

And this is why it is probably no accident that Derrida's death leaves no organised institution of deconstruction whatsoever, no department or school or institute, no institution *of* deconstruction, and at most, at best, but it *is* best, institutions *in* deconstruction, something along the lines of what he sometimes called the 'New International', something that certainly involves the plurality of languages that deconstruction also always affirms, *plus d'une langue* – one of his 'definitions' of deconstruction, meaning both 'more than one language' and 'no more of (only) one language' – a 'New International' that will certainly never be *achieved*, but which we nonetheless embody here and now, today, for the moment, in this our fragile and precious institutionality, thanks to his legacy, and thanks to your hospitality.

Notes

1. See for example 'Circonfession', in Bennington and Derrida, *Jacques Derrida* (Paris: Seuil, 1991), period 32.
2. This paper was originally written for the conference 'Derrida: pasiones institucionales', held in Mexico City, November 2005. This revised version was presented at the University of Pécs (Hungary) in November 2006 as the second annual Jacques Derrida memorial lecture. Previously published in Spanish as 'Fundaciones' (translated by Marionela Santoveña), in Esther Cohen (ed.), *Jacques Derrida: Pasiones Institucionales*, 2 vols (México: Universidad Nacional Autónoma, 2007), I, pp. 119–51, and in Hungarian as 'Alapok' (translated by Jolan Orban), in *Replika*, 61 (2008), 21–34
3. See 'Mochlos, ou le conflit des facultés', in *Du droit à la philosophie* (Paris: Galilée, 1990), pp. 397–438 (p. 422), and 'Ulysse Gramophone: l'oui-dire de Joyce', in *Ulysse gramophone: deux mots pour Joyce* (Paris: Galilée, 1987), pp. 94ff.
4. *De la grammatologie* (Paris: Minuit, 1967), p. 69.
5. *Marges de la philosophie* (Paris: Minuit, 1972), p. 73.
6. Here as elsewhere in Derrida, it is interesting to compare these insights with what is to be found in Rousseau: in the latter's *Discourse on the Origins of Inequality*, Rousseau presents an interestingly sceptical account of the relation between the origin of language and the origin of society, and puts the

problem of the origin of the institution of language thus: 'The first language of man, the most universal and energetic, and the only one he needed until he had to persuade an assembly, is the cry of nature. As this cry was dragged out only by a kind of instinct on occasions of urgency, to implore help in great danger, or relief in violent pain, it was not of any great use in the ordinary course of life, when more moderate sentiments reign. When men's ideas began to spread and multiply, and a tighter communication was established among them, they sought for more numerous signs and a more extensive language: they multiplied the inflexions of the voice, and joined to it gestures that are by their nature more expressive, and whose meaning depends less on an anterior disposition. So they expressed visible and mobile objects by gesture, and those that strike the hearing by imitative sounds: but as gesture can scarcely indicate any but present objects, or ones easy to describe, and visible actions; and as it is not always of use, since darkness or the interposition of a body render it useless, and as it demands attention rather than exciting it; one came round in the end to substituting for it vocal articulations which, without having the same relation to certain ideas, are better able to represent them all, *as instituted signs* [my emphasis]; a substitution that can only happen with common consent, and in a manner difficult to realise for men whose coarse organs had as yet not been exercised, and more difficult still to conceive for itself, since this unanimous agreement had to be motivated, and speech seems to have been very necessary to establish the use of speech.' Jean-Jacques Rousseau, *Oeuvres complètes*, 5 vols (Paris: Gallimard, 1958–96), Vol. III, pp. 148–9 (my translation).

7. Ferdinand de Saussure, *Cours de linguistique générale*, ed. T. de Mauro (Paris: Payot, 1976), p. 26. All translations mine, especially in view of the notorious inaccuracies and wilful distortions of the published translations of Saussure's *Cours*.
8. Saussure, p. 31.
9. Saussure, p. 32.
10. Saussure, p. 104.
11. Saussure, pp. 107–8.
12. Saussure, p. 110.
13. *De la grammatologie*, p. 65.
14. *Du droit à la philosophie*, pp. 434-5.
15. *Force de loi*: *le 'fondement mystique de l'autorité'* (Paris: Galilée, 1994), p. 34.
16. In the only example of which I am aware of Derrida himself using the syntagm 'institution de l'institution', this 'paradox' is clearly linked to the later thematics of messianicity, justice, faith and the performative. See *Foi et savoir*, §§21–22, and especially the following: '**First name:** the *messianic*, or messianicity without messianism. This would be the opening to the future or to the coming of the other *as* advent of justice, but without horizon of expectation and without prophetic prefiguration . . . An invincible desire for justice is linked to this expectation. By definition, it is and should be certain of nothing, through no knowledge, no consciousness, no foreseeability, no program as such . . . This messianicity stripped of everything, as it should be, this faith without dogma that moves forward in the risk of absolute darkness, will not be contained in any received opposition

of our tradition, for example the opposition between reason and mysticism. It announces itself everywhere that, reflecting without wavering, a purely rational analysis shows up this paradox, namely that the foundation of the law – the law of the law, the institution of the institution, the origin of the constitution – is a 'performative' event that cannot belong to the set of events that it founds, inaugurates or justifies. Such an event is unjustifiable in the logic of what it will have opened up. It is the decision of the other in the undecidable.'

17. 'Law is always the law of a repetition, and repetition is always subjection to a law', *La dissémination* (Paris: Seuil, 1972), p. 141.
18. See my *Frontières kantiennes* (Paris: Minuit, 2000), chapters 1 and 2.
19. Rousseau, *Oeuvres complètes*, III, p. 363.
20. More radically still: 'If it were possible that the Sovereign, considered as such, should have the executive power, right and fact would be so confused that one would no longer know what is law and what is not, and the body politic would soon fall prey to the violence against which it was instituted' (ibid., p. 432). Politics, we might want to say, lives *and* dies in the separation of fact and right.
21. *Lettres écrites de la montagne*, in *Oeuvres completes*, III, p. 815.
22. *L'Université sans condition* (Paris: Galilée, 2001).
23. Cf. too: 'All of this refers, beyond the nature/culture opposition, to a supervening opposition between *physis* and *nomos*, *physis* and *tekhnè* the ultimate function of which is perhaps to *derive* historicity; and, paradoxically, to recognize the rights of history, production, institution, etc., only in the form of the arbitrary and against a background of naturalism. But let us leave this question provisionally open: perhaps this gesture that in truth presides over the institution of metaphysics is also inscribed in the concept of history and even in the concept of time' (*De la grammatologie*, p. 50); 'This explanation of the "usurpation" is not only empirical in its form, it is problematic in its content, referring to a metaphysics and an old physiology of the sensory faculties which is constantly belied by science, as it is by the experience of language and of the body proper as language. It imprudently makes of visibility the sensory, simple and essential element of writing. Above all, by considering the audible as the *natural* milieu in which language must *naturally* carve out and articulate its instituted signs, thus exercising its arbitrariness in that milieu, this explanation removes all possibility of any natural relation between speech and writing at the very moment that it asserts it. It thus scrambles the notions of nature and institution that it uses constantly, instead of deliberately dismissing them, which one should no doubt begin by doing' (ibid., pp. 62–3); and, most trenchantly perhaps: 'If "writing" signifies inscription, and first of all durable institution of a sign (and this is the only irreducible nucleus of the concept of writing), writing in general covers the whole field of linguistic signs. In this field there can subsequently appear a certain species of instituted signifiers, 'graphic' in the narrow and derived sense of this word, ruled by a certain relation to other instituted signifiers which are, then, 'written' even if they are 'phonic'. The very idea of institution – and thus of the arbitrariness of the sign – is unthinkable before the possibility of writing and outside of its horizon' (ibid., p. 65).

24. *Voyous*, p. 210.
25. Partially published as 'Je suis en guerre contre moi-même', *Le monde*, 19 August 2004. The full text of the interview was subsequently published as a booklet: *Apprendre à vivre enfin: entretien avec Jean Birnbaum* (Paris: Galilée, 2005).
26. *Voyous*, pp. 178–9.

In The Event

I

One way of talking about 'Derrida's event' is to try to understand the event *of* Derrida, the perhaps philosophical or perhaps more broadly 'cultural' event that he was.[1] It seems to be no accident that we might be inclined to do this upon the fact or event of Derrida's death, on the basis of his now (and henceforth) 'being' dead, to understand the philosophical or cultural event that he was, in the past, or perhaps more properly that he *will have been*, in a projected future past, a future perfect that is also a perfect future in which things will finally have been what they always were to be. That's certainly one kind of approach one might be inclined to make, and it seems to be invited by the event of Derrida's death: now that Derrida is dead, the thought would go, the time has come to have an at least preliminary stab at *putting him in his place*, assigning him his rightful position and importance in the philosophico-cultural history of, say, Modern French Thought, or maybe Modern European Thought, or even just Modern Thought, or Western Thought, or (why not?) just Thought.

This kind of assessment, which seems to be essentially related to the fact (if not quite the event) of Derrida's death, appears to be fundamentally necrological, and wants, *post-mortem*, to get things straight, ordered and hierarchised, to deal with the estate and the legacy. It's no accident that its most appropriate tense should be the future perfect, the tense of what will have been, what will have turned out to be in some projection or fantasy of a Last Judgement, and one of the favourite adverbs of this type of assessment is indeed 'ultimately'. 'Ultimately, then, Derrida . . .'.[2] Nothing was more common in the notices and obituaries immediately provoked by the event (or at least the news) of Derrida's death, even when (perhaps especially when) those pieces had been (or may as well have been) prepared long in advance. (It was at least five years earlier that the London *Times* had approached me to write such an anticipatory obituary of Derrida: I never replied, I'm afraid.)

Let's say that that's one way of approaching Derrida's event. Derrida *will have been* such and such a figure, and the event that he was or will have been is, as it were, rounded off or completed by his death. Thinkers, like other cultural figures, die, and their death provokes a flurry of activity seeking to order, assess, classify and thereby, I'd be tempted to say, to forget and to neutralise. One thing that seems certain to survive the death is just this kind of talk, a sort of discursive machinery that assumes certain ways of processing events and writing them down, writing them up and writing them off into the great, ongoing and ultimately ultimate History of Everything.

II

We might imagine in this vein that sooner or later some form of 'biography' of Derrida might get written, but it would seem difficult in this case to imagine a biography that managed to take into account what the subject of that biography thought and wrote. What would a biography of Jacques Derrida have to look like to be a Derridean biography? I have tried to argue elsewhere that biography is itself a fundamentally philosophical concept, so that a biography of a philosopher is in some senses the most biographical biography imaginable.[3] It is easy to show, on the basis, say, of Plato's *Phaedo*, that the character we call 'the philosopher' is in part defined by leading a life that will have been philosophical enough to warrant a biography, and that life is philosophical enough insofar as it is oriented towards death, a preparation for or pedagogy of death.

This essential relationship between philosophy and death, or the philosophical life and death, is also what calls for biography, rather than autobiography. Autobiography ('the least inadequate name for what I do', as Derrida says somewhere) is a tricky way for a philosopher to deal with death: writing my autobiography, the story of my life, I pretend to be gathering my life up into a totality, rounding it off in preparation for death, but by the very fact of writing the autobiography I am adding a new event to my life (to parody Lyotard in *Le différend*, the synthesis of all the syntheses that make up my life is a further synthesis in my life), a new event which may be the most important event of my life, which by definition the autobiography can never catch up with – by becoming the narrator of my own life, I am enacting a fantasy of immortality, insofar as, structurally speaking, narrators cannot die. But biography, at least in its classical forms, waits for the death of its subject before telling his (usually his) life and gathering it up into a meaningful whole. *Tel qu'en lui-même enfin l'éternité le change*. Biography fulfils the philosophical programme of the philosopher by being predicated on his death: the biography of the philosopher, his written life, is written *from* his death, writing his life out in the future perfect tense that it *will have been*. But only this death confirms that the philosopher really was a philosopher in the philosophical sense of that term: the death of the philosopher allows for his life in the sense of the written account that will consecrate him as a philosopher and thereby consecrate philosophy as philosophy. Real life is always elsewhere, and the philosopher's real life comes after his death. Diogenes Laertius gives us some precious indications about this in the Introduction to his book: the distinction between a sage and a philosopher, due, according to Diogenes, to Pythagoras, is that the latter merely *seeks to attain* wisdom during his life (whereas the sage claims to have achieved it). The written life can then be the account of that search, and, because it is predicated on the idea that the search is not quite fulfilled in life (but only in death), the writing can include all sorts of elements which are *not yet* of the order of wisdom. If the philosopher *is* a philosopher only to the extent that he has *not yet* achieved wisdom, then his biography, teleologically dedicated to charting the path of philosophy towards the wisdom achieved only in death, can allow itself to recount all manner of more or less unedifying anecdotes along the way, and these anecdotes will tend to confirm *a contrario* the ontological status of the philosopher himself. Socrates is still the clearest example of this set-up, if I can use the notion of example here: let's say that Socrates is the *exemplary* philosopher.

What I have called elsewhere the ontologico-biographical supplement, then, is constitutive of the philosophical concept of biography, and indeed the philosophical concept of philosophy. Without it, that is without philosophy's giving rise to philosoph*ers*, philosophy would not quite be philosophy. But this supplement which makes all the difference to philosophy, and which as such, in the case of individual philosophers, is the proper domain of the biographer, *is not itself philosophical* in any obvious sense at all. Biographies of philosophers, even when written by philosophers, are not in principle works of philosophy, or destined solely for philosophical reading. The feature of a philosopher which most saliently makes him into a philosopher is not itself philosophical, but of the order of the anecdote, and it is not clear what philosophy (as opposed to biography) can have to say about it. For philosophical biography (or the biography of philosophers) is not primarily concerned to give a genealogical account of the thought of the philosopher concerned, not simply to document facts about the philosopher's *philosophical* life, but deals with his life as a whole insofar as that life is not philosophy but should bear some relation to philosophy. This means that philosophical biography always teeters on the brink of triviality or the merely anecdotal (if only because it is predicated on the idea that the reader of the biography does not understand the thought of the philosopher concerned), but also that philosophy is constitutively compromised by this more or less unhappy relationship with philosophical biography – for philosophy cannot do without the ontological supplement documented in biography – and therefore cannot do without potential triviality. Any biography that tried to escape its normal teleological form would have, perhaps, to refigure this whole economy.

I think there is something very unsatisfactory about this whole set-up and its generally presupposed culturalist historicism. It's not just that those of us who were more or less close to Derrida, intellectually and personally, experienced his death in a way that makes this type of recuperative bio-philosophical assessment difficult to want to do (and difficult to stomach), leaving us very far from the *ultimatelys* and the *in the last analyses* and the *future-historians-will-tell-us-thats*, and the *Derrida's-main-contribution-will-have-beens*, in a state that makes even an event such as this, 'Derrida's event', a challenge, more of a challenge than previous non-posthumous Derrida events, at any rate, so that it feels harder to know what's going to happen next – not just that, then, but rather that Derrida's event, the event of Derrida in the sense of the event as thought about by Jacques Derrida, seems to be more or less radically incompatible with that type of reaction.

For part of the event that Derrida is, and not the least important part, will have been a way of thinking about and writing about the event that makes it, and him, difficult to process in the ways I've been describing.

III

One way of casting this difficulty is in terms of mourning. As those of us who are in mourning try to mourn Derrida's death, maybe it is time to look again at some of the things Derrida said, at least from *Glas* (1975), but more especially in later texts, about death and mourning. Broadly speaking, the problem is this: so-called 'normal' or 'successful' mourning consists in a process of *getting over it*, of recovering from the loss of the other by withdrawing one's investments or cathexes in that other back into the self, back into the service of the self, the ego. Whether at a personal level or at the level of the kind of reaction I have just been mentioning, this is a teleological process the outcome of which is to *lose the loss*, to turn the loss into a profit, to come back to oneself, to *show a return*, in spite of the other's definitive departure. However 'healthy' we might want to think this process is, this model of mourning seems extraordinarily self-involved and self-interested (even jubilant in the case of several of the pieces published since Derrida's death), part of a more general take on what we all now call 'the other' that is precisely concerned to neutralise alterity in the interests of identity. (A lot of the recent talk about 'the other', in all its supposedly 'ethical' piety, is in fact a fairly transparent alibi for just this kind of self-interest.) And indeed this whole set-up is part of an age-old philosophical conception about life and death, and about philosophy as a process of 'learning how to die' which is of a piece with the 'biography' conceptuality I was mentioning earlier. It is against just this conception that Derrida protests in a lot of late texts, often reflecting on the death of friends and colleagues, and perhaps most strikingly in the interview given to the French newspaper *Le monde* less than two months before his death.

For example, in *Béliers*, originally written in homage to Hans-Georg Gadamer, after the latter's death, and which opens explicitly on the question of melancholia, Derrida is prepared to say that some *failure* of this structure of 'normal' mourning, something more of the order of what Freud calls, then, 'melancholia' (broadly speaking, the state of one who does not achieve the goal of mourning, but remains attached to the lost other), is in some important, 'ethical', sense *preferable* to mourning 'proper'. In fact, he thinks that only something that looks more like melancholia, as a kind of protest against mourning, a militant melancholia, then, gives any 'ethical' dimension to mourning. For example, as part of a meditation on Celan's enigmatic line 'Die Welt ist fort, ich muss dich tragen' [literally: 'the world is gone, I must carry you']:

> According to Freud, mourning consists in carrying the other in oneself. There is no world any more, it is the end of the world for the other when the other dies, and I take into myself this end of the world, I must carry the other and the other's world, the world in me: introjection, interiorisation of memory (*Erinnerung*), idealization. Melancholia is supposed to be the failure and pathology of this mourning. But if I *must* (this is ethics itself) carry the other in myself in order to be faithful to that other, to respect its singular alterity, *a certain melancholia must still protest against normal mourning* [my emphasis]. It must never resign itself to idealizing introjection. It must rail against what Freud says about it with such calm certainty, as though to confirm the norm of normality. The 'norm' is nothing other than the good conscience of amnesia. It allows us to *forget* that keeping the other inside oneself, *as oneself*, is already to *forget* the other. Forgetting begins right there. So melancholy *is necessary*.[4]

This is part of a movement of thought whereby the death of the other is always, rather literally, each time singularly, *the end of the world*, as the French title of what was first published in English as *The Work of Mourning* has it, and as Derrida also says much earlier in *Béliers*:

> For each time, and each time singularly, each time irreplaceably, each time infinitely, death is nothing less than an end of *the* world. Not *only one* end among others, the end of someone or something *in the world*, the end of a life or a living being. Death does not put an end to someone in the world, nor to *a* world among others, it marks each time, each time defying arithmetic, the absolute end of the one and only world, of what each opens as a one and only world, the end of the unique world, the end of the totality of what is or can present itself as the origin of the world for such and such a unique living being, human or not. (ibid., pp. 22–3)

But this 'melancholic' state of half- or semi-mourning (*demi-deuil*, as Derrida also sometimes calls it,[5] trying to capture, as is often the case in deconstruction, a kind of inhibition, arrest or interruption of what might otherwise seem to be a 'normal' teleological process pursuing its course to the end) does not in fact wait for the event of death to kick in. Rather it marks one's relation to the other *from the start*, just because the radically interruptive structure of any relation to any other is a measure of that other's very alterity.[6] My relation to the other is marked from the start by the asymmetry, distance, separation and interruption that makes ethics possible (while making any certainty that I am ever in fact behaving ethically quite impossible) as it respects precisely what makes the other other (and not me). And so one can speak of an 'originary mourning', or rather originary half-mourning or originary melancholia, as Derrida does in that last interview, an originary melancholia that then defines living itself, *vivre*, as a survival, a *survivre*, that would have a conceptual priority over one's usual (metaphysical) notions of life and death.

IV

Once we've complicated the status of the event of death in this way, with all that it entails, what is there left of the event in Derrida? What is an event worth calling an event in Derrida's work? Or, to use an idiom that returns almost obsessively in his later writing, what is an event *worthy of the name*?[7] We call all manner of things events, after all, but maybe something about why we do so can be brought out by trying to isolate the features of an event that's a *real* event, that's really worth calling an event.

One predicate Derrida insists on is this: an event worthy of the name must be radically unpredictable or unforeseeable. An event that arrives on cue, as predicted or programmed, loses its edge as an event just because you saw it coming. A real event (worthy of the name, then) seems to derive its eventhood from some quality of out-of-the-blueness. Events in this sense befall us, surprise us, don't politely announce their arrival and then arrive as announced: rather they land on us, hit us, appear out of nowhere, from above, below, from the side or from behind, rather than from up ahead. Derrida often stresses that events in this strong sense (and thereby the eventhood of events more generally, what makes events events) cannot adequately be thought of in terms of a horizon of expectation – what you see coming against the horizon is not an event (or at least, what in an event you could see coming was not its eventhood). This never-any-certainty-about-an-event means that I am never in control of it, and never sure of it, never sure it will happen. And this leads Derrida to what looks like a modulation in his thinking: from an earlier position where there was a kind of unconditional affirmation of the event in this sense, a kind of call on the event to come and happen in its unpredictability,[8] there seems to be a shift of emphasis at least to a formulation of a kind of transcendental 'perhaps-ness'. No event would not be marked by this 'perhaps-ness' of its very happening.[9]

Whence too the explicit suggestion in some of Derrida's late work that events are always in some sense *traumatic*. This is probably less a psychological remark than an attempt to borrow something of the thought that in trauma there is a kind of overwhelming of a system caught short in its preparation, something of an inability to process what befalls, advenes or supervenes – and this would be true of so-called happy events as well as unhappy ones.[10]

Some rather paradoxical consequences flow from this thought of the event (which is also an event of thought, perhaps).

1. How simple is it to think in this perspective of events happening in their place and time? If I don't, and can't see it coming, and if I can't process it in its arrival, then when exactly can it be said to happen? Freud famously used the term *Nachträglichkeit* (in an early text Derrida says that this is Freud's real discovery, though it seems clear that Freud himself did not think so: as a student of mine recently pointed out, *Nachträglichkeit* itself only became an important or even thematised concept after the event, *nachträglich*[11]) – Freud used that term to try to capture something of this structure ('deferred action' seems a poor translation of this: rather *Nachträglichkeit* seems to suggest a kind of intrinsic after-the-eventness of the event

in this sense, i.e. that of an event worthy of the name and thereby in some sense traumatic). If events are traumatic and therefore marked as events by a kind of after-the-eventness, then events in the strong sense Derrida is trying to bring out can be said to be events that don't entirely or simply happen in their happening or at the moment of their happening. In the kind of cases described by Freud, at any rate, it often makes more sense to say that the event happens as an event only in a strange kind of repetition after the event (sometimes long after the event), or at any rate that the eventhood of the event cannot be given a simple date and time, and defies simple insertion into a continuity.

2. Second paradoxical consequence. If an event worthy of the name is marked as radically unpredictable, irruptive, and not integrable into any straightforward temporal or causal continuum, then an event worthy of the name must presumably also exceed or interrupt the name and concept of event itself. Just as a singularity, if it is really to be singular, has to resist in some sense being recognised *as* a singularity (as merely an instance of the general concept of singularity), so an event should each time be a challenge to the very concept of event that we've been using more or less confidently. At which point the 'worthy of the name' part becomes complicated too – an event *really* worthy of its name would seem to have to be *so* worthy of its name that its name would no longer be so worthy of *it*. As Derrida puts it in an interview just after and about the event now known as '9/11', an event in the strong sense we have been following entails failure of comprehension and appropriation (so that an event is by definition something I don't quite understand, marked by the fact that I don't understand it), and that really ought to put questions to the concept of event itself (and by extension, perhaps, to philosophy and talk of essences and truths and concepts more generally), so that, he asks: 'Would an event that still confirmed to an essence, a law or a truth, or even to a concept of the event, be a major event? A major event ought to be unforeseeable and irruptive enough to unsettle even the horizon of the concept or the essence from which one believes one can recognize an event *as such*.'[12]

V

An event so worthy of its name that it would suggest a kind of impossibility (Derrida sometimes defines deconstruction as 'an experience of the impossible') or unthinkability (and so, I'd like to say, always a kind of unworthiness to go with its worthiness) may, in a sense, never quite *happen*. An event so 'pure' as to escape recognition altogether might not even be worth calling an event. In fact, Derrida's work, from the start, stresses an economy of the kind of pure or radical event we've been sketching with all the things that seem determined to deprive it of its eventhood. Events are always also involved in some type of repetition or repeatability, reproducibility or recognisability. A logic of the event as singularity always goes along with what Derrida also recently calls a 'logic of the machine', of mechanical repetition or reproduction.

This is of course why the kind of recuperative cultural-historical reactions to Derrida's event, with which I began, can even get started. The suspicion, however, would be that those reactions are not given sufficient pause by the eventhood of the event that I've been trying to suggest is what Derrida is trying to bring out. Repetition may be compulsive, but there's still repetition and repetition. What Derrida famously calls *iterability*, in one of his earliest explicit discussions of the event,[13] may affect the event from the start, dividing its uniqueness and giving rise to the possibility of different versions and accounts of the 'same' event, but iterability also entails alteration and difference, so that something new, a new event, also takes place in every account of an event. If we take seriously the after-the-eventness structure of *Nachträglichkeit*, then it ought perhaps to be harder than is often thought to carry on in the massively culturalist and historicist mode that is unfortunately still (and perhaps increasingly) the norm in this domain.

I'd like to suggest in conclusion that Derrida's work in general, 'deconstruction', if that's what we want to call the series of events signed with his name, consistently exhibits and performs just the kind of complex after-the-eventness that he also thematises and describes. One way of bringing this out consists in asking the question: 'When is the deconstruction?' of any of Derrida's texts. A spectacular example here is the reading of Plato published in 1972 as 'Plato's Pharmacy', in which Derrida brings out of Plato's texts a way of thinking about writing quite different from the view that Plato most obviously seems to be putting forward. Derrida is certainly not just reporting the received Platonic view and then disagreeing with it or putting forward an alternative theory – rather claiming to read in and out of Plato (perhaps *through* Plato would be a more Derridian way of describing it)[14] another way of construing writing. This 'other view' is at least as much 'in' Plato as it is 'in' Derrida. It does not seem a satisfactory description of this situation to say simply that 'Derrida deconstructs Plato' (in 1972, then), nor that 'Plato deconstructs himself' (in fifth-century BC Athens, then). Rather the event of deconstruction seems to happen disconcertingly across or between these two dates (and in fact across a wide range of intervening dates too, the whole history of the 'reception' of Plato). And this seems to be what Derrida is trying to bring out when he says in a slightly different context that 'Plato's signature is not yet complete', the event 'signed' Plato being ongoingly and more or less unpredictably countersigned by any number of subsequent events that become, after the event, components of the supposedly 'original' Plato event.[15] And it looks as though this situation can be generalised across the whole of Derrida's work, the whole of 'deconstruction' as it carries through and interrupts the 'tradition'. The undeniable event of Derrida's reading of Plato happens, then, but exactly when and where it happens is probably impossible to say, and insofar as we are still here trying to figure that out, it seems also that, like Plato's signature, the event of Derrida's reading is also not complete, but open for reading and rereading in the future. This structure of reading, which is absolutely fundamental to deconstruction, is something that cultural and historical approaches will never in principle understand.

All of which tends to dissolve or explode 'Derrida's event' into a kind of scattering or dispersion of its eventhood across a range that defies any simple accounting or accountability. The irreducible multiplicity entailed by that thought of scattering also (but that's another story I try to tell elsewhere) defines deconstruction as irreducibly 'political'. To the extent that it still seems important to gather that dispersion or scattering enough to identify a 'Derrida event' at all, we might want to say that Derrida's own work, in its constant reprises and displaced repetitions, its constant re-readings of itself, constantly tries to find ways of thinking together, in the same thought, singularity and repetition, the singular repeating as the same each time differently. Quite a good name for this might still be 'thought'. Derrida's event is an ongoing series of after-the-event reprises and iterations of an event of thought about the event and its constitutive after-the-eventness. And one thing this means is that Derrida's event never quite or entirely happened, or finished happening, and is to that extent still to come, yet to happen, here today in London, for example, and then again elsewhere, tomorrow.

Notes

1. This is an expanded version of an informal talk given in the 'For Derrida' series at the Tate Modern in London in February 2005, for the session entitled 'Derrida's Event'. Previously published in S. Glendinning and R. Eaglestone (eds), *Derrida's Legacies* (London: Routledge, 2008), pp. 26–35.

2. I reserve for a future occasion a discussion of the function of the word 'ultimately' in philosophical argument and in cultural criticism.
3. See 'A Life in Philosophy', in my *Other Analyses: Reading Philosophy* (e-book available from bennington.zsoft.co.uk), pp. 405–25, from which I excerpt a couple of pages here.
4. Jacques Derrida, *Béliers: Le dialogue interrompu entre deux infinis, le poème* (Paris: Galilée, 2003), p. 74.
5. For example in 'Circonfession' (in Bennington and Derrida, *Jacques Derrida* (Paris: Seuil, 1991)), especially period 32.
6. See most recently Derrida's clarifications in Mustapha Chérif, *L'Islam et l'Occident: Rencontre avec Jacques Derrida* (Paris/Alger: Odile Jacob/ Editions Barzakh, 2006), especially pp. 102–3 (where, however, 'rapport de nos rapports' on p. 103 is clearly a mis-transcription of 'rapport du sans-rapport'), but already 'En ce moment même dans cet ouvrage me voici' (in *Psyché: inventions de l'autre* (Paris: Galilée, 1987), pp. 159–202 (especially pp. 176–81)), and the insistent allusions to Blanchot's 'rapport sans rapport' (for example in *Parages* (Paris: Galilée, 1986), pp. 188, 207, 277), and its radicalisation as a 'sans sans sans' (ibid., p. 151).
7. I first drew Derrida's attention to his frequent use of this idiom at another event involving Simon Glendinning, namely the conference entitled 'Derrida's Arguments', held at Queen Mary, London, in 2001, explicitly following up on the 2000 University of Reading conference 'Arguing with Derrida' that Glendinning had organised. (See my ' . . . you meant', in *Other Analyses: Reading Philosophy* (op. cit.), pp. 83–94 (p. 92)). We subsequently discussed it on a number of occasions, notably at the SUNY Stony Brook '*Politics and Filiation*' conference (New York, November 2002): in *Voyous* (Paris: Galilée, 2003), p. 28, Derrida says that this is 'a turn of phrase I use so often and that will one day lead me to provide a long justification'.
8. Cf. the analyses of an irreducible affirmation preceding any possible question in, for example, *De l'esprit: Heidegger et la question* (Paris: Galilée, 1987); *Ulysse Gramophone: deux mots pour Joyce* (Paris: Galilée, 1987), and, for the 'call' on the event, Jacques Derrida, *D'un ton apocalyptique adopte naguere en philosophie* (Paris: Galilée, 1983).
9. See the analysis of the 'perhaps' in *Politiques de l'amitié* (Paris: Galilée, 1994), pp. 58ff., and the more informal presentation in the discussion with Alexander Garcia Düttman, 'Perhaps or Maybe', *PLI: Warwick Journal of Philosophy*, 6 (1997), pp. 1–18.
10. Cf. Jacques Derrida, *Papier machine: le ruban de machine à écrire et autres réponses* (Paris: Galilée, 2001), p. 114: ' . . . always essentially *traumatic*, even when it is happy: an event is always traumatic, its singularity interrupts an order and, like any decision worthy of the name, tears a normal tissue of temporality or history'.
11. Cf. 'Freud et la scène de l'écriture', in *L'ecriture et la différence* (Paris: Seuil, 1967), pp. 303, 314, 317. I am grateful to Susi Schink for pointing out to me the *nachträglich* nature of the concept of *Nachträglichkeit*.
12. Jacques Derrida and Jürgen Habermas, *Le 'concept' du 11 septembre: dialogues à New York, Octobre–Décembre 2001, Avec Giovanna Borradori* (Paris: Galilée, 2004), pp. 138–9.

13. See 'Signature, evénément, contexte', in *Marges de la philosophie* (Paris: Minuit, 1972), and more generally Jacques Derrida, *Limited Inc.* (Paris: Galilée, 1990).
14. Cf. *La voix et le phénomène* (Paris: PUF, 1967), p. 98: '*Through* [the] text, i.e. in a reading that can be neither simply that of commentary nor that of interpretation.'
15. Cf. Jacques Derrida, Claude Lévesque and Christie McDonald, *L'oreille de l'autre: otobiographies, transferts, traductions: textes et debats avec Jacques Derrida* (Montréal: VLB, 1982), p. 119.

That's Life, Death

> What laws are followed by re-naissances, re-discoveries, occultations too, the distancing or re-evaluation of a text that one would like naïvely to believe, on the faith of a signature or an institution, that it remains the same, constantly identical to itself? A 'corpus', in sum, the self-identity of which is supposedly even less threatened than that of a body proper? What must a text be if it can, of its own accord as it were, turn to shine again, after an eclipse, with a different light, at a time that is no longer that of its productive source (was it ever contemporaneous with it?), then repeat this resurgence again after several deaths including among others that of the author, and the simulacrum of a multiple extinction?[1]

> The modality of the possible, the insatiable *perhaps* would destroy everything, implacably, through a sort of auto-immunity from which no region of being, *physis* or history would be exempt. [. . .] A time said to be contemporary that would be anything but contemporary. [. . .] If it presented itself, and with some word said 'I', [this time] could only speak like a madman, and if it said it was alive, this would be perhaps again, and more probably than ever, a sign of madness.[2]

> Here: a bit *sans queue ni tête* . . .[3]

I

Talking about life here, we'll (always) be talking about life *after* . . . What kind of life is this, here and now, that we're living? Inheritance and legacy ('to be is to inherit' (*Spectres de Marx*)), mourning and melancholia (a mourning *digne du nom* would look somewhat more like melancholia than 'normal' mourning). There seems to be something very specifically *difficult* and maybe daunting in what we're doing here, in what Peggy's wonderful initiative, Michael's great idea for a subject, and the generosity of the Borchard Foundation have made possible.

Talking about Jacques Derrida and life, after his death, after his life, we're enjoined to think about this very situation in which we find ourselves *en ce moment même* . . . What kind of 'community' (lots of good Derridean reasons for scare-quotes here, especially from *Politiques de l'amitié*) do we want to be, what kind of institution is called for by what we've been reading and rereading?[4] It seems clear that if we read what JD wrote, we must read (or perhaps hear?[5]) a call to some more inventive type of being-together than is perhaps usual in academic circles. I'm sure we can all think of lots of more or less unpleasant models and examples as to what might typically happen after the death of a figure such as JD (assuming there ever was any other such figure): I am imagining that part of our task is to be smart enough to avoid simply following (or falling into) those models and examples.

It's still a new experience, at any rate, to find ourselves not only at a 'conference' (that may already be far from the right word to describe what is happening here . . .) *on* JD without JD's tutelary presence, but in the knowledge that never again will we find ourselves at a conference *with* that presence, or with that presence in quite the same way (because of course I'm sure we all feel that JD *is* nonetheless present here today, watching us in a way that is clearly different (but perhaps *economically* different, within a general spectrality) from when he was apparently more straightforwardly 'present' and able to respond). As JD himself points out in 'Devant la loi', reading the Freud of *Totem and Taboo*, the dead father may be more alive than the living father – but that might just mean that the *last* way for us to think of JD is as our father (living *or* dead). Part of our question, at any rate, must be that of life, now, as an after-life that would certainly not be inventively faithful to the legacy bequeathed to 'us' (*qui ça, nous*'?, always a good question, *n'est-ce pas*?) if we did not try to figure that after-life, our sur-vival, otherwise than in terms of the model of patrilinear descent that is at the centre of the question of life as thought by the tradition that JD will have spent forty years and more 'deconstructing'. I, for one, am hoping that we'll figure out, if only ephemerally, for these few days, some way of being together (some kind of 'New International', maybe) that will be at least attentive and responsive to everything that JD's legacy will have given us to think, and more especially given us to think *about* legacies, inheritance, and living on or survival. Maybe it would be not much of an exaggeration to say that *all of JD's work* is there to prepare us for this very moment, for which, however, it seems so hard to be prepared.

Here, for a famous example, from *Spectres de Marx*:

> An inheritance is never gathered, it is never one with itself. Its presumed unity, if there is one, can only consist in the *injunction* to *reaffirm by choosing*. *You must* [il faut] means you must filter, select, criticize; you must sort out among several of the possibilities that inhabit the same injunction. And inhabit it in contradictory fashion around a secret. If the legibility of a legacy were given, natural, transparent, univocal, if it did not simultaneously call for and defy interpretation, one would never have to inherit from it. One would be affected by it as by a cause – natural or genetic. One always inherits a secret, which says 'Read me, will you ever be up to it?' The critical choice called for by any reaffirmation of the inheritance is also, like memory itself, the condition of finitude. The infinite does not inherit, is not inherited from. The injunction itself ('choose and decide in what you inherit', it always says) can be one only by dividing, tearing itself, differing/deferring itself, speaking both several times and in several voices. (p. 40)

Will I ever be up to it? Of course not. So rather than *reading* here, I'd rather be *reading out*, happy to quote and do little more than quote (not, I think, that I ever really did anything else, even when I 'quoted' not at all . . .), and especially quote some passages I'm tempted to call 'magnificent', from texts (especially 'early' texts) that I fear are no longer being read so much these days, and that I'm anxious not be forgotten.

(For me, here, at least, this situation has seemed to bring me to something like 'childhood memories', and so I found myself ineluctably brought back to my early readings of some of JD's 'early' texts. How deconstructive is it, I can only wonder, to want to bring the whole thing back to its origins, to tend to think that it all flows in some way from an (I imagine blinding) originary moment of insight into the non-simplicity of origins . . . ? And yet, note how JD in later texts increasingly refers to, and quotes, his earlier ones. JD is a fantastic reader of what is bequeathed by the metaphysical tradition, but also of his own earlier texts. JD's work constantly loops back through itself, finding itself in itself as other than itself, re-vitalising itself, keeping itself alive (maybe re-inseminating (re-disseminating) itself?) What kind of life-form is that? In any case, rereading, it seems possible to claim, as JD often did of himself, 'La vie? Mais il n'a jamais parlé que de ça!')

II

One of our questions here might, then, be this: how are we to think of the form of 'life' that deconstruction *is*? What is at stake in saying that deconstruction is *alive* (or even, as we might wish to say, 'alive and well'?) What kind or type of *vivant* is it if it is alive? Living organism (but organisms always seem to call for teleological judgement . . . ?); *oeuvre*?;[6] *corpus*?[7]

Or maybe, more probably, the form of life that deconstruction is might be something, as in *La pharmacie de Platon* or *Donner le temps*, that would be *sans queue ni tête:*

> In order to be 'acceptable', a written discourse ought to be subjected, like living discourse itself, to the laws of life. Logographic necessity (*anankè logographikè*) ought to be analogous to biological or rather zoological necessity. Without which, of course, it has neither head nor tail. We are indeed dealing with *structure* and *constitution*, in the risk run by *logos* of losing through writing both its head and its tail. [. . .]
>
> Socrates: But here's a thing that you would at least agree to, I think: that every discourse (*logon*) must be constituted (*sunestanai*) after the fashion of a living being (*ôsper zôon*): have a body that is its own, so as to be neither without head nor without feet, but to have a middle at the same time as two ends, written so as to fit with each other and with the whole. (264 b c)[8]

And in *Donner le temps*, apparently content to quote the Baudelaire of the *Spleen de Paris*:

> To Arsène Houssaye.
>
> My dear friend, I am sending you a small work of which one could not say without doing it an injustice, that it has neither head nor tail, since the whole thing, to the contrary, is both head and tail, alternatively and reciprocally. Consider, I pray you, the admirable convenience this combination offers us all: you, me and the reader. We can cut it off where we will: me my reverie, you the manuscript, the reader his reading; for I do not suspend the latter's restive will on the interminable thread of a superfluous plot. Take out a vertebra, and the two pieces of this tortuous fantasy will join up effortlessly. Chop it into many fragments, and you will see that each can exist on its own. In the hope that some of these sections will be alive enough to please and amuse you, I dare to dedicate the whole snake to you. (Baudelaire, quoted [but with surprisingly little commentary on the 'tête' and 'queue'] in *Donner le temps*, pp. 116–17)

III

More specifically, what has to have happened to the inherited concept of 'life' (but also the concept of 'concept', *and thereby all others*) for it to have an after-life in deconstruction? What is at stake in continuing to use the language of life (and inheritance) about objects that are not 'literally' living? Whatever 'literally' means here, it looks as though we're very soon engaged in a kind of tropic or metaphorical drift (itself maybe a form of life?). This issue of literal/metaphorical senses of 'life' is itself an important part of JD's 'early' discussions: so, for example, in the 'Hors livre' section of *La dissémination*, this, on Hegel:

Engendering and enjoying itself, the concept sublates its preface and plunges into itself. The Encyclopedia gives birth to itself. The conception of the concept is an auto-insemination.[30]

This return to itself of the theological semen interiorises its own negativity and its own difference from itself. The Life of the Concept is a necessity which, by including the scatter of semen, by making it work for the profit of the Idea, excludes by the same token any loss and any chance productivity. The exclusion is an inclusion. In opposition to the seminal differance thus repressed, the truth that speaks itself in the logocentric circle is the discourse of what *returns to the father.* (See too *Donner le temps,* p. 68)

[30] [Derrida's note:] Life, an essential philosophical determination of the concept and of spirit, is necessarily described according to the general features of vegetal or biological life, the particular object of the philosophy of nature. This analogy or this metaphoricity, which poses formidable problems, is possible only according to the organicity of encyclopedic logic. Read from this point of view the analyses of the 'return to self' of the 'seed' (§347 et §348), of 'internal chance' ([. . .] §351), of 'lack' and 'copulation' (§369) and more generally of the *syllogism* of life, the life of spirit as truth and death (term) of natural life that carries in it, in its finitude, its '*originary illness* and its innate *seed* of death'. [. . .] Is the preface the *nature* of the logos? The natural life of the concept?[9]

And here too, the important discussion of the 'metaphor' of paternity in *La Pharmacie de Platon*, which is the fuller context for the 'sans queue ni tête' remarks earlier:

What we are continuing, provisionally and for convenience, to call a metaphor belongs in any case to a system. If the logos has a father, if it is a *logos* only assisted by its father, this is because it is always a being (*on*) and even a genus of being (*Sophist* I 260 a), and more precisely a living being. The *logos* is a *zoon.* This animal is born, grows, belongs to *physis.* Linguistics, logic, dialectics and zoology are hand in glove.

In describing the *logos* as a *zoon*, Plato is following certain rhetors and sophists who before him opposed to the cadaverous rigidity of writing the living speech, infallibly adjusting itself to the needs of current circumstances, the expectations and demands of the interlocutors present, sniffing out the place to present itself, pretending to bend to circumstance at the very moment it is becoming both persuasive and constraining.

The *logos*, a living and animate being, is therefore also an engendered organism. And *organism*: a *proper* differentiated body, with a centre and extremities, joints, a head and feet. In order to be 'acceptable', a written discourse ought to be subjected, like living discourse itself, to the laws of life. Logographic necessity (*anankè logographikè*) ought to be analogous to biological or rather zoological necessity. Without which, of course, it has neither head nor tail. We are indeed dealing with *structure* and *constitution*, in the risk run by *logos* of losing through writing both its head and its tail . . . [. . .]

> Like every person, the *logos-zoon* has a father.
> But what is a father?
> Should we assume that we know this and with this – known – term illuminate the other term in what it would be precipitous to describe as a metaphor? In that case one would say that the origin or cause of the *logos* is compared to what we know to be the cause of a living son, i.e. his father. One would understand or imagine the birth and the process of the *logos* on the basis of a domain foreign to it, i.e. the transmission of life or relations of generation. But the father is not the generator, the 'real' procreator before and outside any language-relation. For how is the father/son relation distinguished from the cause/effect or engenderer/engendered relation if not by the agency of the *logos*? Only a power of discourse has a father. The father is always the father of a living/speaking being. In other words, it is on the basis of the *logos* that something like paternity shows up and gives itself to be thought. If there were a simple metaphor in the expression 'father of the *logos*', the first word, which seemed the most familiar, would nonetheless receive from the second more meaning than it would transmit to it. The first familiarity always has some relation of cohabitation with the *logos*. Living beings, father and son come to us, relate to each other in the domesticity of the *logos*. From which one does not emerge, in spite of appearances, to transport oneself by 'metaphor' into a foreign domain in which one would come across fathers, sons, living beings, all sorts of convenient beings for explaining to someone who did not know, and by comparison, how it is with the *logos*, that strange thing. Although this *hearth* is the heart of all metaphoricity, 'father of the logos' is not a simple metaphor. There would be one if one were to state that a living being incapable of language, if one wanted stubbornly to go on believing in such a thing, had a father. So we must proceed to a general inversion of all the metaphorical dimensions, and not ask whether a *logos* can have a father but understand that what the father claims to father cannot go without the essential possibility of the *logos*.[10]

IV

In a slightly less obvious way, perhaps, this question of life is at the *absolute centre* of the argumentative structure of *La voix et le phénomène*, which goes something like this (quotes provided as *aides-memoires*, with crucial moments in bold):

1. **All the faults and perversions denounced by Husserl come down to a failure to appreciate the absolute originarity of the form of the 'living present' in its transcendental 'life':**

> One could bring out the unique and permanent motif of all the faults and all the perversions that Husserl denounces in "degenerate" metaphysics, across many domains, themes and arguments: it is always a blindness to the authentic mode of *ideality*, the one that is, can be, repeated indefinitely

in the *identity* of its *presence* by virtue of the fact that it *does not exist*, is not *real*, is *unreal* not in the sense of fiction but in another sense which can have many names, whose possibility will permit one to speak of the non-reality and the necessity of essence, noema, intelligible object and non-mundanity in general. As this non-mundanity is not another mundanity, and as this ideality is not an existent fallen from the sky, its origin will always be the possibility of the repetition of a productive act. In order for the possibility of this repetition to open *idealiter* to infinity, an ideal form must ensure this unity of the *indefinitely* and the *idealiter*: this is the present, or rather the presence of the *living presence*. The ultimate form of ideality, in which in the last instance one can anticipate or recall every repetition, the ideality of ideality is **the *living present*, the self-presence of transcendental life.** Presence has always been and always will be, to infinity, the form in which – one can say this apodeictically – the infinite diversity of contents will occur. The opposition – inaugural for metaphysics – between form and matter, finds in the concrete ideality of the living present its ultimate and radical justification. **We shall return to the enigma of the concept of *life* in the expressions 'living present' and 'transcendental life'.** (*La voix et le phénomène*, pp. 4–5)

2. But, wonders JD, what is the value of the term 'life' here? That is, how does transcendental (non-real, ideal) 'life' relate to 'real' life?

Ideal presence to an ideal or transcendental consciousness. Ideality is the salvation or the mastery of presence in repetition. In its purity, this presence is not the presence of anything that *exists* in the world, but is in correlation with acts of repetition that are themselves ideal. Does this mean that what opens repetition to infinity or opens to it when the movement of idealization is assured is a certain relation of an 'existent' to its death? And that 'transcendental life' is the scene of this relation? It is too soon to say. We must first pass through the problem of language. Nothing to be surprised at there: language is indeed the medium of this play of presence and absence. **Is there not in language, is language itself not first of all the very thing in which *life* and *ideality* might seem to come together?** Now we must consider the fact *on the one hand* that the element of signification – or the substance of expression – which seems best to preserve both ideality and living presence in all its forms is living speech, the spirituality of breath as *phonè*; and that, on the other hand phenomenology, a metaphysics of presence in the form of ideality, is also a philosophy of *life*.

A philosophy of life, not only because at its heart death is only granted the empirical and extrinsic signification of a mundane accident, but because the source of meaning in general is always determined as the act of a *living*, as the act of a living being, as *Lebendigkeit*. Now the unity of living, the hearth of the *Lebendigkeit* that diffracts its light in all the fundamental concepts of phenomenology (*Leben*, *Erlebnis*, *lebendige Gegenwart*, *Geistigkeit*, etc.) escapes the transcendental reduction and, as unity of mundane life and transcendental life, even clears its path. When empirical life or ever the region of the pur psychic are bracketed, it is still a transcendental *life* or in the last instance the transcendentality of a *living* present that Husserl discovers. And that he thematizes without for all that posing the question of the unity of the concept of life. The 'soul-less (*seelenloses*) consciousness', the essential possibility of which is established in *Ideas* I (§54), is nonetheless a consciousness that is transcendentally *alive*. If one were to conclude, with a gesture that is in indeed very Husserlian in its style, that the concepts of empirical (or in general mundane) life and transcendental life are radically heterogeneous and that the two nouns entertain a relation that is purely indicative or metaphorical, then it is the possibility of this relation that bears the whole weight of the question. The common root making possible all these metaphors still appears to us to be the concept of *life*. In the last instance, between the pure psychic – a region of the world opposed to transcendental consciousness and discovered by the reduction of the totality of the natural and transcendent world – and pure transcendental life, there is, says Husserl, a relation of *parallelism*. [. . .]

But the strange unity of these two parallels, what relates them the one to the other, cannot be divided by them and, dividing itself, finally welds the transcendental to its other, is *life*. One indeed notices very rapidly that the only nucleus of the concept of *psychè* is life as relation to self, be it or not in the form of consciousness. **'Living' is thus the name of what precedes the reduction and finally escapes all the divisions that it makes visible. But this is because it is its own division and its own opposition to its other.** By determining 'living' thus, we have therefore just named the resource of insecurity of the discourse, the point where, precisely, it can no longer *assure in a nuance its possibility and its rigour*. **This concept of *life* is then grasped anew in an instance that is no longer that of pre-transcendental naivety, in the language of everyday life or of biological science. But if this ultra-transcendental concept of life allows one to think life (in the common sense or the sense of biology) and if it has never been inscribed in language, perhaps calls for an *other name*.** (*La voix et le phénomène*, pp. 8–10, 14)

3. **So: the unity of (transcendental) life and (psycho-empirical) life is still provided by the concept of . . . *life,* or perhaps now 'life' or Life. But *that* concept of life is also as much its own division as its own unity. This 'ultra-transcendental'[11] sense of 'life' 'appelle peut-être un *autre nom*' . . . and my thought today would be: maybe 'auto-immunity' just is that (or one such) *autre nom,* already called for here from this 1967 text.)**

4. **If this concept of 'life' or 'living' is its own *partage* or division, this is because (jumping forward almost 50 pages):**
   (a) **of the way it relates to 'death' (mortality):**

   What is meant by the value of originary presence to intuition as the source of meaning and evidence, as *a priori* of *a prioris*? It means first of all **the certainty, itself ideal and absolute, that the universal form of all experience (*Erlebnis*) and therefore of all life, has always been and will always be the present.** There is never and there never will be anything but the present. Being is presence or modification of presence. The relation to the presence of the present as ultimate form of being and ideality is the movement whereby I transgress empirical existence, factuality, contingency, mundanity, etc. And first of all *my own.* **To think presence as the universal form of transcendental life is to open myself to the knowledge that in my absence, beyond my empirical existence, before my birth and after my death, *the present is.*** I can empty out all empirical content, imagine an absolute upheaval of the content of any possible experience, a radical transformation of the world: the universal form of presence – I have a strange and unique certainty of this since it concerns no determinate being – will not be affected by it. **It is therefore the relation to *my death* (to my disappearance in general) that is hidden in this determination of being as presence, ideality, absolute possibility of repetition. The possibility of the sign is this relation of death. The determination and effacement of the sign in metaphysics is the dissimulation of this relation to death that nevertheless produced signification.**

If the possibility of my disappearance in general must in a certain way be lived for a relation to presence in general to be able to be instituted, one can no longer say that the experience of the possibility of my absolute disappearance (of my death) comes to affect me, supervenes on an 'I am' and modifies a subject. As 'I am' is lived only as an 'I am present', it presupposes in itself the relation to presence in general, to being as presence. The appearing of the I to itself is thus originarily a relation to its own possible disappearance. **'I am' thus originarily means 'I am mortal'.** 'I am immortal' is an impossible proposition. We can then go further: as language, 'I am that I am' is the avowal of a mortal. The movement that leads from the I am to the determination of my being as *res cogitans* (and therefore as immortality), is the movement whereby the origin of presence and ideality conceals itself in the presence and ideality it makes possible. (*La voix et le phénomène*, pp. 60–1)

(b) because of the temporality of the trace:

Without reducing the abyss that might indeed separate retention from re-presentation, without hiding from the fact that **the problem of their relations is none other than that of the history of 'life' and the becoming-conscious of life,** one must be able to say *a priori* that their common root, the possibility of re-petition in its most general form, the trace in the most universal sense, is a possibility that must not only inhabit the pure actuality of the now, but constitute it through the very movement of *différance* that it introduces into it. Such a trace is, if one can use this language without immediately contradicting it and crossing it through, more 'originary' than phenomenological originarity itself. (*La voix et le phénomène*, p. 75)

And

(c) **because 'I am' makes sense only as 'I am dead':**

My death is structurally necessary to the pronouncement of the I. That I be 'living' too and certain of that fact comes on top of the fact of meaning-to-say. And this structure is active, it retains its original efficacy even when I say 'I am living' at the very moment when, if this is possible, I have the full and actual intuition of it. The *Bedeutung* 'I am' or 'I am living', or else 'my living present is', is what it is, has the ideal identity proper to every *Bedeutung,* only if it is not affected by falsehood, i.e. if I can be dead at the moment when it functions. No doubt it will be different from the *Bedeutung* 'I am dead', but not necessarily from the *fact* that 'I am dead'. **The utterance 'I am living' is accompanied by my being-dead and its possibility requires the possibility that I be dead; and conversely.** This is not an extraordinary tale by Poe, but the ordinary story of language. (*La voix et le phénomène,* p. 108)[12]

(d) **which means, among other things, that phenomenology (and thereby presumably metaphysics more generally), falls foul of an essentially paradoxical structure:**

In its ideal value, the whole system of 'essential distinctions' is therefore a purely teleological structure. By the same token, the possibility of distinguishing between sign and non-sign, linguistic sign and non-linguistic sign, expression and indication, ideality and non-ideality, subject and object, grammaticality and non-grammaticality, pure grammaticality and empirical grammaticality, pure general grammaticality and pure logical grammaticality, intention and intuition, etc. – this pure possibility is deferred to infinity. Given this, these 'essential distinctions' are caught in the following aporia: *de facto, realiter*, they are never respected, as Husserl recognizes. *De jure* and *idealiter*, they efface themselves because they live, as distinctions, only on the difference between right and fact, ideality and reality. Their possibility is their impossibility.

But how is this difference given to be thought? What does 'to infinity' mean here? What does presence as differance to infinity mean? What does the life of the living present mean as differance to infinity?

The fact that Husserl always thought of infinity as an Idea in the Kantian sense, as the indefiniteness of an *ad infinitum*, makes one think that he never *derived* difference from the plenitude of a parousia, the full presence of a positive infinite; that he never believed in the accomplishment of an 'absolute knowledge' as self-presence of an infinite concept in the Logos. And what he shows us as to the movement of temporalisation leaves no doubt about this: although he did not thematise 'articulation', the 'diacritical' work of difference in the constitution of meaning and sign, he deeply recognized its necessity. And yet the whole discourse of phenomenology is caught, as we have amply seen, in the schema of

> a metaphysics of presence that tirelessly exhausts itself deriving difference. Within this schema, Hegelianism appears to be more radical: most notably at the point at which it shows that the positive infinite must be thought (which is possible only if it thinks *itself*) for the indefinity of differance to appear *as such*. Hegel's critique of Kant would no doubt work against Husserl too. But this appearing of the Ideal as infinite differance can only happen in a relation to death in general. Only a relation to my-death can bring out the infinite differance of presence. By the same token, compared to the ideality of the positive infinity, this relation to my-death becomes an accident of finite empiricity. **The appearing of infinite differance is itself finite. At which point differance, which is nothing outside this relation, becomes the finitude of life as essential relation to self as to one's death. *Infinite differance is finite.* One can no longer think it in the opposition of finity and infinity, of absence and presence, of negation and affirmation.** (*La voix et le phénomène*, p. 114)

('La différance infinie est finie':[13] why? Because *infinite* 'différance' would be presence again . . .

Compare in the *Grammatologie*:

> The subordination of the trace to full presence resumed in the logos, the abasement of writing below a speech dreaming of its plenitude, these are the gestures required by an onto-theology determining the archeological and teleological meaning of being as presence, as parousia, as **life without differance: another name for death, the historial metonymy in which the name of God keeps death at bay.** (*De la grammatologie*, p. 104)

and:

> This whole structure appears as soon as a society begins to live as a society, i.e. from the origin of life in general, when, at very heterogeneous levels of organization and complexity, it is possible to *defer presence*, i.e. *expenditure* or consumption, and to organize production, i.e. the *reserve* in general. This happens well before the appearance of writing in the narrow sense, but it is true, and one cannot neglect this fact, that the appearance of certain writing systems, three or four thousand years ago, is an extraordinary leap in the history of life. The more extraordinary for the fact that, at least during these few millennia, no noteworthy change in the organism went along with this prodigious increase in the power of differance. **It is precisely what is proper to the power of differance to modify life less and less as it expands. If it became infinite – which its essence excludes *a priori* – life itself would be returned to an impassive, intangible and eternal presence: infinite differance, God or death.** (*De la grammatologie*, pp. 190–1))

I want to say that this general argument is *already* the whole structure of (auto-)immunity, 'life' mutating into an *economie de la mort,* something that calls for that *autre nom* . . . .

> Death is the movement of differance insofar as it is necessarily finite. Which means that differance makes possible the opposition of presence and absence. Without the possibility of differance, the desire for presence as such would have no room to breathe. This means by the same token that this desire bears within itself its destiny as non-fulfillment. **Differance produces what it forbids, makes possible the very thing it makes impossible.** (*De la grammatologie*, p. 206)

V

We could illustrate at much greater length still the insistence of these motifs in all the 'early' texts. Life is an 'economy of death' because otherwise life *just is* (immediately or *ipso facto*) death. Life as either complete self-enclosure or as complete exposure is just death. So life begins by *dying a little* so as not to just *die immediately*. Some kind or some measure of death protects life from life itself, i.e. from death. If we had time, I'd quote at even greater length from the *Grammatologie* (and especially pp. 326, 344, 347–8, 388 and 411); or still more from 'La Pharmacie de Platon' (and more especially the great passage on pp. 165–7 which picks up from the filiation language and does a reading of democracy and its relations to *différance* and writing that is already close to 'Voyous'); from 'Freud et la scène de l'écriture', or from 'Spéculer – sur "Freud"' on an originary death constituting life as life in its essential finitude. Metaphysical life/death *mutates* into deconstructive life-death.

VI

I'd like to think that this at least sketches the 'genealogy' of the later 'auto-immunity'. (Of course, if the deconstruction of the metaphysics of presence necessarily passes through the deconstruction of the unity and coherence of the concept of 'life', and accessorily of all the attendant metaphorics of *logos* and paternity, and eventually fraternity too (*Politiques de l'amitié*), then I can't really say 'genealogy' here . . .) So I probably want to say that 'auto-immunity' would be the latest in the sequence of 'non-synonymic substitutions' that began with terms like *différance*, dissemination, trace, *pharmakon*, and so on.

With maybe this difference . . . The 'early' work did its deconstructive thing by apparently playing previously devalued terms (most obviously 'writing') against what metaphysics seemed most clearly to want to value (most obviously 'presence', but in this context also essentially 'life'). If there were a 'turn' in JD's work, might it not be towards a kind of 'retrieval' (not a resurrection, at any rate) of some of the terms that metaphysics had seemed to appropriate? So just as the 'Envois' to *La carte postale* say that JD really was only interested in voice and presence, just as 'experience' returns as a valorised term after the quite severe mise-en-garde in the *Grammatologie*, so the later work might make it clear that the deconstruction of life is nonetheless done *in the name* of life, and more especially in the name of a *life worthy of its name*. A life worthy of the name would have to be not only involved in the economy of death that the 'early' texts elaborate, but would, more especially, have to be 'open' (i.e. *alive*) to the event of the other in the radical sense of event that the later work spends a lot of time describing. So the deconstruction of life leads nonetheless to something like an affirmation of life, or an affirmation *in the name of life*.

And indeed this seems pretty clear in the second essay in *Voyous*:

> It is reason that puts reason into crisis, in autonomous and quasi-auto-immunitary fashion. One could show that the ultimate 'reason', in the sense of cause or foundation, the *raison d'être* of this transcendental phenomenological auto-immunity, is to be found lodged in the very structure of the present and of life, in the temporalisation of what Husserl calls the Living Present (*die lebendige Gegenwart*). The Living Present occurs only by altering and dissimulating itself. I do not have the *time* precisely, to go down this route but I wanted to mark its necessity, where the question of becoming and therefore of the time of reason appears indissociable from the immense, old and entirely new question of life (*bios* ou *zoe*), at the heart of question of Being, of presence and beings, therefore of the 'being and time' question, of *Sein und Zeit* – a question with the accent this time placed on the side of life rather than the side of death, if, as I am tempted to think, that still makes any difference. (*Voyous*, pp. 178–9)

However thoroughly the terms life and death have been mixed up together, then, something still seems to emerge from that mix on the side of life, as it were, something that's different from what emerges on the side of death. That something seems to be along the lines of: that something always might happen is a good; that nothing ever could happen is bad. That the possibility of the event (an event worthy of the name) be held open, *whatever that event may be*, is unconditionally 'good'. And this is apparently why, in spite of some appearances in Derrida's later work, 'auto-immunity' as the very structure of deconstructed life, or at least as a kind of radical possibility 'before' any 'actual' auto-immune phenomenon, cannot be all bad:

> If an event worthy of the name is to happen, it must, beyond all mastery, affect a passivity. It must touch an exposed vulnerability, without absolute immunity, without indemnity, in its finitude and in non-horizontal fashion,

> where it is not yet or no longer possible to face up to, to put up a front, to the unforeseeability of the other. In this respect, auto-immunity is not an absolute evil. It allows exposure to the other, to *what* is coming and *who* is coming – and must therefore remain incalculable. Without auto-immunity, with absolute immunity, nothing would ever happen. One would no longer wait, expect, each other, or any event. (*Voyous*, p. 210)

To say that 'l'auto-immunité n'est pas un mal absolu' seems, however 'negative' some of its later characterisations in terms of cruelty or suicide, to be a complex gesture to say the least. It may be that, as *Foi et savoir* seems to suggest, auto-immunity has something to do with what Kant calls 'radical evil': but on a Derridean construal, radical evil may well be radical, but is not so much evil as the positive condition, the *chance* of the good in an ethical sense. Whence, I think, the insistence on 'pervertibility' rather than 'perversion' at certain points. Always-necessarily-pervertible (following the general logic from, say *Limited Inc*, on the necessary possibility of mis-), is the positive condition of the chance of the ethical.

VII

Final (or always only penultimate) thought. It seems to me to be no accident that these formulations are always and everywhere struggling with teleological structures – exemplarily at the end of *La voix et le phénomène*, and elsewhere in the repeated discussions of the 'Idea in the Kantian sense' (most recently the *mise au point* in *Voyous*), which begins with a curious gesture:

> The fact remains that, for want of something better [*faute de mieux*], if one can say 'for want of something better' of a regulative Idea, the regulative Idea remains perhaps an ultimate reserve. This last resort might well run the risk of becoming an alibi, but it retains a dignity. I would not swear that I never give in to it. (*Voyous*, p. 122)

'Une ultime réserve'. What would it mean for the 'ultimate' itself to be of the order of a *reserve*? And for that 'ultime réserve' to be of the order of *dignity*? I'm guessing that this would be the place to look into JD's very insistent and (for me at least) enigmatic use of the idiom 'digne de ce nom'.[14] I want to say that 'auto-immunity' is an attempt to capture a structure whereby a teleological tendency (drive? urge? movement?), here registered in the refusal of a *simple* refusal of the Idea-in-the-Kantian-sense, is registered *in its very inhibition* or holding short of itself. This is, I think, the sense of the 'infinite différance is finite' remark in *La voix et le phénomène*, and the glosses in the *Grammatologie* to the effect that *différance* cannot by definition be or become infinite. 'Life', on this suggestion, would be described as an inhibited tendency towards an *autos* or *ipse* that would, however, if achieved, be the end of life. The 'auto-' in auto-affection, auto-nomie, auto-biography would then be affected by a +R effect, part of the hospitality of the host to the guest or the ghost: *autro-affection*, *autro-nomy*, *autro-biography*. With this effect, auto-affection is *already* auto-immunity. And even *autro-immunity*.

> Now auto-affection is a universal structure of experience. Any living being has the power of auto-affection. And only a being capable of symbolizing, i.e. of auto-affecting itself, can let itself be affected by the other in general. Auto-affection is the condition of an experience in general. This possibility – another name for 'life' – is a general structure articulated by the history of life and giving rise to complex and hierarchized operations. Auto-affection, the as-for-oneself or the for-oneself, subjectivity gains in power and mastery of the other as its power of repetition becomes idealized. Idealization is here the movement by which sensory exteriority, the one that affects me or serves me as a signifier, subjects itself to my power of repetition, to what from then on appears to me as my spontaneity and escapes me less and less [. . .]. Auto-affection constitutes the same (*auto*) by dividing it. (*De la grammatologie*, pp. 236–7)

And that's life, death.

Notes

1. Jacques Derrida, 'Qual Quelle: les sources de Valéry', in *Marges de la philosophie* (Paris: Minuit, 1972), pp. 325–63 (p. 331).
2. *Politiques de l'amitié* (Paris: Galilée, 1994), p. 94.
3. This text was distributed, along with those of the other participants, in advance of a small three-day seminar organised by Peggy Kamuf and funded by the Borchard Foundation, entitled (on Michael Naas's suggestion) 'Jacques Derrida and the Question of Life', Château de la Bretesche, France, in July 2005. The point of the papers presented was as much to lay out some materials for discussion as to make an argument. The other participants were Thomas Dutoit, Marian Hobson, Peggy Kamuf, Elissa Marder, Ginette Michaud, Michael Naas, Elizabeth Rottenberg, Nicholas Royle, Elisabeth Weber and David Wills.
4. Cf. 'Mochlos, ou le conflit des facultés', in *Du droit à la philosophie* (Paris: Galilée, 1990), pp. 397–438 (p. 422), and 'Ulysse gramophone: l'oui-dire de Joyce', in *Ulysse gramophone: deux mots pour Joyce* (Paris: Galilée, 1987), pp. 94ff. for the argument that all texts call for an institution devoted to their interpretation.
5. Cf. 'Introduction' to Edmund Husserl, *L'origine de la géométrie* (Paris: Presses Universitaires de France, 1961), p. 155: 'The Idea is that on the basis of which a phenomenology establishes itself in order to accomplish

the final intention of philosophy. The fact that a phenomenological determination of the Idea is henceforth radically impossible perhaps means that phenomenology cannot reflect itself as a phenomenology of phenomenology, and that its *Logos* can never appear as such, never give itself to a philosophy of seeing, but only, as with any Speech, to be heard through the visible. The *Endstiftung* of phenomenology, its ultimate critical jurisdiction, the thing that tells it its meaning, its value and its rights, is thus never directly within the scope of a phenomenology. At least it can give access to itself in a philosophy to the extent that it *announces itself* in a concrete phenomenological self-evidence, in a concrete *consciousness* that makes itself *responsible* for it in spite of its finitude, and insofar as it grounds a transcendental historicity and intersubjectivity. Husserlian phenomenology sets off from this *anticipation lived* as a radical responsibility. This does not seem to be literally the case with Kantian critique'; and ibid., p. 156, n. 2: 'Husserl rigorously distinguishes the *Idea* from the *eidos* (cf. *Ideas* . . . I, Introduction). The Idea, then, *is* not the essence. Whence the difficulty – already pointed out – of an *intuitive grasp* and an *evidence* of what is neither a being nor an essence. But one must also say of the Idea that it *has no* essence, for it is only the opening of the horizon for the appearance and determination of any essence at all. As the invisible condition of *evidence*, it loses, while saving *sight*, the reference to *seeing* implied by the *eidos*, a notion from which is nonetheless comes, in its mysterious Platonic heart. The Idea can only be *heard*.'

6. On the notion of the *œuvre*, cf. in *Voyous*, on *Being and Time*: 'One must think the event otherwise to welcome into thought and history such a "work" [« œuvre »]. *Sein und Zeit* seems to belong neither to science, to philosophy or poetics. Maybe this is the case for any *œuvre* worthy of the name: what puts thought to work [*en œuvre*] in it exceeds its own frontiers or what it itself proposes to show of them. The work gets outside itself, overflows the limits of the concept of itself that it claims to have properly of itself as it presents itself. But if the event of this work thus exceeds its own frontiers, i.e. those that its concept seems to give itself – for example those of an existential analytic of *Dasein* in the transcendental horizon of time – it does so in that place wherein it *faces the test of aporias*, and perhaps of its premature interruption, its very prematuration' (*Voyous* (Paris: Galilée, 2008), pp. 64–5). Or, in *Papier machine*: ' . . . I insist in this seminar [on *pardon*, *perjury*, and *capital punishment*], on a certain irreducibility of the *work* [*l'œuvre*]. As possible inheritance of what is initially an event, the work has a virtual future only by surviving its signature and cutting itself from its supposedly responsible signatory. It *thus* presupposes, however implausible this may appear, that a logic of the machine go along with a logic of the event' (*Papier machine: le ruban de machine à écrire et autres réponses* (Paris: Galilée, 2001), p. 38).
7. Cf. especially in *Marges*, and more especially still 'La mythologie blanche': 'The names we have just associated show this clearly and, what is more, the divisions to be defined or maintained pass inside discourses signed with a single name. A new determination of the unity of corpuses ought to precede or accompany the elaboration of these questions' (p. 255); 'Through an empiricist and impressionist precipitation towards supposed differences, in

fact towards divisions that are in principle linear and chronological, one seems to go from discovery to discovery. A rupture under every step! For example, one might present as the physiognomy proper to the rhetoric of the 18th Century a set of features (such as the privilege of the noun) which are inherited, although not in a straight line, with all sorts of discrepancies and inequalities in the transformation, from Aristotle or the Middle Ages. We are here brought back to the program, which is entirely still to be worked out, of a new delimitation of corpuses and a new problematic of signatures' (p. 275: clearly with Foucault in mind); 'This implies that one critique *both* the model of the transcendental history of philosophy and that of systematic structures perfectly closed on their technical and synchronic arrangements (heretofore only recognized in corpuses identified by the proper name of a signature)' (p. 304); 'If one tried for example to fix the diagram of the metaphorics proper (or supposedly proper) to Descartes, even supposing, *concesso non dato*, that one can rigorously delimit the metaphorical corpus coming under this signature alone . . . ' (p. 318). See too the remarks on Rousseau in the *Grammatologie*, e.g. p. 231.

8. *La dissémination* (Paris: Seuil, 1972), pp. 89–90. And, a little later in the same text: 'This parricide, which opens the play of difference and writing, is a fearful decision. Even for an anonymous Stranger. It requires superhuman strength. And one must risk madness or risk passing as mad in the wise and sensible society of grateful sons. And so the Stranger is still afraid of not having the strength, of playing the fool, of course, but also of holding a discourse that would be genuinely without head nor tail; or else, if you like, to start out down a road he could only walk down on his head. This parricide, in any case will be as decisive, cutting and fearsome as capital punishment. With no hope of going back. In it, one is playing – if one wishes to give it this name – for one's head at the same time as the head of state [le chef]' (*La dissémination*, pp. 190–1). There would be a lot more to say about this figure of the *Etranger,* of course, also in the work on hospitality.
9. *La dissémination*, p. 56.
10. *La dissémination*, pp. 89–91.
11. On the 'ultra-transcendental' see too *De la grammatologie* (Paris: Minuit, 1972), p. 90: 'For there is, we think, a this side and a beyond of transcendental critique. Seeing to it that the beyond does not return to the this side involves the recognition, in contortion, of the necessity of a crossing. This crossing must leave a wake in the text. Without this wake, abandoned to the simple content of its conclusions, the ultra-transcendental text will always look just like the pre-critical text.'
12. Cf. too in 'Signature, événement, contexte': 'All writing must therefore, in order to be what it is, be able to function in the radical absence of any empirically determined addressee in general. And this absence is not a continuous modification of presence, it is a rupture of presence, the "death" or possibility of the "death" of the addressee inscribed in the structure of the mark (this is the point, I note in passing, at which the value or the "effect" of transcendentality is necessarily bound to the possibility of writing and death thus analysed)' (*Marges de la philosophie*, p. 375). Or, from the *Grammatologie*: 'Now spacing as writing is the becoming-absent and the

becoming-unconscious of the subject. Through the movement of its drift, the emancipation of the sign constitutes in return the desire for presence. This becoming – or this drift – does not supervene on the subject either choosing it or letting itself be passively drawn into it. **As relation of the subject to its death, this becoming is the very constitution of subjectivity. At all levels of organization of life, i.e. of the *economy of death*. Every grapheme is essentially testamentary.** And the original absence of the subject of writing is also that of the thing or the referent' (*De la grammatologie*, pp. 100–1, my emphasis).

13. On the understanding of this sentence, see also 'Handshake', below.
14. I first drew JD's attention to his use of this locution at the Queen Mary conference, London, in March 2000 (see my ' . . . you meant', in *Other Analyses*, which is essentially a commentary on §38 of *Foi et savoir*). He subsequently sent me some notes he had made on the question, and the issue was the subject of conversations between us at the SUNY Stony Brook 'Politics and Filiation' conference in November 2002, and at another Queen Mary event (on the occasion of JD's receiving an honorary doctorate) in July 2004.

Handshake

> 'I used to be a mason, but I canna mind the grips.' (Para Handy, Master Mariner)

What kind of greeting does Derrida give to his friend Jean-Luc Nancy in *Le Toucher, Jean-Luc Nancy*?[1] What kind of address, salutation, salute and welcome? There is of course the slightly lurid dream Derrida reports of kissing Nancy on the mouth (*Le Toucher*, p. 339). We could also easily imagine something involving hugging, cheek-kissing and possibly some back-slapping, a classic French *accolade fraternelle,* although the blurb for this conference invites us – I'm afraid I might not manage this – to think 'beyond the intimacy of the fraternal relation between Derrida and Nancy'. There is also a strange passage in *Le toucher* that, perhaps inadvertently, Derrida repeats *in extenso* and almost unchanged (pp. 125 and 160) in which he reflects dialogically on the strangeness of his own gesture, of his own 'drôle de salut', the first time because it looks as though he is trying to render the whole vocabulary of touch useless or forbidden, the second, slightly modified and expanded version, because it looks as though he is trying to reappropriate that vocabulary for the tradition or for a filiation, or to cordon it off in that tradition as though it were a principle of contamination or even a virus.[2] So, for now at least, rather than jumping straight into the complexities of that configuration, trying as usual to keep things simple, as simple as possible, let's just start by imagining them doing that very French thing: exchanging (if 'exchange' is the appropriate verb here, which I doubt) – exchanging or giving each other [*se donnant*] a handshake.

A handshake is of course not a simple thing, either historically or phenomenologically. Somewhere between the 'blow' and the 'caress' that will occupy Derrida later in *Le Toucher*, supposedly a gesture of trust and confidence, whereby I extend my empty right hand (usually the right hand) toward the other's empty right hand, originally it would appear as proof that it is not holding a weapon, but which I then still use, in the very clasp and shake (if there is a shake: in French one does not 'shake' hands (though my hand may of course shake with fear or anxiety as I extend it toward yours), one 'squeezes' or 'clasps' hands or even gets a fistful of hand [*serrer la main à quelqu'un*; *une poignée de main*]) – which I might still then use somewhat as a weapon, perhaps trying to intimidate my interlocutor by the firmness of my grasp, while simultaneously measuring it against the firmness of his (usually his: the paradigmatic handshake of course takes place between two men).[3] Not a simple thing, then, a handshake, as rapidly becomes clear from any self-help manual for businessmen (of the type one sees being read in planes by those businessmen still unsuccessful enough to be travelling economy, back with the academics, who then surreptitiously try to read their self-help manuals). The site askmen.com, for example, distinguishes between the 'wet' handshake (referring to sweaty or clammy palms, which apparently are a widespread problem and do not go down at all well in the business world), the 'softy' handshake (elsewhere referred to as the 'wet fish' or 'dead fish', perhaps a little like the handshake of the Autodidacte in Sartre's *La Nausée*, the hand like 'a fat white worm' (*Livre de poche*, p. 14)),[4] the 'tipsy finger' handshake (prissily squeezing the fingers rather than getting a good virile palm grip), the 'squeeze' grip (sometimes known, I believe, as the 'bonecrusher') and the 'homey' grip, which seems to refer to a variety of more or less showy, exotic, acrobatic or merely complex handshakes, apparently best avoided in the boardroom.[5] This last category, like the supplementary signifier in Levi-Strauss (or perhaps one of the entries in Borges's Chinese encyclopaedia),[6] is really a placeholder for *all the rest*, all the other possibilities, the 'etc.'s that the rest of the classification has not exhausted. (So other sources, for example, make a separate category for the 'glove' handshake, when one of the shakers uses both hands to enclose the one hand of the other, whereas we assume that the 'glove' is simply part of the 'homey' category in the askmen.com classification I have taken as my guide, and others still distinguish a kind of handshake called the 'pumper', enthusiastically moving the hand some distance up and down several times.) This remainder or 'reste', as usual, rapidly also opens abyssally onto the world of the secret, here secret handshakes and signs of recognition, secret signs exchanged, perhaps openly, but all the more secretly for that fact, conspiratorial possibilities opened behind a gesture which is, after all, one of *closure*[7] as much as one of opening. By definition, I cannot tell you the meaning of secret handshakes *in general*: we can never tell for sure whether a secret has or has not been exchanged in a handshake that happens in plain view, and in shaking hands neither of us could ever know for certain whether a secret has in fact been transmitted or failed to be received. But insofar as some secrets can be and have been revealed or unveiled (in at least a formal sense, so that I can know something of the secret even if I still don't know exactly what the secret is), we might look briefly at an example from a 'well-known' repertoire of secret handshakes, or grips, namely that of the freemasons. Here for example:

> The hand is taken as in an ordinary hand shake, and the Mason presses the top of his thumb against the space between the first and second knuckle joints of the first two fingers of his fellow Mason; the fellow Mason also presses his thumb on the corresponding part of the first Mason's hand.
>
> The name of this grip is 'Shibboleth'. When a candidate is imparted with this grip and its usage it is done in this manner:
>
> First, the Worshipful Master says to the candidate:
>
> 'I now present my right hand in token of the continuance of friendship and brotherly love, and will invest you with the pass-grip, pass-word, real grip and word of a Fellow Craft. As you are uninstructed, he who has hitherto answered for you, will do so at this time. Give me the grip of an Entered Apprentice.'
>
> As previously explained from the Entered Apprentice degree, he then has this exchange with the Senior Deacon, who is standing next to the candidate, who is still kneeling at the altar, after having assumed the obligation of this degree):
>
> WM: Brother Senior Deacon.
> SD: Worshipful Master.
> WM: Will you be off or from?
> SD: From.
> WM: From what and to what?
> SD: From the grip of an Entered Apprentice to the pass-grip of a Fellow Craft.
> *(At this time, the candidate is shown the Pass Grip)*
> WM: Pass. What is that?
> SD: The pass-grip of a Fellow Craft.
> WM: Has it a name?
> SD: It has.
> WM: Will you give it to me?
> SD: I did not so receive it; neither will I so impart it.
> WM: How will you dispose of it?
> SD: Letter or syllable it.
> WM: Syllable it and begin.
> SD: You begin.
> WM: Begin you.
> SD: Shib

> WM: bo
> SD: leth
> WM: Shibboleth, my Brother, is the name of this grip. You should always remember it, for should you be present at the opening of a Fellow Crafts Lodge, this pass-word will be demanded of you by one of the Deacons, and should you be unable to give it, it would cause confusion in the Craft.[8]

'Shibboleth is the name of this grip', although it would seem that the *pronouncing* of the word 'shibboleth', which is of course a word made for pronouncing if ever there were one, is reserved for this occasion of initiation, and prepared by the syllabic version of it (other such names are first given backwards or in some other order) when the candidate is 'imparted' with his grip: and one might imagine that a tendency to speak the name of the grip when performing it might undermine its purpose as a discreet sign of mutual recognition between masons when among non-masons.

'Shibboleth', to be distinguished from other more or less complex and unpronounceable grips, such as the 'Boaz', 'Jachin', the 'Tubalcain' or the 'Ma-Ha-Bone'.

* * *

In *Le Toucher*, among those apparently more exciting forms of contact, such as kissing or the mysterious touching of eyes that opens the book, Derrida mentions the handshake in the course of the *Tangente* devoted to Merleau-Ponty (the central section of the book, and the longest of the five *tangentes*). In a footnote, he points out that 'Just as he [. . .] denies any anthropological presupposition, Merleau-Ponty everywhere accords an exemplary importance to the experience that consists in shaking [*serrer*] the other's hand', and goes on to point out that this is a culturally limited 'ritual gesture', presumably thus casting doubt on its general phenomenological pertinence. This note is provoked by a passage from Merleau-Ponty which presents itself as a reading of Husserl, and which, as is the rule in Derrida's relatively few explicit discussions of Merleau-Ponty, Derrida will suggest is a misreading,[9] even though (or perhaps especially because) one might be tempted to see in Merleau-Ponty's apparent attention to a certain implication of alterity within the selfsame a gesture of thought that would be at least Derrida-friendly, worthy of some kind of acknowledgement or *salut*, perhaps itself in the form of a handshake.

Put briefly, the point of contention is this: Merleau-Ponty argues, with explicit and apparently precise reference to Husserl, including page-references and words in German, for a kind of continuity between the experience in which I touch one of my hands with the other (this moment of the *touchant-touché* having become a kind of Merleau-Pontyan signature, although it is first discussed, and at some length, by Husserl himself),[10] and the experience in which I shake another's hand. In Merleau-Ponty's phrase here quoted by Derrida (from 'Le philosophe et son ombre'), '*Ce n'est pas autrement* que le corps d'autrui s'anime devant moi, quand je serre la main d'un autre homme ou quand seulement je le regarde' [It is not otherwise that the body of another person comes to life before me, when I shake another man's hand or when I merely look at him]. So do I experience the other (in the handshake) the same way I experience myself (when I touch my right hand with my left), or do I experience myself (when I touch my right hand with my left) the way I experience the other (in the handshake)? These apparently symmetrical options and the ways in which they are not in fact entirely symmetrical will become the difficulty that is here concentrated in the handshake as a kind of *shibboleth* between phenomenology and deconstruction.

Derrida wants to make two moves in this situation, in a way that seems entirely characteristic: first, to re-establish a more accurate, even rather literal, reading of the Husserl passage to which Merleau-Ponty is rather ostentatiously referring; and then on the basis of that to propose what he thinks is a more radical or irreducible version of the self–other relation here being described by Merleau-Ponty. The first move is dictated in part by 'a concern for philological integrity or discipline', but also because of what Derrida calls 'some of its paradoxical and typical consequences' (p. 216). The thought seems to go something like this: Husserl could never have agreed that 'ce n'est pas autrement' in the experience of the *touchant-touché* and that of the other man's hand, just because I have a relation to my own body (and hand), as indeed does the other to *his* own body and hand, that is in some sense immediate and 'without introjection', as Husserl puts it: but my access to the other always and irreducibly has to go via introjection and appresentation. Derrida has always been impressed by Husserl's insistence on the fact that any access I might claim to have to the other is *always* of this appresentative nature, that there is a really radical interruption which just is the structure of the alterity of the other, an interruption without which there simply would be no other and therefore no possibility of a relation to him (her, it . . . : for the intrinsic non-humanity or ahumanity of the other in 'its' alterity is provided for by this same structure).[11] What looked as though it might be a 'Derrida-friendly' gesture on Merleau-Ponty's part, in that it seemed to suggest that there was a kind of similarity or continuity between on the one hand the kind of access I have to my own embodied self (through the experience of one hand touching the other), and the kind of access I have to the other (through the experience of shaking his hand), turns out, 'paradoxically' but 'typically' (both Derrida's words here), to end up comforting and supporting the sameness of the same, allowing in something that might look like alterity, but doing so in such a way that that alterity is always in fact on the way to being subsumed under a sameness. This is an absolutely fundamental point in Derrida's work in general, and engages a sort of 'less is more' logic that is one of the features that distinguish deconstructive from dialectical thought. Here is how he puts it in *Le Toucher*:

> Typical because [these consequences] have often given rise to similar gestures, especially in France. Paradoxical because, just when they send Husserl in the direction of taking the other into account more audaciously (of an other originarily in me or for me, etc.), to the detriment of a Husserl who is more classical, more egocentered, etc., one runs the risk of arriving at exactly the opposite result. One runs the risk of reconstituting an intuitionism of immediate access to the other, as originary as my access to my most proper proper – and by the same token, doing without appresentation, indirection, *Einfühlung*, one also runs the risk of *reappropriating* the alterity of the other more certainly, more blindly and even more violently that ever. In this respect, Husserl's prudence will always remain *before us*, as a model of vigilance. One must watch over the alterity of the other: it will always remain inaccessible to an originary presentive intuition [*intuition donatrice*], to an immediate and direct presentation of the *here*. (p. 191)

Derrida's measured defence of Husserl on this point (and, as usual, it *is* only a measured defence, because as Derrida also says on this same page, this thought of the radically-only-appresentational status of the other is difficult for phenomenology itself 'to assimilate to its intuitionist "principle of principles"', and is indeed a kind of ongoing internal ruin of phenomenology) – this measured defence can be seen to communicate with more obviously Derridean themes in the immediately following paragraph, because this structure of the alterity of the other as thought in terms of a radical interruption with respect to all my powers of presentation or intuition just is the structure of what we are familiar with Derrida calling elsewhere 'originary mourning' or, as he does here, 'pre-originary mourning', i.e. the structure whereby the other is, structurally speaking, even when alive, already in a relation to death as part of his (her or its) alterity. And this seems even to have given a certain principle to Derridean ethics, around a refusal of the supposedly normal structure of mourning, the work of mourning as 'normally' and normatively conceived, and gives it a character that one might be more tempted to associate with melancholia:

> If I have often spoken on this matter of pre-originary mourning, linking this motif to that of an *ex-appropriation*, this was to mark the fact that in this mourning before death, interiorisation, and even the introjection that is often granted to normal mourning, *cannot and should not* [or must not: *ne peut pas et ne doit pas*, my emphasis on this crucial point of what I call interrupted teleology] be accomplished. Mourning as impossible mourning. And, moreover, a-human, more than human, pre-human, other than the human 'in' the human of humanism [*humainisme* for the *main*, the hand]. Well, in spite of all the differences that separate the discourse I am holding at the moment from a Husserlian-style discourse, and doubtless too the great mountain-ranges of phenomenology, I find that it has more affinity with the discourse that Husserl obstinately maintains on the subject of appresentation (and that I am tempted to extend and radicalize, at the price of the necessary displacements, but this is not the place to insist on this), then with the discourse of a *certain* Merleau-Ponty: the one whose *typical* gesture at least we are following here – typical because it recurs often in his work and in that of others even if, whence my respectful prudence, it is far from exhausting or even dominating his thought through and through. (pp. 218–19; see too the explicit association with melancholia in *Béliers*)[12]

[Parenthetical 'methodological' remark: this is also a 'typical gesture' on Derrida's part. Identifying and formalising a 'typical gesture' (even if this is not always what he calls it) in the text being read (what he famously calls Saussure's 'propos déclaré', for example, as opposed to 'un autre geste'; or what he says Rousseau *voulait dire*, even if Rousseau also says more or something other than that) – this gesture, 'typical' of Derrida, is also what regularly provokes protests from his readers (Paul De Man a propos of Rousseau; Barbara Johnson a propos of Lacan; Gillian Rose or Slavoj Žižek a propos of Hegel; I imagine any number of phenomenologists here a propos of Merleau-Ponty) on the grounds that Derrida is somehow in so doing limiting the author concerned to this typicality which is, after all, simply the most obvious or surface aspect of the text, and saving for himself the credit for more complex insights that, so the reproach goes, are really already 'in' the author concerned. There are several ways to respond to this widespread (indeed 'typical') objection, which is in principle *the* objection of hermeneutics to deconstruction. (1) Derrida in fact reserves no credit at all for himself, and regularly finds deconstructive insights in the texts he is reading (so, for example, the whole of deconstruction may be said to be 'in' Plato when Plato is read a certain way, against the grain of Platonism, for example, as in 'La Pharmacie de Platon'). (2) But this apparent 'credit' given to the text of the other also involves the necessity of an activity of *reading* that draws from that text (through the operation of what Derrida famously in *La voix et le phénomène* says is no longer of the order of commentary nor that of interpretation (p. 98)) material that its signatory never signed (and perhaps never would sign), through the counter-signing operation in which 'counter' has a sense of contestation as much as of endorsement, and which must in principle break the horizons of hermeneutics in an operation I have been tempted on occasion to call 'pure reading'. As always in Derrida, this 'methodological' remark is not to be separated from the 'substance' of his thought (and this inseparability already in fact flows from the apparently methodological remark itself): here, for instance, just the insistence on the irreducibly appresentative relation to the other as a condition of the other's alterity, the very fact, explicitly thematised here, that I cannot directly intuit the other *qua* other, already entails the fact of what I have just called reading. I read the other in general just because I cannot intuit him (her, it . . .) directly. Only the alterity of the other, maintained thus as radical and irreducible (if not 'absolute'), provokes the operation worthy of the name 'reading' in the sense that exceeds the resources of hermeneutics – and simultaneously the 'activity' of reading in this sense always already bears witness to the irreducible alterity of the other. End of 'methodological' parenthesis.]

Derrida goes on immediately to say that this 'typical' gesture does not exhaust or even dominate Merleau-Ponty's thought through and through, and that it is also, simultaneously, 'exposed' (the word is significant and precious) 'to an antagonistic necessity, to the other law' (p. 219). And this too would be characteristic of the configuration I've just been describing, as the 'autre geste' in Saussure or what Rousseau 'dit sans vouloir dire'. This 'autre loi' is not just, or not entirely, idiomatic to Merleau-Ponty, but (and this would be partly its law-character) in part at least a general law of metaphysics itself, which 'is' 'itself' (though of course this law is the law whereby it never is quite itself) only to the extent that it is inhabited or haunted by this other law, to which it is not only exposed, but which is a law of exposure, of the intrinsic exposure of metaphysics to its other(s), what will later usually get called 'auto-immunity'.

Insofar as it looks as though Merleau-Ponty is doing his best to think and formulate explicitly something of this exposure, one can see why it might be thought that Derrida is being a little parsimonious in the credit he is prepared to give him. After all, the Merleau-Pontyan thought might go, here is Merleau-Ponty describing the constitution of the same, the *propre* as *corps propre*, in terms of an originary implication of the other, of the outside, so that my being myself as *corps propre* involves an external surface exposed to touch, be that touch my own in the never quite self-coincident, never quite completely reflexive example of the *touchant-touché*, or that of the other whose hand I grasp, or whose hand grasps me, in the handshake.

And it is true that Derrida's difference with Merleau-Ponty here is subtle, and is reminiscent of other gestures made with respect to authors one might suspect of being close to him. In terms of a semi-serious taxonomy I once proposed,[13] this would be characteristic of Derrida's dealings with those who look as though they might be his friends or his brothers, i.e. texts or authors who look as though they are more or less radically contesting 'metaphysics', but who, on Derrida's reading, turn out still to rely at least to some extent on insufficiently thought through or deconstructed metaphysical schemas. For example, in *Spectres de Marx*, Derrida finds Heidegger thinking about justice as always involving a discord or an out-of-jointness, an *Un-fuge*, but then says that nonetheless (in spite of the 'credit' he gets for this perception), he tends still to resolve things towards a gathering, a fit or a harmony, and thus to lose the edge of the very *Un-fuge* he is credited also for having thought.[14] This general schema, one might suspect, is one that could also be recognised more generally in Derrida's relations with Hegel and the speculative dialectic: in a very general and schematic way, what Hegel calls 'the negative' looks just like something for which Derrida might have to give him what I've been calling 'credit', to the extent that it seems to disturb the identity of the same or the self-same – but of course that negative is from the start and to the end destined for the complex kind of recovery called *Aufheben*. In the particular case before us, here is how Derrida in *Le toucher*, sums up this issue around Merleau-Ponty:

> What is it that makes reading Merleau-Ponty so uneasy (for me)? What is it that makes the interpretation of his mode of philosophical writing something that is both gripping and difficult, but also sometimes irritating or disappointing? Perhaps this, in a word: the movement we mentioned, this experience of coincidence *with* non-coincidence, of the coincidence of coincidence *with* non-coincidence[15] can be seen again transferred into the (non-consequent) consequence or the (interrupted) continuity of the philosophical statements, and not always diachronically, following the evolution or the mutation of a thought, but sometimes synchronically. Should we give the philosopher credit for this [*faut-il en créditer le philosophe*], as I am most often tempted to do, or on the contrary regret that he was unable to proceed to a more powerful reformalization of his discourse to thematize and think the law under which he was thus placing himself, always *preferring*, at the end of the day, *in fact*, the 'coincidence' (of coincidence with non-coincidence) to the 'non-coincidence' (of coincidence with non-coincidence)? (pp. 238–9)

This is a subtle, almost enharmonic, distinction at a second level – and perhaps this second-level distinction could be used a principle of formalisation to describe Derrida's relation to texts of this type (where 'of this type' refers to the 'fraternal' relation he might be thought to have with texts or authors who might seem to be his friends, texts, then, that *appear* to be anti- or at least not-so-simply metaphysical, not so straightforwardly founded on the value of presence; and indeed the problem Derrida has *with the very concept of fraternity*, and notably in the work of Jean-Luc Nancy, would then be emblematic or strongly *exemplary* of this configuration, so that we might be tempted to say that what *comes between* Derrida and those we might think of as his brothers is precisely this concept of brotherhood, what separates the members of this apparent fraternity is the concept of fraternity itself, what sets Derrida apart is the insistence on the Husserlian sense of the radical apartness of the other as really and radically not available to me in intuition, but at best in analogical appresentation, that alterity of the other constantly belying the claim to fraternity, constantly making the handshake the mark of separation as much as and in fact more than that of joining, the place of the *shibboleth* as also the irreducibility of *reading*, which then becomes another name for just that irreducible alterity of the other that the motif of fraternity is always reducing. I have to read, and I have to read just where it is unreadable, precisely because of this structure, which constantly, in the fact of reading itself, brings back the priority of non-coincidence over the coincidence that, *in reading*, Derrida finds thematically prioritised by Merleau-Ponty. Reading in the strong sense practised by Derrida, even when it is not being thematised, is the proof, *in actu*, as it were, of the priority of non-coincidence over coincidence that is the undoing of the 'principle of principles' of phenomenology even as it is drawn from a phenomenological insight. And this would then go too for Derrida's reflections on Didier Franck (whose claim as to an originary impropriety of the proper looks at first blush fairly Derridean) and Jean-Louis Chrétien (whose insistence on interruption and interval can also have a deconstructive feel).

* * *

What kind of handshake might Nancy give, or be giving, in return? Even a 'normal' handshake must involve two hands and two shakes, as it were (this being one of the reasons why in fact my shaking the other's hand is an experience incommensurable to my touching my right hand with my left: just because I have one right and one left hand I cannot really shake hands with myself, in that a handshake involves usually two right hands (or occasionally, as I believe is the case in the boy scout movement, two left hands)). So nothing prevents (and in fact all the self-help business world discussions more or less secretly presuppose) some asymmetry at work in the handshake. The 'wet fish' handshake is, one imagines, identified as such by and from a handshake of a different type. The 'pumper' is usually pumping a non-pumper (two pumpers pumping each other is really not a pretty sight). The 'glove' is by definition not quite reciprocal: there are enclosing hands and a hand enclosed by them. So however we characterise the handshake Derrida gives Nancy, in *Le Toucher* or in *Voyous*, we might expect to find a different handshake coming back from Nancy to Derrida. How does it look when we consider the shaker shaken?

One element of a response to this quite difficult question would, I think, come from looking at the fate of what I'm tempted to call a 'line' from Derrida, in Nancy's hands. This 'line', from *La voix et le phénomène*, and which we might also call a slogan, a motto, a maxim, a sentence, even perhaps a witticism, is one that I was once moved to call, about twenty years ago, 'one of the most enigmatic statements in the whole of Derrida',[16] and reads simply: 'La différance infinie est finie' ['Infinite *différance* is finite'].[17] This difficult claim, in which we might suspect that a lot of Derrida is packed, or tightly curled up around itself like those extra spatial dimensions that string-theory postulates, shows up at least three times in Nancy,[18] once before Derrida's death (and indeed before *Le Toucher*), and twice since. The most recent of these occurrences is in the short piece Nancy wrote in *Libération* after the very recent death of Philippe Lacoue-Labarthe.

> One day I happened to use the word 'syncope', and you liked it too. This is probably where we best touched each other and that we were given the chance of a singular sharing of life and thought. Between us, yes, a suspense, a holding-back of presence, numerous and strong signs exchanged from one bank to the other, and the crossing always necessarily deferred. But *différance*, memory between us of this word of Jacques's and of Jacques himself, the *différance* from one to the other differs little, in the end, from the *différance* from oneself.
>
> Today infinite *différance* is finite [or: finished, over]; the caesura becomes eternal, the syncope remains open. This is not without beauty, in spite of everything, you know that: that's even your most intimate knowledge.[19]

'Aujourd'hui la différance infinie est finie'. There's obviously a strange effect in adding the specific 'aujourd'hui' to what elsewhere looks rather like a general claim, perhaps even a definition, although in a sense all it does is remind the reader of the finitude in the definition itself: if we take seriously the thought that 'infinite' difference is finite, then that finitude or perhaps becoming-finite of the infinite *différance* might be thought to entail something of the order of a now or an *aujourd'hui* in general, if I can put it that way, that would here be being re-marked by Nancy. *Différance*, we might want to say, brings with it an each-time-nowness that would bear some measured cross-reading with the each-time-mineness, the *Jemeinigkeit*, that Heidegger famously attributes to *Dasein* in *Being and Time*, and that Nancy himself comments on at some length at the beginning of *L'Expérience de la liberté*.[20]

Moving back in time, the next reference is in the address Nancy gave to the event organised by the Collège international de philosophie after Derrida's death, in October 2004.[21] Here, under the title 'Trois phrases de Jacques Derrida', Nancy again quotes the sentence ('La différance infinie est finie'), and tells an anecdote about once talking with Derrida about this line, with Derrida reportedly replying: 'You know, I'm not certain I really understand it myself' ['Tu sais, je ne suis pas certain de très bien comprendre moi-même'] (p. 69). Whatever we might make of that anecdote (so that we always might wonder, alterity-of-the-other *oblige*, whether Derrida 'really meant' it when he said it, assuming he said it, in the proto-fictional structure that Derrida finds at work in any act of witnessing or testimony)[22], which we should also put in the perspective of a relative paucity of *viva voce* philosophical discussion between Derrida and Nancy,[23] there is something striking about it, a kind of humanising gesture with respect to a difficult thought, perhaps, but also something of a self-protective gesture on Nancy's part, perhaps, a kind of avowal of non-comprehension that then needs to support itself or cover itself with the idea that *even Derrida himself* did not understand it. Nancy says firmly of this sentence (for this, rather than the slogan itself, is one of the 'trois phrases' that Nancy is reporting, as we know from the fact that he opens his remarks with the observation that the three sentences in question are all spoken rather than written) that, in saying it, Derrida 'Was smiling, but was not joking' [*Il souriait, mais ne plaisantait pas*] (How could one be sure?). Nancy then reports of his reaction to Derrida's saying this:

> That day I understood that for him too thought got away: one's own thought overran, necessarily, by some extremity – and I felt that thought always has to do with this escape, this inaccessibility in the very event of access. Jacques never thought he had finished a thought. And just that is 'differ*a*nce': not a simple distinction between Being and beings, but the thought of Being differed/deferred in beings. (p. 69)

This sense of a perhaps slightly recuperative need to protect or cover something can be given further support by the fact that, although to my knowledge neither Derrida nor Nancy ever publicly refers to this fact (though this could perhaps have been the reason for their conversation that day, that Nancy has just been reporting), this same motto or slogan shows up earlier still in Nancy, this time in the preface to *Une pensée finie* (1991), where, however, it is *misquoted* as 'La différence finie est infinie' (p. 20 n.).[24] Here Nancy is again glossing, in a footnote, Heidegger's ontico-ontological difference, and suggesting (not uncontroversially, I think, given what Derrida says himself, for example in the *Grammatologie*)[25] that Derrida's *différance* is an attempt to capture the Heideggerian sense in which that difference involves a self-differing and deferring of Being, and goes on:

> This is what Jacques Derrida wanted to bring to light with the neither-word neither-concept 'différance'. And as he wrote in *La voix et le phénomène* (Paris: PUF, 1967, p. XXX [*sic*: one imagines that Nancy had meant to correct this in proof and forgot to do so or was perhaps prevented (by illness?) from doing so]: 'Finite différence [with an e, so this is also a misquotation] is infinite.' – 'This sentence, I fear, is meaningless', he said one day [perhaps this refers to the same incident differently reported in the 'Trois phrases' piece?]. Perhaps, but meaning is in it. (p. 20 n.)

This misquotation is, in a sense, less being corrected than being repeated and justified in the 'Trois phrases' piece (even though there Nancy does not mention his own earlier misquotation and is this time very careful to quote the sentence correctly, even insisting with an almost parodic scholarly care and accuracy, rather like Merleau-Ponty quoting Husserl: 'I reread it yesterday, it is on page 114' (p. 69)). This very precise reference is then pursued as follows: ' . . . it is on page 114, and I saw that the sentence, printed in italics, follows these words: "the finitude of life as essential relation to self as to one's death".' And Nancy proceeds, after closing the quotation marks, by way of commentary: 'And that very thing *is* the infinite or else *makes* the infinite' [*Et cela même* est *l'infini ou bien* fait *l'infini*]. This seems a little like a repetition or justification of the earlier misquotation, still making Derrida's slogan turn toward the infinite, whereas Derrida seems to have it always turn or fold back to the finite.[26] And this motif of the infinite, or this turn to the infinite on Nancy's part, returns in the third of these 'three sentences':[27] this one is about Derrida in hospital, after an operation, just a day or so before his death, and saying to Nancy, with reference to the latter's heart transplant: 'Now I have a scar as big as yours'. Nancy comments:

> Beyond the humour, [this sentence] touched me: as though there were a friendly rivalry in the suffering, incision and inscription of the body. As though from the one scar to the other there could be competition – for what? For the incision and inscription of what? Of our finitude the tracing of which makes our infinitude appear in 'the *sans* of the pure cut' as he wrote earlier.

And Nancy ends this part of his short text with a little one-sentence paragraph: 'But I don't want to make him say more than he said' [*Mais je ne veux pas lui faire dire plus qu'il n'a dit*].

I don't want to make Nancy say more than he said either, of course (although there would be a good deal more still to say about what *that* would mean, and how reading may also *always* involve having the text say more than it says), but I want to suggest in conclusion that this somewhat anecdotal thread can help us approach something of the difference between Derrida and Nancy more generally. In *Le Toucher* itself, Derrida is concerned to bring out and even celebrate an aspect of Nancy's thinking that tends to distinguish him from the configurations he sketches out in the five 'Tangents' that form the middle portion of the book, and that are concerned essentially to pursue the fate of a certain reading of Husserl, and more specifically the Husserl of *Ideen II*, in twentieth-century French thought. What Derrida likes in Nancy's account of touch and space and corporality is that, unlike the Merleau-Pontyan drift we have been following, it seems to stress the 'non-coincidence' part of the second-level equation of coincidence and non-coincidence, and in so doing more radically *exposes* the thought of touch to the type of alterity we have been talking about, especially in the directions of exteriority, the inhuman, the inorganic, the graft and (thereby and essentially) the technical (see among other examples pp. 205–6, but more especially the 'precision' on pp. 322–3).

But let's imagine here that there's an even more refined version of the 'second-level' structure I laid out earlier, and that we're here in a 'third-level' logic, which can only be paradoxical. On the 'second level', dealing with Merleau-Ponty exemplarily here for us, Derrida takes propositions that might look somewhat 'deconstructive' (or at least not standardly metaphysical), and shows how, even if they stress something of the order of non-coincidence at the first level, they still, on a second level of the relation between coincidence and non-coincidence, tend to *prefer* the coincidence of coincidence and non-coincidence to their non-coincidence (or, in the Heidegger example, prefer the jointedness of the jointed and the out-of-joint to their out-of-jointness: or, perhaps more generally, prefer the gathering of gathering and dispersion to their dispersion, etc.).[28] Nancy helps Derrida make these second-level points, for example through his insistence on the *partes extra partes*, a kind of non-gatherable exteriority that would open up to the 'technical' and also be the condition of 'freedom'.

And yet, on what I am here pretending to isolate as a 'third level', the thought would be that Nancy still, in spite of everything, for example in the motif of fraternity in the freedom book, or more generally in his *attachment* to Christian motifs, or here, more symptomatically, in his repeated and insistent difficulty with the slogan about infinite *différance* being finite, *in the end*, 'ultimately' (the ultimate here being very precisely part of the problem)[29] – Nancy 'prefers' the infinite to the finite even as he thinks the finite more finitely, more 'exactly', than the phenomenologists. Nancy's initial misquotation of Derrida's slogan as to the finitude of infinite *différance*, and then his complex countersigning of that misquotation in the 'Trois phrases' essay, in which in spite of the letter of Derrida's text what emerges is a somewhat un-Derridean emphasis on the infinite, shows that even as Nancy holds thought open beyond the already complex phenomenological closure, at what I am artificially here calling the 'third level', he closes it again, paradoxically enough, by 'preferring' the infinite to the finite, preferring to read the always radically finite trace as still a trace of an infinite, rather than, as in Derrida himself, the always finite opening of the finite itself as (infinitely) finite, or more properly, as the same passage from *La voix et le phénomène* goes on to make clear, as neither straightforwardly finite nor infinite.[30]

This extremely subtle ('third-level') difference (which it would be nice to be able to articulate with the difference Derrida himself proposes between the 'Il n'y a pas "le" . . .' of Nancy and his own 'S'il y en a . . .' (pp. 323–4)) is the very surface of the difference in the handshake, the trace of non-reciprocity that the thought of exposure entails, the shibboleth that always might go unrecognised in the grip but that reading can perhaps bring out as at least a possibility, the residual possibility of a violence that the concept of fraternity violently denies. If I'm not mistaken, this is also what Derrida calls 'salut', in the non-soteriological sense he briefly develops at the very end of the first essay in *Voyous*, the 'salut sans assurance à l'autre qui vient ou qui part' (*Voyous*, p. 160), salute without safety or salvation, always shibboleth perhaps, some more or less secret grip I'll never be certain of having really grasped, and which makes perhaps its first appearance here, at the very end of *Le Toucher*, before the longer development in *Voyous*, last wave or handshake still with the dignity of the name, 'un imprésentable salut qui d'avance renonce, comme il se doit pour être un salut digne de ce nom, au Salut.'[31]

Notes

1. This paper was presented to the March 2007 conference '*The Future Matters: Apropos of Derrida's Touching on the Technology of the Senses to Come in a Post-global Horizon*' at the University of Leeds. Previously published in *Derrida Today*, vol. 1, no. 2 (2008), pp. 167–89.
2. Jacques Derrida, *Le Toucher, Jean-Luc Nancy* (Paris: Galilée, 2000). (1) Page 125: '(– And you say to yourself, internally: this is a funny admiring and grateful salute you're addressing here to Jean-Luc Nancy, a curious

way of claiming to touch him while doing everything as though you wanted to take his vocabulary of touching out of service from now on. Or put it on the banned list, even. Or as though you were stubbornly recalling that this vocabulary should always already have been out of service, even if we like it, touching, precisely when it is impossible-forbidden, and that we even like to call that loving – abstain. Like the messiah. Funny present, indeed, what an offering! Just as if, right when you are calling on others to get ecstatic about this great work and this immense philosophical treatise on touching, you were murmuring in his ear: "Now, Jean-Luc, that's enough, don't touch that word again, it's forbidden, you hear me, abstain from this 'touching', don't ever use this incredible vocabulary again, this concept with nothing definite corresponding to it, these figures without figure and thus without credit. Moreover did you not say yourself, I'll remind you again, 'there is not "the touching"'"? So don't keep on pretending to believe, stop making believe you want us to believe there is something that might be called touching, a "thing-itself" about which we could pretend to agree, just where, touching on the untouchable, it remains untouchable. Knowing you as I do, this objection won't stop you – I tell myself. No, you carry on, and me too, and gratefully I follow you.'). (2) Page 160: '(And you say to yourself, internally: this is a funny admiring and grateful salute you're addressing here to Jean-Luc Nancy, a curious way of claiming to touch him while doing everything as though you wanted to put his vocabulary of touching back into the service of a tradition, or worse, of a filiation, even. Or recall that this vocabulary ought always already have been referred to usages or even an ageless usury, even if we like that, touching, anew, precisely, when it is impossible-forbidden and even that we like to call that loving – abstain. Funny present, indeed, what an offering! Just as if, right when you are calling on others to get ecstatic about this great work and this immense philosophical treatise on touching, you were murmuring in his ear: "Now, Jean-Luc, that's enough, give that word up, it's forbidden, you hear me, leave it to the ancestors, no longer compromise yourself with it, don't let yourself get contaminated by this megalovirus, don't ever use this incredible vocabulary again, this concept with nothing definite corresponding to it, these figures without figure and thus without credit. Don't keep on, like them, pretending to believe, stop making believe you want us to believe there is something that might be called touching, a thing itself about which we could pretend to agree, and say something new, just where, touching on the untouchable, it remains untouchable. Touching is finitude, period. Did you not say yourself 'there is not "the" touching'"? Knowing you as I do, this objection won't stop you – I tell myself.

– You neither. Would you like to touch him, as you say, the way one touches someone in a duel, with a covered sword-point? "Touché", as the Americans say in French, with a funny accent, when they score a point.

– On the contrary, it is his singularity, his "being singular plural" that matters to me here above all, even when I'm talking to the others about the others. It is this absolute singularity of his signature that I am striving to get at here.

– You're striving? What does that mean?)'

3. I remember too from schooldays that there was reputed to be a way of giving a very specific and well-timed shake of the hand that would dislocate the other's shoulder. Remember too OddJob's literally bone-crushing handshake in the movie *Goldfinger*.
4. Jean-Paul Sartre, *La nausée* [1936] (Paris: le livre de poche, 1963), p. 114.
5. Of course the language of handshake and handshaking extends in a way I am sure Derrida would be cautious about calling metaphorical to other types of situation. Do not get me started, for example, on the computer science network protocol use of the term, which would, however, comfort the 'technological' drift of Derrida's argument. Or how about this, from an article by John G. Cramer called 'The Quantum Handshake': 'The absorber theory description, unconventional though it is, leads to exactly the same observations as the conventional one. But it differs in that there has been a two-way exchange, a "handshake" across space-time which led to the transfer of energy from emitter to absorber. This advanced-retarded handshake is the basis for the transactional interpretation of quantum mechanics. It is a two-way contract between the future and the past for the purpose of transferring energy, momentum, etc. It is nonlocal because the future is, in a limited way, affecting the past on the same basis that the past affects the future. When you stand in the dark and look at a star a hundred light years away, not only have the retarded light waves from the star been travelling for a hundred years toward your eyes, but also advanced waves from your eyes have reached a hundred years into the past to encourage the star to shine in your direction' (http://www.npl.washington.edu/av/altvw16.html).
6. See Derrida's quoting and commenting on Foucault's use of this in the Preface to *Les mots et les choses*, in 'Et Cetera . . . ', in N. Royle (ed.), *Deconstructions: A User's Guide* (Basingstoke and New York: Palgrave, 2000), pp. 282–305 (pp. 284–8). The original French text was subsequently published in the special *Jacques Derrida* issue of the *Cahiers de l'Herne* published in 2004 (pp. 21–34).
7. The handshake is the sign of *closing* a deal as well as of opening negotiations.
8. See http://www.ephesians5-11.org/handshakes.htm.
9. See, for example, the 'Introduction' to *L'origine de la géométrie*, pp. 71–2 and 116–22, and *L'Ecriture et la différence* (Paris: Seuil, 1967), p. 245, n. 1. A couple of pages earlier in *Le Toucher*, Derrida has reflected more generally on this tendency in Merleau-Ponty (and elsewhere), after quoting a passage from 'Le philosophe et son ombre': 'on this passage and so many others, we would have to locate the moment when, by a simple rhetorical slippage, the accompaniment of the commentary, the pedagogical restitution, without simply betraying the other's intention, begins to inflect it discreetly to lead it elsewhere. Moreover, the precaution that consists in giving a precise reference and in sheltering behind a literal quotation, in German, sometimes betrays the betrayal – and not only in Merleau-Ponty' (p. 214).
10. In, *Ideen II* (The Hague: Martinus Nijhoff, 1952), §§36ff.
11. See, for example, *La Voix et le phénomène* (Paris: PUF, 1967), pp. 5, 42ff., 94 n. 1; *L'Ecriture et la différence*, 181ff. Recalled also in *Politiques de l'amitié* (Paris: Galilée, 1994), p. 73 and *Adieu à Emmanuel Levinas* (Paris: Galilée, 1997), p. 96.

12. Cf. too *Le Toucher*, p. 65: 'If Psyché is life itself, the mourning of Psyché will not be one mourning among others. It is mourning itself. It is absolute mourning, mourning of life itself, but a mourning that this time could not be *borne* (no life can bear this mourning any longer), nor do its 'work'. Mourning without work of mourning, mourning without mourning. Mourning on the threshold of mourning. Our life itself, no?' See too p. 66: 'There is no autobiography, there never was a "I touch myself" for Psyché, for a psyche entirely exposed to the outside and the other. No signed autobiography for she who, untouchable to herself, feels or knows nothing of herself. The mourning of autobiography is not an autobiography among others, any more than the mourning of Psyché lets itself be preceded or properly figured by any other. As much as to say that, because it is unimaginable, it can give rise only to figures, tropes, allegories or metonymies opening the ways of a *technique*. Because it is undeniable, it can only give rise to negation. And then mourning without mourning will never be overcome in any "work of mourning", be it successful or a failure.' (See too a slightly different derivation of this 'technical' moment on p. 206.) This passage occurs shortly after a complex sequence in which Derrida notes that 'Touch remains for Nancy the motif of a sort of absolute, irredentist and post-deconstructive realism' (p. 60), and then returns to Aristotle to show how death supervenes immediately in the absence of touch, but also in the face of too great an intensity of touch (p. 61): touch must then take place in a kind of *measure*, a self-restraint or *tact*. See too the development around tact and the law, pp. 81–2.
13. See my 'Circanalyse', in R. Major and P. Guyomard (eds), *Depuis Lacan* (Paris: Flammarion, 2000), pp. 270–94; English translation in my *Interrupting Derrida* (London: Routledge, 2000), pp. 93–109.
14. 'Does not Heidegger, as always, dissymetrise *in favour* of what he indeed interprets as the very possibility of *favour*, favour accorded, namely the accord that gathers or brings together harmoniously (*Versammlung*, *Fug*), even in the sameness of differences or disputes, before the syn-thesis of a sys-tem? [. . .] Beyond right, and still more so beyond juridicalism, beyond morality, and still more so beyond moralism, does justice as relation to the other not presuppose on the contrary the irreducible excess of a dis-jointing or an anachrony, some *un-Fuge*, some 'out of joint' dislocation in Being and in time itself, a disjoining that, even as it always runs the risk of evil, expropriation and injustice (*adikia*) against which there is no calculable assurance, could alone *do justice* or *render justice* to the other *qua* other?' *Spectres de Marx* (Paris: Galilée, 1993), p. 55. See too *Voyous* (Paris: Galilée, 2003), p. 128.
15. This kind of 'second-level' argument might provide a tool for formalising the relations here: cf. Hegel in *Glas*, and the question of the relation between the dialectical and the non-dialectical, which must be dialectical according to Hegel, but perhaps need not be for Derrida.
16. See my 'Deconstruction and the Philosophers: The Very Idea', in *Legislations: The Politics of Deconstruction* (London: Verso Books, 1994), pp. 11–60 (p. 31).
17. Here is some immediate context, even though this sentence has a sententious quality to it and to that extent tends to detach itself from its context:

'The fact that Husserl always thought of infinity as an Idea in the Kantian sense, as the indefinity of an *ad infinitum*, leads one to believe that he never derived difference from the plenitude of a parousia, from the full presence of a positive infinity; that he never believed in the accomplishment of an "absolute knowledge" as presence to itself, in the Logos, of an infinite concept. And what he shows us of the movement of temporalisation leaves no doubt on this subject: although he never made a theme of the "articulation", of the "diacritical" work of difference in the constitution of meaning and the sign, he deeply recognized its necessity. And yet, the whole phenomenological discourse is caught up, as we have sufficiently seen, in the schema of a metaphysics of presence that tirelessly exhausts itself deriving difference. Within this schema, Hegelianism appears to be more radical: par excellence at the point at which it brings out the fact that the positive infinity must be thought (which is possible only if it thinks itself) for the indefinity of differance to appear as such. Hegel's critique of Kant would no doubt also be valid against Husserl. But this appearing of the Ideal as infinite differance can only take place in a relation to death in general. Only a relation to my-death can make the infinite differance of presence appear. By the same token, compared to the ideality of the positive infinity, this relation to my-death becomes an accident of finite empiricity. The appearing of infinite differance is itself finite. Given this, differance which is nothing outside this relationship, becomes the finitude of life as essential relation to self as to one's death. *Infinite differance is finite.* One can thus no longer think it in the opposition of the finite and the infinite, absence and presence, negation and affirmation' (p. 114).

18. Almost four times, perhaps, if one includes the tangential reference in the discussion between Derrida, Nancy and Lacoue-Labarthe transcribed in the 'Penser avec Jacques Derrida' issue of *Rue Descartes*, no. 52 (2006), pp. 86–99, which opens with a reference to a notion of 'finitude infinie [infinite finitude]' that Derrida and Nancy supposedly share (p. 88), whereas, according to Nancy, Lacoue-Labarthe would be on the side of an 'infinitude finie [finite infinitude]'.
19. 'Philippe Lacoue-Labarthe, la syncope reste ouverte', *Libération*, 2 February 2007.
20. Cf. too *Une pensée finie*, p. 19: 'This "single" meaning has neither unity nor singleness: it is a "single" meaning (of a "single" *being*), because it is *each time* meaning.'
21. Published in *Rue Descartes*, no. 48 (2005), 'Salut à Jacques Derrida.'
22. Cf. *Demeure: Maurice Blanchot* (Paris: Galilée, 1998) and *Donner la mort* (Paris: Galilée, 1999).
23. This is something Nancy reports in Safaa Fathy's film *D'ailleurs, Derrida*, and (with Lacoue-Labarthe) in the collective volume *Penser à Strasbourg* (Paris: Galilée, 2004), p. 15: 'Jean-Luc . . . was discovering Jacques Derrida's capacity for silence . . . we were vaguely astonished: we were learning that one does not necessarily talk philosophy with a philosopher, and that the work goes via the texts' (p. 15). Anecdotally again, I along with many others can confirm an experience of that 'capacity for silence'. At Cerisy in 2002, after Derrida's paper (subsequently published as the first essay of *Voyous*) in which there is a long, detailed and intransigent critique

of Nancy's appeal to the motif of fraternity in the Freedom book, I asked Derrida if he and Nancy had ever discussed the matter before: he replied, 'No, in fact we've never talked so much philosophy as we have this week.'

24. If I can again briefly enter the realm of anecdote: when I mentioned this to Derrida, who at the time had not yet read Nancy's book, and saw his look of surprise, I said a little lightly: 'but maybe in the end it comes to the same thing'. Derrida very quickly and seriously said: 'I don't think so', giving me a curious look as though I had just shown myself to be an imbecile after all.
25. See, for example, *De la grammatologie* (Paris: Minuit, 1972), p. 38: 'To get to the point of recognizing, not short of but on the horizon of the Heideggerian paths, and still in them, that the meaning of being is not a transcendental or trans-epochal signified (even were it always dissimulated in the epoch) but already, in a properly unheard-of sense, a determinate signifying trace, is to assert that in the decisive concept of ontico-ontological difference, *everything is not to be thought at once*: entity and Being, ontic and ontological, "ontico-ontological" would be, in an original style, derived with respect to difference, and with respect to what later on we shall call *differance*, an economic concept designating the production of the differing and the deferring. Ontico-ontological-difference and its ground (*Grund*) in the "transcendence of Dasein" (*Vom Wesen des Grundes*, p. 16) would no longer be absolutely original. Differance *tout court* would be more "originary", but one could no longer call it "origin" or "ground", these notions belonging essentially to the history of onto-theology, i.e. the system that functions as effacement of difference. However, difference can only be thought up close to itself on one condition: that one begin by determining it as ontico-ontological difference before crossing this determination out. The necessity of the passage through the crossed-out determination, the necessity of this turn of writing is irreducible. This is a discreet and difficult thought that, through many unnoticed mediations, ought to carry the whole weight of our question, a question that we are still provisionally calling historial. It is thanks to it that later we'll be able to try to make differance and writing communicate.'
26. 'It is precisely what is proper to the power of differance to modify life less and less as it spreads. If it became *infinité* – which its essence excludes a priori – life itself would be reduced to an impassive, intangible and eternal présence: infinité differance, God or death' (*De la grammatologie*, p. 191).
27. The first of the three sentences is a remark from around 1970, 'no doubt', told as follows by Nancy: 'I was in a moment of doubt and discouragement, and I said to Jacques that I thought I didn't have, or no longer had, much to say. He replied the following, brusquely, almost angry: "Yes, I know, these are pretexts one gives oneself to avoid having to write". I was astonished, and that's why I didn't forget what he said (later, he had forgotten)' (p. 68).
28. Cf. Derrida's piece on Bernard Tschumi: 'Point de folie – maintenant l'architecture', in *Psyché, inventions de l'autre* (Paris: Galilée, 1988), pp. 477–93.
29. Just after the footnote in *Une pensée finie*, Nancy explicitly addresses this question, in the context of Heidegger's 'being-toward-death': 'what carries

thought in an expression like "being to death" ["être à la mort"] (*zum Tode sein*) [Nancy here has a note justifying the translation with "à" rather than "pour" on the grounds that "pour" is too purposive], is not primarily "death", but the *to*, about which "death" indicates only that it is maintained, as a structure of being, "to the end" [*jusqu'au bout*] – which is an absence of "end", extremity or finality [*fin*: also just "end"] where the infinite circle of a sense-less appropriation would be closed. [. . .] . . . in "finitude" the question is not that of the "end" [*fin*], neither as aim nor as accomplishment, but only of a suspense of sense, in-finite, each time played anew, re-opened, each time exposed with such a radical newness that it immediately misses itself' (p. 21). The question is simply that of the passage from 'each time anew' to 'in-finite'.

30. This is not just a terminological question, of course. Derrida himself uses the *word* 'infini' (for example in a reference to the 'infini secret de l'autre', in *Voyous* (p. 128)): but most often it is still wrapped in a paradoxical relation to the finite. Cf., still in *Voyous*, p. 211: 'For once reason does not close itself to the event of who or what comes, if it is not irrational to think that the worst can always happen, and well beyond what Kant still contains under the name "radical evil", then only the infinite possibility of the worst and of perjury can grant the possibility of the Good, of veracity and sworn faith. *This possibility remains infinite but as the very possibility of an auto-immunitary finitude*' (my emphasis). See too the important *mise en garde* in the *Grammatologie*, p. 99: 'That the logos be first an imprint and that this imprint be the scriptural resource of language means, of course, that the logos is not a creative activity, the continuous and full element of the divine word, etc. But one would not have taken a single step outside metaphysics if one took from it no more than a new motif of the "return to finitude", of the "death of God", etc. This is the conceptuality and problematic that we must deconstruct. They belong to the onto-theology they contest. *Différance is also something other than finitude*' (my emphasis). In *Le Toucher* itself, in the second version of the repeated passage (pp. 125 and 160), we do find the following, but the context clearly suggests a kind of free indirect discourse: 'Le toucher, c'est la finitude, un point c'est tout' [touch is finitude, period]. Immediately followed by the mention of the English (or American) usage of 'touché' in the language of the duel or of fencing (see note 2 above).
31. 'An unpresentable salute that in advance, as it must in order to be a salute worthy of the name, renounces Salvation.'

The Limits of My Language

'The limits of my language mean the limits of my world', as Wittgenstein notoriously puts it in the *Tractatus*.[1] My interest in this paper is not so much to discuss that assertion itself, as to wonder what to make of the notion of language having limits at all. What sense can we make of the expression 'limits of language'? And this question might itself divide into at least two sub-questions, namely: (1) what kind of limits does language have (assuming it has any)? and (2) does language even have limits?

It might seem at first as though language must have limits, and that those limits must be where it abuts onto 'the world'. Language 'over here', or so the thought would go, is separated from, but in some relation to, the world 'over there'. That relation would be essentially, if we are to follow the tradition, the relation of reference, or at least possible reference. On this view the world, which intuitively existed long before language, sits there waiting, as it were, for language to arrive on the scene and to refer to it. In referring (or at least in successfully referring), language both recognises its limits and transgresses them, in the sense at least that it points beyond those limits (maybe even puts out 'feelers') to reality or the world beyond. On this simple but powerful view of language, reality, whether construed as empirical, as in Locke, or of some higher order, as in Plato, not only comes first in the relationship, but 'wears the trousers', as J. L. Austin might have said. If I can quote David Pears characterising this view (as that of the *Tractatus*) in his magnum opus on Wittgenstein:

> The idea is that in all our operations with language we are really running on fixed rails laid down in reality before we even appeared on the scene. Attach a name to an object, and the intrinsic nature of the object will immediately take over complete control and determine the correct use of the name on later occasions. Set up a whole language in this way, and the structure of the fundamental grid will inexorably dictate the general structure of the logical system.[2]

My intention is not to follow what happens to these questions in Wittgenstein, however, but to see how they fare in the work of Jacques Derrida. It might plausibly be thought, for example, and often indeed has been thought, that Derrida is proposing (however obscurely) a philosophy of language, and one that also attempts to produce a non- or anti-Platonist account of what holds language together in its relations with the world, once the Platonic presumption has been refused, albeit not an account that obviously turns to what Pears calls 'the stability of our own practices' to do the trick.[3] It would also have in common with Wittgenstein that it gives rise to what Pears calls 'the characteristic intellectual giddiness of withdrawal from Platonism'. On this view of Derrida proposing a philosophy of language, Derrida might be thought, and often has been thought, to argue for a kind of radical linguisticism and indeed a kind of ultra-linguisticism, as though there were really no world but *only* language. When Derrida notoriously claims in *Of Grammatology* that 'there is nothing outside the text', or 'il n'y a pas de hors-texte',[4] it is difficult not to think that this amounts to a radical declaration of linguistic imperialism. In common with what is often taken to be the position of Saussure and the whole structuralist and poststructuralist movement inspired by him, reference stops even *being* a question just because, on this view, language constantly and endlessly refers only to itself. Here, the limits of my language are indeed the limits of my world not only because language gives me some kind of privileged access to the world, or maybe even allows me to 'have' a world in the first place, but because my world is in a significant sense entirely language anyway.

I want to argue that this is a mistaken reading of Derrida's thinking. Far from imprisoning us and everything there is in language, or so I shall be suggesting, Derrida certainly questions any simple separation of language and world, certainly pays the closest attention to language in its most irreducible and idiomatic aspects, but in so doing does not so much bring the world into language as he de-linguistifies language and takes it out into the world. In other words, Derrida's concern is to think about the supposed separation of language and world in a way that neither reinforces it nor simply denies it, but that places that separation into a situation of *différance* such that 'language' and 'world' at most name poles of attraction in a more general structure which is neither language nor world (nor their synthesis or amalgam). One way of saying this in Derridean language is that the traditional opposition of language and world is deconstructed. This means coming to some understanding of the claim that there is nothing outside the text that does not simply identify 'text' with 'language', and understands the thought that reality or world is 'textual' not to mean that reality or world is linguistic.

Derrida certainly seems to *begin* this process of deconstruction from the side of language, as it were – whence the (at least superficial) plausibility of the view I am contesting. But his derivation of the quasi-concepts of trace, *différance* and text entails that language, at least as usually understood, dissolves somewhat in the process of the derivation, which I shall now sketch out.

Derrida takes very seriously Saussure's notorious claim that 'language is a system of differences without positive terms', first in order to deconstruct the very notion of the sign to which Saussure is still quite firmly attached, and to do so apparently by prioritising the *signifiant* over the *signifié*. If a view of language that we might think of as broadly 'Platonic' has a clear order of priority beginning with the thing, moving to the idea of the thing (roughly what Saussure calls the *signifié*) and then to the (usually spoken) *signifiant* (and just occasionally to one further remove, i.e. the written signifier of that spoken signifier), then Derrida uses Saussure apparently to invert that order of priority. Saussure, it will be remembered, arguing against his version of the 'Platonic' position (what he calls the view that language is essentially a *nomenclature*), argues that, once the perception that signs are 'arbitrary' is taken seriously and radically (i.e. beyond a merely conventionalist understanding involving a kind of aporetic fiction or fable whereby people must one day have *agreed* on what to call things), then the only thing that can be thought to hold language together in any kind of coherence (as a *system*, what Saussure calls *langue* as opposed to actual uses of language or *parole*) is the differential relationship of elements among themselves. Notoriously, Saussure's view of language pushes 'the world' into the background, and draws attention to the way that linguistic elements relate to each other as a prior condition of their having any chance at all of referring to things. Signs, in Saussure, form a kind of self-supporting network, and it is that network and the intra-linguistic relations of its terms that determine what can be referred to, and perhaps even what can be said to exist. This is a kind of reversal the possibility of which already haunts the 'Platonic' view of language as a possible aberration or pathology to be avoided. I'm thinking here especially of Locke's splendid indignation about ways in which 'words' rather than 'things' can sometimes come to the fore, for example in rhetoric, that 'perfect cheat', and his more deep-seated worry about the terms he calls 'mixed modes', where words can hardly fail to do so.[5] The priority in Saussure clearly goes to sign over referent: and it seems as though the Derridean position, pushing Saussure a little further than the latter most obviously wants to go, must be that the priority goes not just to the sign, but within the sign to the *signifiant*, the so-called 'play' of which (i.e. its dynamic interrelatedness entailed by the differences-without-positive-terms view of language) generates what Derrida calls 'effects' of meaning or of signifieds. The signified becomes no more than a kind of sum of the differences between signifiers, always only, as Derrida puts it, 'a signifier placed in a certain position by other signifiers', or 'a stratum of the signifier that *gives itself* as signified'.[6] That signified could give rise, at least on occasion, to something like a 'world', which on this view would apparently always be in some sense the 'poetic' 'product' of the activity of language itself. On this very plausible and widespread reading of Derrida, he would then line up in a general kind of way with thinkers such as Merleau-Ponty and Heidegger and propose a version of what Levinas memorably characterises as a 'disoriented' 'world' of essentially lateral and fundamentally poetic *significations* intrinsically lacking any orientation or *sens*.[7]

Saussure himself draws back from extending the 'differences without positive terms' argument to the 'sign as a whole' – i.e. he thinks that it is valid at the level of *signifier* taken separately, and at that of the *signified* taken separately, but that at the level of sign 'in its totality', we are dealing, as Saussure says, with 'something positive in its order', and that the appropriate form to look for relationships in this order is that of *opposition* rather than *difference*. One imagines that the paradigmatic opposition for Saussure here is just the very opposition between signifier and signified themselves. Naturally Derrida's reading does not (or at least would not – I don't think he ever in fact makes this argument quite explicit) accept this consequence, just because he is concerned to undermine any thought that there could be a 'sign in its totality' and, apparently at least, to urge the idea that the functioning of the signifier is alone sufficient to account for the operation of language.

Unlike some of the other post-Saussureans, however, Derrida conspicuously and explicitly does not decide to remain here with the signifier (which can be presented as 'floating' with respect to any signified, for example, or can, in some versions, be reclaimed as the 'material' part of the sign as against the 'idealist' attachment to the signified),[8] in spite of the priority it seems to be given in this view of language. This is a slightly tricky point which I think has not always been taken in by the commentators: Derrida certainly casts suspicion on the very idea of a signified, and does so by prioritising the signifier. Look up in the dictionary a word you don't know (i.e. a signifier without a signified), and the dictionary will *never* provide you with more than more signifiers, which may in turn send you elsewhere in the dictionary in search of their signified, which you will never find. It looks, however, as though the reason we do not seem (at least in any simple way) to get stuck in the dictionary, and typically return from it with a sense of having understood *something*, is that at a certain point, a signifier (placed in a certain position) *counts as* a signified or *functions as* a signified. Just because, as I mentioned earlier, and as Derrida says in a different section of the *Grammatology*, something of the signifier *gives itself* or *gives itself out* as a signified, secretes an 'effect'[9] of a signified, so, in a more general way the signifier /signifier/ cannot fail to secrete /signified/ as the-signifier-that-counts-as-its-signified. Or, put another way, even accepting the 'differences-without-positive-terms' argument and deciding that it finally entails the absence of a signified (or the thought, if I can put it in a more Anglo-Saxon idiom, that 'words' don't need to have 'meanings'), *still*, in the interrelatedness that marks language in the 'difference' model, the extreme proximity of the signifier /signified/ to the signifier / signifier/ in the network, and, more importantly perhaps, the millennial tradition of moving from signifier to signified (because the network is never, in spite of what Saussure might sometimes appear to suggest, simply independent of its history) tends to make almost inevitable that, given 'signifier', then 'signified'. In other words, once the deconstruction of the sign proceeds to the point at which the signified falls away and the whole field seems to be covered by the signifier, then the very coherence of the signifier starts to be a question in its turn.

This is one of the reasons why Derrida moves cautiously toward the term 'trace' to capture what the 'difference' view of language entails, if one accepts its more radical implications and refuses the Saussurean 'fall-back' position on signs-as-a-whole and opposition.[10] I want to argue that one advantage of this move (over the temptation to retain the term 'signifier' in the way that Lacan, among others, does) is that it allows a non-reductive extension of the 'difference' argument beyond what would still be, in Saussure at least, a quite subtle form of idealism. This is because (1) maintaining the thought of a 'sign' entails maintaining the distinction between signifier and signified: but the very thought of signified (i.e. of signified thought *as* signified, and no longer as signifier-giving-itself-out-as that we just saw) entails that the signified be ideally and in principle separable from the signifier, and this in turn rapidly entails that there be a transcendental signified, the most perspicuous traditional signifier for which is the name 'God' (this is why the metaphysical concept of sign is the concept of sign-vanishing-in-favour-of, and why, therefore, as Derrida puts it in *Speech and Phenomena*, 'effacing' the classical concept of the sign can involve insisting on it and *maintaining* it against that built-in effacement);[11] (2) Deciding, on the 'difference' argument, that we can advantageously (and possibly even materialistically) *replace* signified with signifier, oddly produces a version of just the same problem. The traditional thought of signified cannot fail to generate a 'transcendental signified': the attempt to think signifier without signified cannot fail to generate a 'transcendental signifier'[12] which is really not so different from a signified –transcendentalised in this way, a signifier *may just as well be a signified* [13] – whence the suspicion that it might be strategically preferable to use another term, i.e. trace. 'Trace', as Derrida derives it in these notoriously difficult pages of the *Grammatology*, is not the *perfect* nor even *the right* term for what is being thought here,[14] but attempts to gather (from its semi-stable but never completely stable 'place' in the language system[15]) some of the possibilities of the elaborated and radicalised 'difference' account. 'Trace' attempts to capture something about that account: namely that faced with a 'given' element of the language system (what we'll still always feel like calling a word or a signifier), and wondering what it is that makes that element the element that it is rather than something else (and this seems to mean wondering first, then, what makes it *different* from all the other elements that it is not), we are driven to the thought that any given element must in some sense *bear the trace* of all those other elements that it is not, so that (to take an almost trivially simple example) in the roman alphabetical system, what it is about the letter 'b', say, that renders it identifiable or recognisable as such (and thereby also repeatable as the same letter on another occasion) is the 'presence' in it of the 'absence' of all the other letters that it is not. On this view, 'b' is not *simply* present *as* itself (i.e. as a letter of the alphabet rather than just a line or set of lines), in that its 'presence' *as* 'b' emerges as the product, as it were, of the 'absence' of all those other letters. And those other letters are not *simply* absent (just because their absence is in some sense 'present' here and now in this 'b' that they define just by the trace of their absence). 'Trace' is the word Derrida proposes, then, to capture something of this set-up which defies simple description in terms of presence and absence, and which can, at the very least, be extended to the whole of what we typically call 'language'.[16] This radicalisation of the 'difference' view of language is also of course what generates Derrida's infamous neologism 'différance', naming that which gives rise to the instantiable differences that Saussure is talking about. As Derrida puts it:

> Now here the appearing and the functioning of difference presuppose an originary synthesis that is preceded by no absolute simplicity. This, then, would be the originary trace. Without a retention in the minimal unit of temporal experience, without a trace retaining the other as other in the same, no difference would do its work and no meaning would appear. We are, then, not here dealing with a constituted difference but, before any determination of content, of the *pure* movement that produces difference. *The (pure) trace is différance.* It depends on no sensory plenitude, audible or visible, phonic

> or graphic. On the contrary, it is their condition. Although it does not exist, although it is never a present-entity outside all plenitude, its possibility is *de jure* anterior to everything that is called sign (signifier/signified, content/expression, etc.), concept or operation, motor or sensory.[17]

So *différance* just is 'trace' when trace is thought along the lines we have indicated, as the condition of possibility for the particular differences that constitute the language system, and, as always in Derrida, the condition of *im*possibility that the sign ever quite settle into the fixed unity of signifier and signified or word and meaning. As is perhaps a little better understood than the general trace argument, Derrida will also call this condition 'writing' or 'archi-writing' or text, on the grounds that the tradition has massively determined 'writing' to mean '(graphic) signifier of a (phonic) signifier', as opposed to speech which is thought to be directly the signifier of a signified. If we're using the traditional terminology, language *in general* now looks better described as 'signifier of a signifier', for, according to the trace-argument, *there is no signified.*

Once this radicalisation of Saussure has taken place, and the sign has been disassembled, as it were ('deconstructed'), then we no longer quite have a sign, of course, nor a signified, *nor thereby a signifier*. Language thought along the (generally anti-Platonic) lines proposed by Saussure leads to the description in terms of trace as complication of presence and absence that rapidly begins to render the 'limits' of language difficult to discern. This is not the same, I think, as annexing certain apparently non-linguistic elements to language by making them significant (so that non-linguistic objects can be counted as signifiers), nor even quite the same kind of thing that Wittgenstein does when, in the *Investigations*, he counts certain non-linguistic elements (colour-samples, say) as part of the language-game being described. Rather, on the basis of Saussure's insight that if language is not a nomenclature then it will require the 'differences-without-positive-terms' characterisation, it seems as though a regular and coherent conceptual derivation has produced a description of language which has a kind of dissolving virtue with respect to the idea that language has limits, or at least that it is simply distinguishable from something other than it (such as the world, say).

For once we have 'trace', it seems, then we also have a way of thinking about more than just 'language', as Derrida claims in a famously dense and perhaps rather excitable page of the *Grammatology*, and which I am really trying to do no more than approach:

> The 'immotivation' of the sign [i.e. what Saussure calls its 'arbitrary' nature] requires a synthesis in which the absolutely other announces itself ['s'annoncer' also means something like 'to loom up': we might want to say

> that in the trace the other *looms* without ever quite showing up in person or presence] as such – without any simplicity, identity, resemblance or continuity – in what is not it. Announces itself as such: that is the whole of *history*, from what metaphysics determined as the 'not-living', up to 'consciousness', passing through all levels of animal organisation. The trace, in which the relation to the other is marked, articulates its possibility on the entire field of entities, which metaphysics has determined as being-present on the basis of the occulted movement of the trace. The trace must be thought before the entity. But the movement of the trace is necessarily occulted; it produces itself as the occultation of itself. When the other announces itself as such [when it looms, then], it presents itself as dissimulation of itself. [So, in our alphabetical example, the 'a' and the 'c' and all the other letters *loom* in the 'b' but never *appear* in the 'b', which just appears *as* a 'b'.] This formulation is not theological, as one might think somewhat precipitously. The 'theological' is a determinate moment in the total movement of the trace. The field of entities [i.e. 'the world' in terms of the standard opposition between language and the world], before being determined as field of presence, is structured according to the diverse – genetic and structural – possibilities of the trace. The presentation of the other as such, i.e. the dissimulation of its 'as such', has always already begun and no structure of being escapes this.[18]

'Trace', then, says something about what Derrida also sometimes calls an 'originary synthesis' whereby anything at all is what it is only in its relational difference from its others in general, of which it bears the non-present but also non-absent trace from the start. In terms of his later work, we can say that the trace entails a general 'spectrality': any apparently 'present' element is 'haunted' by the others of which it bears the trace, but this haunting also spectralises it, renders it less than fully present. This is what leads him to describe the trace as 'originary trace', and then point out that the very notion of the trace disrupts the concept of origin, so that if at the origin 'there is' trace (but then, the trace 'is' not), then it is no origin.[19] Once what is, is an effect of the trace, then the trace is only ever the trace of (another) trace, and so on, without ever reaching any final or first 'presence'.

'Trace', then, derived here from the reading of Saussure's account of language, and radicalised as the quasi-originary possibility of any effect of identity whatsoever, has overrun any notional 'limits of language' with which we might have begun. 'Language' is an 'abstraction' with respect to the trace, and so, presumably, is the 'world'. Derrida is perfectly explicit about this, writing on this same page that

> the general structure of the unmotivated trace causes to communicate in one and the same possibility and without their being separable except by abstraction, the structure of the relation to the other, the movement of temporalisation and language as writing.[20]

Or else, writing in the slightly later essay 'Signature, événement, contexte':

> I should like to show that the features that can be recognized in the classical and narrowly defined concept of writing are generalisable. [In my view] they would be valid not only for all orders of 'signs' and for all language in general but, beyond semio-linguistic communication, for the whole field of what philosophy would call experience, or even the experience of being: so-called 'presence'.[21]

How, then, are we to account for the privilege that language still seems to have? For example, in 'Cogito and the History of Madness' Derrida says that language is no doubt the fact that always resists transcendental suspension or *epoche*.[22] I imagine that Derrida would want to say that *différance*, implied by the originary non-simplicity or again 'originary trace' (where 'trace' crosses through 'origin') that is the upshot of his reading of Husserl as much as the reading we have followed of Saussure, gives rise to language (or perhaps 'something like language') just through the differentiation that it is from the start. In the order of 'analysis', at least, once the sign is deconstructed along the lines I have indicated – giving rise not to any finally-discovered nucleus or atom (and this is why deconstruction is not quite analysis, of course[23]) but to the originary and endless complexity that 'trace' or 'text' attempts to capture, but by definition never can quite capture – then the differential relationship which is the 'principle' of the ensuing 'ontology'[24] *already contains* – in the referral that is part of what the trace is, or that is *just* what the trace is – the possibility of a signifying relation which is continuous with what we would more normally be inclined to call language. If we saw him, in the difficult passage about the trace from the *Grammatology*, insisting on the whole field and history of mineral, vegetable and animal existence, this is not only to ask hard questions of the traditionally massive distinction that metaphysics (up to and including Lacan, Heidegger and Levinas at least) needs to draw between the human and the animal, with all that flows from it (so that on Derrida's view the metaphysical need to deny the capacity of language to animals *in general* reflects an insufficiently critical approach),[25] but also to suggest that the continuity that 'text' suggests extends across everything that is. In other words, the thought of the trace and of the text affirms that in the 'first' distinction between anything and anything, in the minimal referral (not yet a reference in the normal sense of the term) that the trace involves, the possibility of what we come to think of as language is already given.

On this view, what philosophers often take to be the 'normal' function of language, i.e.., reference to the world, is a derivative possibility of this generalised trace-structure. Reference in this 'normal' sense is a special case of referral or *renvoi* in the sense specified by trace and text. Language and world have, if you will allow me, the same general *texture*. This is why, in the infamous 'Question of Method' section of the *Grammatology*, in which the 'nothing outside the text' remark is originally made, Derrida, discussing the status of the apparently extra-textual referent of Rousseau's *Confessions*, to which a reading might claim to gain some kind of access, says this:

> The fact that reading should not be content to double the text does not mean that it can legitimately transgress the text toward something other than it, toward a referent (a reality, be it metaphysical, historical, psycho-biographical, etc.) or toward a signified outside the text, a signified the content of which could take place, could have taken place outside language, i.e., in the sense we are here giving to this word, outside writing in general. This is why the methodological considerations we are risking here around one example are strictly dependent on the general propositions we elaborated earlier, as to the absence of the referent or the transcendental signified [i.e. the arguments about the trace that I have been rehearsing]. *There is no outside-the-text.* [Il n'y a pas de hors-texte]. And this not because the life of Jean-Jacques does not primarily interest us, nor the existence of Maman or Thérèse *themselves*, nor because we have access to their so-called 'real' existence only in the text and have no means to do otherwise [I think that this last is often presented as though it were Derrida's own position . . .], nor any right to neglect this limitation. All reasons of this type would already be sufficient, of course [i.e. sufficient to render illegitimate the claim to transgress the text and get to the signified or the referent], but there are more radical ones. What we have tried to demonstrate following the guiding thread of the 'dangerous supplement', is that in what is called the real life of these existences 'in flesh and blood', beyond what one thinks can be circumscribed as Rousseau's oeuvre, and behind it, there has only ever been writing; there have only ever been supplements, substitutive significations which could emerge only in a chain of differential referrals [*renvois*], the 'real' supervening or adding itself only by making sense on the basis of a trace and a call for a supplement, etc. And thus *ad infinitum* . . . [26]

And, returning to this slogan in the 'Hors-Livre' section of *La dissémination*, and modifying it a little, so that now we have, for example, 'il n'y a pas de hors-texte *absolu*'[27] Derrida wants to stress that this apparent refusal of the 'outside' does not amount to a simple generalisation of the 'inside': 'If there is nothing outside the text, this implies with the transformation of the concept of text in general, that text no longer be the comfortable inside of an interiority or self-identity (. . .) but a different set-up of effects of opening and closing'.[28] Which will lead (via a reading of Lautréamont's *Les chants de Maldoror*, which for some reason I do not imagine is common reading among students of philosophy these days) to formulations such as 'Il n'y a que du texte, il n'y a que du hors-texte', these now being the same thing, or differentiations of the same 'thing'.[29]

This confirms the thought I have been urging upon you: in Derrida there is no outside, no inside, no limits or frontier between language and something else, rather a differentiated (by definition . . . I want to say more or less differentiated, differently differentiated) *milieu of difference* which Derrida also sometimes calls simply 'the Same', and which has something to do with his abiding interest in Plato's *Khora*.[30] 'The limits of my language are the limits of my world' not because, or not only or primarily because, as in the so-called Sapir-Whorf hypothesis, the language I happen to speak conditions and even creates the parameters of my reality (however true that may also be), but because language and world are the same, text and trace, which is neither simply language nor world.

Notes

1. Ludwig Wittgenstein, *Tractatus Logico-Philosophicus*, trans. D. F. Pears and B. F. McGuinness (New York: Routledge, 2001), 5.6. This chapter was given as a plenary lecture in April 2006 to the Boston College Graduate Student Philosophy Conference 'On Language', and was previously published in J. Burmeister and M. Sentesy (eds), *On Language: Analytic, Continental, and Historical Contributions* (Cambridge, MA: Cambridge Scholars Press, 2007).
2. David Pears, *The False Prison: A Study of the Development of Wittgenstein's Philosophy* (New York: Oxford University Press, 2004), Vol. I, p. 10.
3. Pears, *The False Prison*, Vol. I, p. 12.
4. *De la grammatologie*, p. 227.
5. See my discussions in 'The Perfect Cheat: Locke and Empiricism's Rhetoric', *Legislations: The Politics of Deconstruction* (New York: Verso, 1994), pp. 119–36. See also *Sententiousness and the Novel* (New York: Cambridge University Press, 1985), an e-book reprint at bennington.zsoft.co.uk.
6. *De la grammatologie* (Paris: Minuit, 1972), p. 229.
7. Emmanuel Levinas, 'La signification et le sens', in *Humanisme de l'autre homme* (Montpellier: Fata Morgana, 1972), pp. 17–63 (especially pp. 34, 42–5, 48–50).
8. Although Derrida would certainly agree with questioning any particular attachment to the signified (because that is just what he calls 'logocentrism'), he more than once points out that the signifier can in no simple sense be thought of as simply 'material' – its intrinsic repeatability as the same signifier entails a measure of ideality that this self-proclaimed 'materialist' view cannot account for: see, for example, *De la grammatologie*, pp. 20, 45, 138: see also ibid., p. 32, n. 9: 'The "primacy" or the "priority" of the signifier would be an untenable and absurd expression in that it is formulated illogically in the very logic that it wishes, legitimately no doubt, to

destroy. The signifier will never precede *de jure* the signified, because otherwise it would no longer signify and the signifier "signifier" would no longer have any possible signified.' See too the much more recent and playful remark about Hélène Cixous: 'She knows just when to stop at the limit of crafty artfulness, when the signifier no longer signifies because it is merely a signifier' (Jacques Derrida, *Genèses, généalogies, genres, et le génie: les secrets de l'archive* (Paris: Galilée, 2003), pp. 44–5).

9. Derrida says that this use of 'effect' is not quite that of cause-and-effect, nor quite that of 'illusion' . . . See Jacques Derrida, *Positions* (Paris: Minuit, 1972), p. 90.
10. See, most recently, the remarks in the posthumously published seminar *La Bête et le souverain I* (Paris: Galilée, 2008), p. 181: ' . . . I substituted the concept of trace for that of signifier . . . '.
11. This is almost a rule that determines which concepts retain Derrida's attention, at least in his earlier work: so metaphor, for example, and its two 'deaths' laid out at the end of Jacques Derrida, 'La mythologie blanche', in *Marges de la philosophie* (Paris: Minuit, 1972), pp. 320–21, or 'Hors livre, préfaces', in *La dissémination* (Paris: Seuil, 1972), p. 14.
12. Such as the phallus in Lacan, at least as Derrida reads him: but our logic here is that the signifier /signifier/ is *already* occupying this place as a paradoxical consequence of its being cut free from 'signified'.
13. See *La dissémination*, p. 32, discussing the psychoanalytic interpretation of castration: 'The void, the lack, the cut, etc., have here received the value of a transcendental signified or, what comes to the same thing, a transcendental signifier: self-presentation of the truth (veil/ not-veil) as *Logos*.'
14. In general, there is never a 'right' term in Derrida, no true or proper name for his object, whence his series of more-or-less contextually motivated 'non-synonymic substitutions'. This type of situation is why Derrida sometimes and rather mysteriously suggests the need to maintain a 'non-classical' separation between thought and language, as for example in the following perhaps rather obscure comments from a note to 'Cogito et histoire de la folie': 'So it is necessary, it is perhaps time to return to the ahistorical in a sense that is radically opposed to that of classical philosophy: not in order to misrecognize but this time in order to **avow** – in silence – negativity ['avow in silence' to avoid the trap of the false or dishonest avowal of philosophy that claims to avow out loud a negativity that in fact it recuperates and thus forgets]. It is this negativity and not positive truth which is the non-historical fund of history. We would be dealing in that case with a negativity so negative that it could no longer even be named thus. Negativity has always been determined by dialectics – i.e. by metaphysics – as *labour* in the service of the constitution of meaning. **Avowing** negativity in silence means acceding to a dissociation of a non-classical type between thought and language. And perhaps between thought and philosophy as discourse: knowing that this schism can only be said, while effacing itself, in philosophy' (*L'Ecriture et la différence* (Paris: Seuil, 1967), p. 55n.). See also 'Write, He Wrote', below.
15. Synchronic *and* diachronic, so Derrida is led in the *Grammatology* to motivate to some extent his use of this term in the light of other uses he finds around him: 'If words and concepts take on meaning only through linkings

of differences, one can justify one's language and the choice of terms only through within a topic and a historical strategy. Their justification cannot ever, then, be absolute and definitive. It responds to a state of forces and translates a historical calculation. In this way, beyond those we have already defined, a certain number of factors belonging to the discourse of the time, progressively imposed this choice upon us. The word "trace" must of itself make reference to a certain number of contemporary discourses the force of which we intend to take into account. Not that we accept all of them. But the word "trace" establishes with them what seems to us the most secure communication and allows us to save time on developments that have shown up their efficacy in them. In this way, we liken this concept of "trace" to the one that is at the centre of the latest writings of E. Levinas and his critique of ontology' (*De la Grammatologie*, p. 102).

16. Derrida of course thinks that it is no accident that graphic examples seem more promising that phonic ones to illustrate this argument about difference and the trace, and it is this that will in part justify the later extension of the term 'text'.
17. *De la grammatologie*, p. 92.
18. ibid., p. 69.
19. Derrida here writes 'aucune structure de l'étant' rather than 'de l'être'. Trace needs to be thought before the 'étant' (the entity, or a being with a lower-case 'b', *das seindes*), but perhaps not before 'l'être' (Being, *Sein*). The reference to Heidegger, unmistakable here, would refer us to the earlier discussion in the *Grammatology* where Derrida suggests a kind of ambiguity in Heidegger's *Sein*, whereby on the one hand it still has at least a foot in the metaphysics of presence and functions as an 'originary word' and a transcendental signified, even as it also questions and even deconstructs any such understanding. Derrida's gesture in these pages, curiously like the one he makes with respect to Husserl in the Saussure chapter, is that it is absolutely necessary to *pass through* Heidegger's thinking of the ontico-ontological difference (the difference, then, between 'être' and 'étant'), even as he asserts that what he, Derrida, will call 'différance' is 'more originary' still: 'To get to the point of recognizing, not short of but on the horizon of the Heideggerian paths, and still in them, that the meaning of being is not a transcendental or trans-epochal signified (even were it always dissimulated in the epoch) but already, in a properly unheard-of sense, a determinate signifying trace, is to assert that in the decisive concept of ontico-ontological difference, *everything is not be be thought at once*: entity and Being, ontic and ontological, "ontico-ontological" would be, in an original style, derived with respect to difference, and with respect to what later on we shall call *differance*, an economic concept designating the production of the differing and the deferring. Ontico-ontological-difference and its ground (*Grund*) in the "transcendence of Dasein" (*Vom Wesen des Grundes*, p. 16) would no longer be absolutely original. Differance *tout court* would be more "originary", but one could no longer call it "origin" or "ground", these notions belonging essentially to the history of onto-theology, i.e. the system that functions as effacement of difference. However, difference can only be thought up close to itself on one condition: that one begin by determining it as ontico-ontological difference before

crossing this determination out. The necessity of the passage through the crossed-out determination, the necessity of this turn of writing is irreducible. This is a discreet and difficult thought that, through many unnoticed mediations, ought to carry the whole weight of our question, a question that we are still provisionally calling historial. It is thanks to it that later we'll be able to try to make differance and writing communicate' (Derrida, *De la grammatologie*, p. 38). Compare on the use of the concept of experience and the need to 'pass through' transcendental phenomenology and 'leave a track' [*sillage*]: ibid., pp. 89–90.

20. *De la grammatologie*, p. 69. See also twenty pages later: 'Because archi-writing, the movement of differance, irreducible archi-synthesis, opening together, in one and the same possibility, temporalisation, the relation to the other and language, cannot, as a condition of any linguistic system, form part of the linguistic system itself, be situated as an object in its field.' (ibid., p. 89). The 'relation to the other' part of this description is what justifies Derrida in saying that his later interest in more apparently ethical and political questions is not the result of some 'turn' on his part.
21. *Marges de la philosophie*, p. 377.
22. 'Because this difficulty or this impossibility must rebound on the language in which this history of madness is written, Foucault indeed recognizes the necessity of maintaining his discourse in what he calls a "relativity without recourse", i.e. without support from the absolute of a reason or a logos. Necessity and at the same time impossibility of what Foucault elsewhere calls a "language without support", i.e. refusing in principle if not in fact to articulate itself on a syntax of reason. In principle if not in fact, but the fact here does not easily let itself be bracketed. The fact of language is no doubt the only one that in the end resists all bracketing. "Here, in this simple problem of elocution", says Foucault, "the greatest difficulty of the undertaking was hidden and expressed"' (*L'Écriture et la différence*, p. 60).
23. See Jacques Derrida, 'Lettre à un ami japonais', *Psyché. Inventions de l'autre* (Paris, Galilée, 1987), p. 392, and especially Jacques Derrida, 'Résistances', in *Résistances de la psychanalyse* (Paris: Galilée, 1996), pp. 10–53.
24. 'Ontology' in quotation marks: cf. *La dissémination*, p. 65: 'The beyond of the totality, another name of the text insofar as it resists all ontology . . . '. See too the remarks on ontology in response to Antonio Negri, in Michael Sprinker (ed.), *Ghostly Demarcations: A Symposium on Jacques Derrida's* Specters of Marx (London: Verso Books, 1999), pp. 257–62.
25. See especially the texts collected in the posthumous volume *L'Animal que donc je suis* (Paris: Galilée, 2006).
26. *De la grammatologie*, pp. 227–8.
27. *La dissémination*, p. 42, my emphasis.
28. ibid.
29. ibid., p. 50.
30. See especially *Khôra* (Paris: Galilée, 1993).

Derrida's 'Eighteenth Century'

Mais ni Descartes ni Hegel ne se sont battus avec le problème de l'écriture. Le lieu de ce combat et de cette crise. c'est ce qu'on appelle le XVIIIe siècle. [But neither Descrates nor Hegel grappled with the problem of writing. The place of this combat and this crisis is what is called the eighteenth century.]

. . . le 'XVIIIe siècle français' par exemple et si quelque chose de tel existe . . . [. . . the French eighteenth century', for example and if any such thing exists.]

Un texte a toujours plusieurs âges, la lecture doit en prendre son parti. [A text always has several ages and reading must take account of that fact.]

(Jacques Derrida, *De la grammatologie*)

'*Ce qu'on appelle* . . . .' 'What we call,' 'what one calls,' 'what is called' – the Eighteenth Century.[1]

These brief remarks bear the same title as the volume as a whole, with, however, this very slight difference: that the words 'Eighteenth Century' are now enclosed in quotation marks. So not 'Derrida's Eighteenth Century', but 'Derrida's "Eighteenth Century"'. These quotation marks are supposed to function as 'scare-quotes', first, suspending a potentially problematic term or concept, 'mentioning' it rather than 'using' it, not quite wanting to subscribe to it, but they also function as 'real' quotation marks, because I am quoting Jacques Derrida's use of the words 'Eighteenth Century' (or at least « XVIIIe siècle »).[2] And then they have to be doubled up quotation marks, double *and* single, because I am especially quoting his use of those words *already in quotation marks*, more than once, several times, probably more often than not, in fact, in more than one text, the words « XVIIIe siècle » enclosed in what seem to be scare-quotes, and more explicitly still suspended in Derrida's reference to 'what we call' or 'what one calls' the Eighteenth Century, 'if any such thing exists.' My real point here will be to insist on those quotation marks and to wonder what they might do to the object of our study. What, for example, would it mean if the American Society for Eighteenth-Century Studies were to place quotation marks round the 'Eighteenth-Century' in its title?

So: what he calls 'what we call' the Eighteenth Century.

Now Derrida might reasonably be thought to have a certain affection for what he calls 'what we call' or 'what one calls' the Eighteenth Century. Among the very many centuries across which his work ranges, the eighteenth might not be the one most insistently discussed, but it could certainly be thought at least to hold its own. Jean-Jacques Rousseau, perhaps most obviously, is given (for reasons we shall probably see in due course) a very central role in Derrida's 'early' developments around the problem of writing – developments that are arguably absolutely crucial to his thinking in general; Kant, too, occupies an important place in Derrida's understanding of deconstruction, if perhaps somewhat negatively, both in that one of the things that deconstruction must most saliently be compared to and distinguished from – in other words one of the things it might most obviously be, and has been, mistaken for – is *critique*,[3] and in that the 'Idea in the Kantian sense' (usually, though not always, filtered through Husserl's idea of Kant's Idea) is also something I believe to be a real crux of Derrida's thinking from the very first to the very last. In addition, Derrida famously asserts an interest in and affection for the so-called 'mechanical' materialists when interviewed by a pair of Parisian dialectical materialists in 1972,[4] and also writes directly and one might say enthusiastically about figures such as Condillac or Warburton.

As the quotation I used as my first epigraph makes clear, this interest in the eighteenth century (or at least what Derrida calls more saliently in the *Grammatology* the 'époque de Rousseau' (p. 145)) has its initial reason in that that age or era is the one in which a certain set of problems about writing comes to the fore in an original way. In the section from which I take that epigraph, Derrida draws a very broad and quite dense picture of the history of metaphysics as the metaphysics of presence or as logocentrism. He suggests one major point of articulation in that history around Descartes, at which point presence takes on the form of self-presence, internalising possibilities of repetition and mastery already given by the ancient forms of *ousia* and *eidos*, and reinforces them into an unassailable power of auto-affective ideality, which power can be called 'God' without in principle compromising the integrity of consciousness, and this inaugurates a subsequent period (defined as that in which 'God's infinite understanding is the other name for the logos as self-presence' (*De la grammatologie*, p. 146) – a subsequent period that stretches from Descartes to Hegel. That period identifies consciousness with *voice* (necessarily according to Derrida), or more precisely with hearing-oneself-speak, as the only possibility whereby this idealising mechanism of auto-affection can seem to function without the need to compromise itself with alterity or mundanity. With its inherent phonocentrism, this Descartes-to-Hegel period has within it a new articulation, defined as the moment when writing is confronted and dealt with *as such* in these terms of self-presence. The story of *that* articulation, which Derrida wants to concentrate on Rousseau, is a story whereby the apparently inevitable tendency of the self-presence of consciousness to experience itself via voice and 'hearing-oneself-speak' finds itself needing to expel writing from its central concerns; and needing to do so *explicitly* and vigorously in the wake of an event Derrida describes as follows: 'attempts of the Leibnizian type had opened a breach in logocentric security' (*De la grammatologie*, p. 147) operated by projects for a universal characteristic. Rather than centre his story *on* Leibniz say (or, one might think, Wilkins, or even the earlier exchanges between Mersenne and Descartes on the possibility of an essentially written Universal Language, which Derrida does discuss to some extent in the *Grammatology* and again at greater length in seminars some fifteen years later),[5] he here chooses the slightly earlier moment at which the logocentric closure (in its 'modern' or post-Cartesian form, then) is being *repaired* or *reinforced* in *reaction* to such a potential breach, and that repair or reinforcement must take the form of a reassertion of the foundational values of consciousness (or sentiment, adds Derrida perhaps a little rapidly, remembering that Rousseau is going to be his man here), and that repair (given the claimed centrality of the experience of hearing-oneself-speak to the new form taken by metaphysics in the whole Descartes–Hegel tranche of its history) must then take the form of an explicit grappling with and reduction of writing. This configuration would then organise the 'age of Rousseau', and Rousseau would be the central figure or hero of that age just because he happened, or so Derrida claims, to be the one who most obviously stepped up to the breach, as it were, and tried to repair it. Rousseau would then seem to define or sum up 'Derrida's Eighteenth Century' because he is the one who most clearly or at least most energetically takes on this task of fighting off the threat that a certain kind of thinking about writing poses to the closure of metaphysics as defined in this its Descartes-to-Hegel period.

On this reading then, 'Derrida's Eighteenth Century' is defined not so much as an 'age of Enlightenment' or 'age of Reason', but as the age in which a certain unfolding story of metaphysics as presence and then self-presence has its specific crisis as a moment of recovering the foundational privilege of voice from the threat of writing. And this privilege is asserted more forcibly still elsewhere in the *Grammatology*, when in the chapter dealing with grammatology 'as a positive science' Derrida writes:

> The extent to which the eighteenth century, here marking a break, attempted to allow for these two exigencies [i.e. that investigation of writing allow a theory to guide a history], is too often ignored or underestimated. If, for profound and systematic reasons, the nineteenth century has left us a heavy heritage of illusions or misunderstandings, all that concerns the theory of the written sign at the end of the seventeenth century and during the eighteenth centuries has suffered primarily. (p. 111)

All of which might reasonably lead us to suppose that 'Derrida's Eighteenth Century' is almost simply 'Derrida's Century', the one that he would be the most inclined to celebrate and investigate, and those of us who have kept at least part-time day jobs as 'dix-huitièmistes' might feel inclined to be pleased about that.

And yet the tranquillity (as Derrida might have said) with which these characterisations are made – forgetting the 'ce qu'on appelle', and those persistent quotation marks around the words 'XVIIIe siècle' – that tranquillity is one we might do well to question, before settling back more or less comfortably in the *dix-huitièmiste* armchairs of our supposed specialty. We would hardly be reading Derrida seriously if we thought it appropriate, or even really possible, to assume the reality and consistency of anything like an 'eighteenth century' as a referent about which he might have said certain specific things (as opposed to other things he might have said about the sixteenth or nineteenth or fifth BC or any other 'century' at all). A little later I'll be suggesting that the mere fact and act of *reading* (its very possibility) is itself already sufficient to undo the largely unquestioned historicism that still, I fear, affects most work in the humanities and that haunts any periodising effort. But in any case, the very passage I have been looking at in the *Grammatology*, on the 'age of Rousseau' itself, immediately proceeds to put some preliminary questions to the kind of thing that is at stake in making such assumptions.

> The names of authors or of doctrines have here no substantial value. They indicate neither identities nor causes. It would be frivolous to think that 'Descartes,' 'Leibniz,' 'Rousseau,' 'Hegel,' etc., are names of authors, or the names of authors of movements or displacements that we thus designate. The indicative value that we attribute to them is first of all the name of a problem. If we provisionally allow ourselves to treat this historical structure

> by fixing our attention on philosophical or literary texts, it is not for the sake of recognizing in them the origin, cause, or equilibrium of the structure. But as we also do not think that these texts are the simple *effects* of structure, in any sense of the word; as we think that *all the concepts hitherto proposed in order to think the articulation of a discourse and a historical totality are caught within the metaphysical closure that we are questioning here*, as we do not know of any other concepts and cannot produce any others, and indeed shall not produce any so long as this closure limits our discourse; as the primordial and indispensable phase, in fact and in principle, of the development of this problematic consists in questioning the internal structure of these texts as symptoms; as that is the only condition for determining these symptoms *themselves* in the totality of their metaphysical belonging, we find in this an argument to isolate Rousseau, and, in Rousseauism, the theory of writing. This abstraction is, moreover, partial and it remains, in our view, provisional. (pp. 147–8)

So here we have Derrida arguing that: (1) the only concepts we have available at present for formulating the relationship between a discourse and 'its' historical structure or totality are caught up in the very metaphysics under discussion; (2) we can only hope to begin to get some distance from that metaphysics by first reading the 'internal structure' of texts as symptoms. At which point (or so a historian might suggest), Derrida happily gets into just that 'internal' type of reading (typically, on the evidence of the *Grammatology* at least, in a ratio of several hundred pages as compared to two or three on the history bit) and never really re-emerges again.

The historian, of course, will in general be suspicious of what can only seem to be a somewhat homogenising tendency (so that the history of metaphysics seems to be *kind of all the same thing*, or, even allowing the major articulation around Descartes, is *still pretty much the same kind of thing*, or, if we allow the identification of an 'age of Rousseau' along the lines I've just rehearsed, *still not really so very different*), whereby metaphysics will always say something like 'it all really comes down to presence, innit?,' and deconstruction will reply, 'in fact it's all really text and trace, innit?'). This tendency seems to be confirmed in a passing remark in the course of the essay 'La mythologie blanche',[6] which clearly enough has Foucault in its sights, although Foucault is not explicitly named here.

> As goes without saying, no claim is being made here as to some homogenous continuum ceaselessly relating tradition back to itself, the tradition of metaphysics or the tradition of rhetoric. Nevertheless, if we did not begin by attending to some of the more durable constraints which have been exercised on the basis of a very long systematic chain, and if we did not take the trouble to delimit the general functioning and effective limits of this chain, we would

> run the risk of taking the most derived effects for the original characteristics of a historical subset, a hastily identified configuration, an imaginary or marginal mutation. By an empiricist and impressionistic rush toward supposed differences, in fact toward periodisations that are in principle linear and chronological, we would go from discovery to discovery. A break beneath every step! For example, we would present as the physiognomy proper to 'eighteenth century' rhetoric a set of characteristics (such as the privilege of the noun), inherited, although not in a straight line, and with all kinds of gaps and uneven transformations, from Aristotle or the Middle Ages. Here, we are brought back to the program, still entirely to be elaborated, of a new delimitation of corpuses and a new problematic of the signature. (*Marges*, pp. 274–5; cf. too *Marges*, p. 82)

Derrida's manner here (and this seems to be consistent throughout his work) is to try to combine two gestures: the one will insist on the secular or millennial, quasi- but never quite permanent features of what he calls, for shorthand, 'metaphysics'. *Any* 'century' (or age or epoch or era) will tend in this perspective to lose specificity as it is placed in the extreme long view that doesn't even begin with Plato. On the other hand, specific texts will be read with that famously minute attention to detail and, more importantly, to their internal coherence, economy or 'syntax' (as Derrida sometimes calls it). This moment corresponds to the 'primordial and indispensable phase' we saw mentioned earlier in the *Grammatology*, which 'consists in interrogating the internal structure of these texts as symptoms'.

In 'La mythologie blanche', Derrida also constantly interrogates this play between a kind of 'internal' articulation of concepts and a historical or genealogical attachment. The relationship between the two, as exemplified by the question of the 'XVIIIe siècle' is precisely our problem here.

> However, the issue is not to take the function of the concept back to the etymology of the noun along a straight line. It is in order to avoid this etymologism that we have been attentive to the internal, systematic, and synchronic articulation of Aristotle's concepts. Nevertheless, none of their names being a conventional and arbitrary X, the historical or genealogical (let us not say etymological) tie binding the signified concept to its signifier (to the language) is not a reducible contingency. (*Marges*, p. 302)

> In recalling here the history of the signifier 'idea,' we are not giving in to the etymologism that we refused above. While acknowledging the specific function of a term within its system, we must not, however, take the signifier as perfectly conventional. No doubt Hegel's Idea, for example, is not Plato's Idea; doubtless the effects of each system are irreducible and must be read as such. But the word *Idea* is not an arbitrary X, and it imports a traditional charge that continues Plato's system in Hegel's system, and must

> also be interrogated as such, by means of a stratified reading; neither pure etymology nor pure origin, neither a homogenous continuum nor an absolute synchronism or the simple interiority of a system to itself. Which implies a *simultaneous* critique of the model of a transcendental history of philosophy and of the model of systematic structures perfectly closed onto their technical and synchronic organization (which until now has been recognized only in corpuses identified by the 'proper name' of a signature). (*Marges*, p. 304; no mention of Kant and *his* idea here)

And this seems to be the point of the quite complex and obscure opening section to the chapter of the *Grammatology* on 'La violence de la lettre', which opens on the question of genealogy. Here Derrida advances a number of difficult points:

1. If in a rather conventional way we here call *discourse* the present, living, conscious *representation* of a *text* within the experience of those who write or read it, and if the text constantly goes beyond this representation by the whole system of its resources and its own proper laws, then the question of genealogy greatly exceeds the possibilities that we are at present given for its elaboration. We know that the metaphor that would describe the genealogy of a text faultlessly is still *forbidden*.
2. In its syntax and its vocabulary, in its spacing, by its punctuation, its lacunae, its margins, the historical belonging of a text is never a straight line. It is neither causality by contagion, nor the simple accumulation of layers. Nor the pure juxtaposition of borrowed pieces.
3. And if a text always gives itself a certain representation of its own roots, those roots live only by that representation, that is by never touching the ground. Which undoubtedly destroys their *radical essence*, but not the necessity of their *enracinating function*. To say that all one ever does is to interweave roots endlessly, bending them to take root in roots, to pass through the same points again, to redouble old belongings, to circulate among their differences, to coil around themselves or to be enveloped one in the other, to say that a text is only ever a *system of roots*, is undoubtedly to contradict both the concept of system and the schema of what a root is. But not being purely apparent, this contradiction takes on the meaning of a contradiction, and receives its 'illogicality,' only by being thought within a finite configuration – the history of metaphysics – and caught within a root system that does not end there and which as yet has no name.
4. Now the text's self-consciousness, the circumscribed discourse in which the genealogical representation is articulated (what Lévi-Strauss, for example, makes of a certain 'eighteenth century,' in

> swearing by it) without being confused with genealogy itself, plays, precisely by virtue of this divergence, an organizing role in the structure of the text. Even if one did have the right to speak of retrospective illusion, this would not be an accident or a piece of theoretical detritus; one would have to account for its necessity and its positive effects. A text always has several ages, and reading must register that fact. And this genealogical self-representation is itself already the representation of a self-representation' what, for example, 'the French eighteenth century,' if such a thing exists, already constructed as its own provenance and its own presence.
>
> (*De la grammatologie*, pp. 149–50)

This methodological point is also made in the famous explicit exchange with Foucault, albeit not now about the 'eighteenth century', but about the history in terms of which anything like an 'eighteenth (or any other) century' might be named. Announcing in a preliminary way the kinds of questions he will be asking of Foucault's 'interpretation', Derrida defines interpretation in 'Cogito et l'histoire de la Folie' as 'a certain semantic relationship proposed by Foucault between, *on the one hand*, what Descartes said – or what he is believed to have said or meant – and *on the other hand*, let us say, deliberately vaguely for the moment, a certain 'historical structure', as they say, a certain historical totality full of meaning, a certain total historical project that it is believed is indicated *in particular* through what Descartes said – or what he is believed to have said or meant'.[7] This unpacks as two sub-questions: first as to 'what-Descartes-said', and second as to its historical significance and its significance as essentially historical. And in a slightly later reference to the *first* of these sub-questions, Derrida says the following, announcing some of the questions he'll be putting to Foucault about the latter's reading of Descartes:

> I do not know to what extent Foucault would agree that the prerequisite for a response to such questions passes first of all through the internal and autonomous analysis of the philosophical content of the philosophical discourse. Only when the totality of this content will have become manifest in its meaning for me (but this is impossible) will I rigorously be able to situate it in its total historical form. It is only then that its reinsertion will not do it violence, that it will be a legitimate reinsertion of this philosophical meaning *itself*. In particular as regards Descartes, no historical question about him – about the latent historical meaning of his discourse, about its place in a total structure – can be answered before making a rigorous and exhaustive internal analysis of his manifest intentions, of the manifest meaning of his philosophical discourse.
>
> We will now turn to this manifest meaning, which is not legible in a passing immediacy, to this properly philosophical. (*L'Écriture et la différence*, p. 70)

'Only when the totality of this content will have become manifest in its meaning for me (but this is impossible) will I rigorously be able to situate it in its total historical form.' So it looks as though we will never get to the 'historical moment' . . . Derrida's reading would then tend to remain at the interminable preliminary stage of decipherment, and endlessly defer the properly 'historical' moment that it might seem ought to follow on. The suspicion would be that the 'new delimitation of corpuses' and the 'new problematic of signatures', announced in 'La mythologie blanche', simply never comes.

And yet Derrida, in spite of certain appearances, really is arguing all this in some sense in the interests of history, of the possibility of history, and is doing so in way that is *already* enacting (or at least beginning to enact) that new delimitation and new problematic. The burden of his argument with Foucault in this respect is that without the moment of 'madness' that the 'internal' philosophical reading finds in Descartes (i.e. that the cogito is valid whether I am mad or not), and which Derrida assimilates to a 'mad' philosophical endeavour to exceed any determinate totality whatsoever, *then there would be no history at all.* When Derrida returns to Foucault many years later, and more specifically to Foucault's treatment of Freud, he finds some comfort for this argument in a later reference Foucault makes to the 'Malin Génie' (a reference which Derrida seems to have overlooked at the time of the 'Cogito and History of Madness' essay) in which Foucault sees the 'Malin Génie' posing an *ongoing* and indeed '*perpetual* threat' to the security of the cogito: what kind of historical status *in general* can the notion of 'perpetual threat' have, asks Derrida:

> One can imagine the effects that the category of 'perpetual threat' (these are Foucault's words) can have on indications of presence, positive markings, the determinations. For in principle, all these determinations are, for the historian, either presences or absences. *They exclude haunting.* They allow themselves to be located by means of signs, one would almost say on a table of absences and presences. They belong to the logic of opposition, in this case, the logic of inclusion *or* exclusion, of the alternative between the inside and the outside, etc. The perpetual threat, that is, the shadow of haunting (and haunting is, no more than the phantom or fiction of an Evil Genius, neither presence nor absence, neither the positive nor the negative, neither the inside nor the outside), does not challenge only some thing or another; it threatens the logic that distinguishes between one thing and another, the very logic of exclusion or foreclosure, as well as the history founded upon this logic and its alternatives. What is excluded is, of course, never simply excluded, neither by the cogito nor by anything else, without this returning – that is what a certain psychoanalysis will have also helped us to understand. [8]

And this point is also just what the famous argument about context is establishing in 'Signature, Event, Context' and 'Limited Inc'. If I can caricature a little and say that the historian will always want to *put it back into its context* (the tiger is out of the cage, the historian always wants it put back inside), then Derrida will always also be urging the question: 'How did it escape in the first place?' And the best proof that it *did* escape seems to be the irreducible (and somewhat mad) fact of reading. *None of these questions could even arise* were it not for reading, reading must by definition entail escape from context, and therefore something of the 'madness' that Derrida is talking about in the 'Cogito' text, something of the 'haunting' he posits in later work, and therefore something of the order of an ongoing unreadability.

Oddly enough, perhaps, this argument could also be illustrated around another pre-eminently Rousseauian theme (albeit not one that Derrida himself focuses particularly on Rousseau), that also happens to be one of the chosen themes of this panel today. Rousseau arguably offers the most coherent and economical account of sovereignty to be found in the tradition, and the account that shows up more clearly than some the inevitability of its deconstruction. Happily enough for our purposes today, the deconstruction of sovereignty is the condition of history itself (for if sovereignty 'worked', as it were, then its temporality would be one of absolutely self-contained instants that would have no link between them: the present would always be radically in the present with no possible link to past or future – whence a profound identity, in spite of some appearances, between a Rousseauian and a Nietzschean or Bataillean version of sovereignty. The same argument of course holds for subjectivity too). What makes sovereignty *not* work, never quite work, and which in Rousseau gives rise to all the strictly *supplementary* features of the state, without which there would be no politics (the legislator, the government, the tribunate, and so on), is what Derrida is increasingly in his later work inclined to call 'auto-immunity', whereby a structure's attempts to secure itself as itself and in itself founder on an irreducible opening to an 'outside' which allows it to be, certainly, but to be only as finite and intrinsically ('perpetually') menaced by unpredictable events without the possibility of which, however, the structure in question would simply *not* be (or would be dead, at best in a kind of living death). In the current case, this means that if the 'Eighteenth Century' ever could be defined in and as itself, it would quite simply become unreadable to us, and that its continued readability and availability for discussion depends on our not quite knowing what it is and in general on its failure to be quite itself. This is also why, for example, Lévi-Strauss is still in some meaningful sense part of the 'age of Rousseau', and why texts have several ages.

In the general case before us, this auto-immunity is just what I call reading, as what opens texts up always beyond their historical specificity to the always possibly menacing prospect of unpredictable future reading. The link between this and madness is something that Rousseau's work as a whole makes very plain. But just that same structure is what gives Rousseau's texts their several ages, why reading is never completed, and why we'll always do well to keep putting the 'Eighteenth Century' in quotation marks.

Notes

1. This paper was presented to a panel organised by Jodie Green under the title 'Derrida's Eighteenth Century' at the American Society for Eighteenth-Century Studies annual conference, Montreal, 2006. Previously published in *Eighteenth-Century Studies*, vol. 40, no. 3 (2007), pp. 381–93.
2. The relevant passages invoking the eighteenth century, or the 'eighteenth century', appear in Jacques Derrida, *De la grammatologie* (Paris: Minuit, 1967), pp. 147 and 150.
3. See my 'Almost the End', in *Interrupting Derrida* (London: Routledge, 2000).
4. See *Positions* (Paris: Minuit, 1972), p. 69.
5. Cf. 'Les romans de Descartes ou l'économie des mots', in *Du droit à la philosophie* (Paris: Galilée, 1990), pp. 311–41.
6. The essay appears in *Marges de la philosophie* (Paris: Minuit, 1972).
7. *L'Écriture et la différence* (Paris: Seuil, 1967), p. 53.
8. *Résistances de la psychanalyse* (Paris: Galilée, 1996), pp. 111–12.

Half-Life

The word *deuil*, mourning, seems scarcely to appear in Derrida's early work.[1] Unless I am mistaken, not once in the 'Introduction' to the *Origine de la géométrie*, not once in *La voix et le phénomène*. Not once in *Marges – de la philosophie*. In *La dissémination*, the word appears, I think, only in quotations of Lautréamont (p. 47, in a note), of Gorgias (pp. 131–2), and in a gloss on the etymology of the word 'hymne' (p. 242). In the 436 pages of the French edition of *L'Écriture et la différence*, the word 'deuil' appears, I believe, precisely twice (once in a quotation of Jabès), and in *De la grammatologie* only once. For a thinker who in a later interview more or less claims that he 'runs on' *deuil* the way a car runs on gas,[2] and whose encounter with the 'singular event of psychoanalysis' seems significantly to involve this concept of mourning, this might seem like an almost unbelievably small amount of fuel (really only two instances of his using the word 'in his own name', as he might have said), an extraordinarily energy-efficient way to cover the several thousand pages that one might otherwise have thought (that I, for one, have tended to think) laid down the bases for much, if not all, of the Derrida to come.

This 'early' work, the work of the first half of Derrida's life, of course already quite clearly registers the importance of psychoanalysis (said, along with linguistics, in the *Grammatology*, to offer some chance of breaking with metaphysical thought,[3] and of course given a long and complex reading in 'Freud and the Scene of Writing'[4]), but a psychoanalysis the philosophical importance of which seems to reside more with the notion of *Nachträglichkeit* (supposedly Freud's true discovery) than with anything else.[5] If *deuil* is so scarce in this early work, and if it is nonetheless a fundamental motif in Derrida's thought in general, as he himself seems to think, then it would seem at first sight as though this motif simply makes its thematic entry after this 'early' swathe of work, perhaps inaugurating a new 'period' of deconstruction – and indeed one might even be tempted to refer its quite dramatic and insistent appearance in texts from the 1970s to some biographical event, most obviously the death of Derrida's father in, precisely, 1970.

It is true that these few, these precious few, these really only two occurrences of *deuil* in that 'early' work are not without their interest, and, promisingly enough for the Derridean fundamentalist that he once accused me of being ('puritanical rigorist') and that I guess I am (by which I mean that I think that in a non-teleological and non-trivial sense all of Derrida is already 'in' the early work, already at least half there, at least half alive, in at the start or the origin, available and already living on for later returns in reading and rereading; that, like in fractal geometry, everything can be unfolded from an arbitrarily small segment of the curve, and that that just is the life of deconstruction, its life as the half-life that is the structure of reading as such, beyond or before any periodising or historicising concern) – promisingly enough for the fundamentalist that I am, then, in both cases these apparently incidental occurrences of *deuil* are attached to recognisably 'important' moments. In the *Grammatologie*, the single occurrence of the word appears as part of the reconstruction of the presuppositions informing Saussure's treatment of so-called phonetic writing as supposedly 'external' to speech, and anticipates on what will be the longer analysis of this 'Platonic' moment in 'La Pharmacie de Platon' a few years later:

> A particular system the *principle* or at least the *declared* project of which is to be external to the system of spoken language. Declaration of principle, pious wish and historical violence of a speech dreaming its own self-presence, living itself as its own resumption: so-called [self-saying] language, self-production of so-called living speech, capable, as Socrates said, of assisting itself, logos that believes itself to be its own father, thus rising above written discourse, *infans* and infirm in that it cannot respond when questioned and which, always 'needing the assistance of its father' (τοῦ πατρὸς ἀεὶ δεῖται βοηθοῦ – *Phèdre* 275 d), must thus be born of a primal cut and *expatriation*, which doom it to wandering, blindness and mourning. (*De la grammatologie*, pp. 58–9)

Writing, then, at least in this initial sense, prior to its generalisation as archi-writing, here less perhaps primarily parricidal than simply orphaned, ex-patriated in the sense of fatherless, less *voyou* than vulnerable and pathetic – writing wanders blindly, in mourning (perhaps, after all, rather like Oedipus arriving at Colonus, as discussed at some length thirty years later in *De l'hospitalité* ([Paris: Calmann-Lévy, 1997] pp. 37ff.)), arriving as a blinded, parricidal, mournful expatriate who also presents himself explicitly as an outlaw and a ghost (we'll see the ghost explicitly in a moment, in *L'Ecriture et la différence*: in the *Grammatologie* itself, Derrida says rather discreetly in the Saussure reading that writing, the wanderer proscribed by linguistics, 'has never ceased *haunting* language as its primary and most intimate possibility' (*De la grammatologie*, p. 64, my emphasis)). And the passage from the *Grammatologie* that mentions *deuil* will go on to make the 'signature' Derrida claim that the fact that supposedly full speech can even begin to lend itself to spacing in written form, 'places it originarily in relation to its own death' (ibid.). Writing, we might be tempted to say on the basis of this description, is not only itself the abandoned wandering mourner, not opposed to, nor really even distinct from speech, but speech 'itself' beside or outside itself, already in originary and endless mourning *for itself*, and thereby (because of the endlessness or the already) not exactly in mourning, but in something more like the melancholia or the 'deuil du deuil', the *demi-deuil*, of later work.

In *L'Écriture et la différence*, the other place where the word or concept of 'deuil' appears in this 'early' work, the word 'deuil' shows up only at the very end of the text, in the curious kind of postscript entitled 'Ellipse': the only part of the book that had not already been published elsewhere, dedicated to Gabriel Bounoure, a friend of Derrida's (but of the generation of his father) who was himself to die shortly afterwards. 'Ellipse' is indeed a rather elliptical text (at seven and a half pages, one of Derrida's shortest ever), and seems to function both as an explicit post-scriptum to the book it (all but) closes, and as a short commentary on Edmond Jabès (the subject, of course, of a much longer treatment earlier in the volume).

[The very figure of the ellipsis in Derrida might also repay some further attention,[6] even though it is only elliptically thematised as such in this text that takes it as its title: ellipsis names both a geometrical and a rhetorical figure, and also shows up, for example, in the title of a subsection of 'La mythologie blanche', and then more or less discreetly or elliptically throughout Derrida's work (in the very title of *Points de suspension* . . . , for example, and quite often in the interviews collected in that volume) up to the late *Voyous*, where the very opening of the first essay goes as follows:

> For a certain sending that awaits us, I imagine an economic formalization, a very elliptical phrase, in both senses of the word *ellipsis*. Ellipsis does not just name the lack. It is also a curved figure with more than one focal point. We are already between the 'one less' and the 'more than one'. [*entre le « moins un » et le « plus d'un »*: between the not half and the no end – GB]
>
> Between the 'one less' and the 'more than one', democracy has perhaps some affinity with this turn or trope called ellipsis. The elliptical sending would come to us by e-mail, and we would read:
>
> '*Democracy to come: it has to give the time that there is not.*'[7]

This elliptical association of democracy and ellipsis, which I cannot develop here, but whose being-elliptical already, one might suspect, has something to do with the structures of living on and mourning, and Derrida's elliptical prolixity more generally, would also perhaps have to take into account the suggestion from the *Grammatologie*, in the course of the Lévi-Strauss reading (just before the famous discussion of the war of proper names), of the need to return to 'Another ellipsis on the metaphysics or ontology of the logos (especially in its Hegelian moment) as impotent and oneiric effort to master absence by reducing metaphor in the absolute parousia of meaning. Ellipsis on originary writing in language as irreducibility of metaphor, that must be thought here in its possibility and this side of its rhetorical repetition.'[8]]

The opening gesture of this little text entitled 'Ellipse' sets up a kind of 'end of the book and beginning of writing' scenario (also of course laid out in the *Grammatology*), in terms of 'book' and 'text':

> Here or there we have discerned writing: a division without symmetry sketched out on one side the closure of the book, on the other the opening of the text. On one side the theological encyclopedia and, modelled on it, the book of man. On the other, a tissue of traces marking the disappearance of a God exceeded [*excédé*: at the end of his rope] or a man effaced. The question of writing could only be opened with the book closed. The joyous errancy of the *graphein* was then without return. The opening to the text was adventure, expenditure without reserve.[9]

But to correct the hasty reading one always might give this kind of assertion (and that was indeed often enough given by early commentators on Derrida, excited or indignant by the prospect of getting to choose one of the famous 'two interpretations of interpretation' formulated in the 'Structure, Sign and Play' essay that immediately precedes this one in the book (see pp. 427–8), despite the precautions Derrida himself always took to try to avoid such haste) – to correct such a hasty reading, Derrida immediately offers the following corrective:

> And yet did we not know that the closure of the book was not just one limit among others? That it is only in the book, ceaselessly returning to it, drawing all our resources from it, that we could indefinitely designate the writing beyond the book?
>
> *The Return to the Book* is then given to be thought.

This leads to an extended gloss on Jabès, from which I'll try to extract some argumentative nuclei, if you'll allow me that unsatisfactory formulation (unsatisfactory for reasons that have absolutely to do with the thought I am trying to unpack here). Writing unsettles the Book (and thereby God[10]) just through its powers of repetition: the return to the book takes the book outside itself just because of the figure of the return itself. The book (the Book) may think that it has an origin and an end, but the very movement whereby it tries to make sure of that fact undoes origin and end, deports identity into a sameness that is not the same as identity, not identical with identity. This power of repetition, without which the Book would not be the Book, but with which the Book cannot quite be the Book either, entails the disappearance of the centre:

> This repetition is writing because what disappears in it is the self-identity of the origin, the self-presence of so-called living speech. The centre. The lure that gave life to the first book, the mythical book, the eve of all repetition, is that the centre was safe from play: irreplaceable, withdrawn from metaphor and metonymy, a sort of *invariable forename* that could be invoked but not repeated. The centre of the first book should not have been repeatable in its own representation. As soon as it lends itself just once to such a representation – i.e. once it is written – , when one can read a book in the book, an origin in the origin, a centre in the centre, then it is the abyss, the bottomlessness of infinite redoubling. The other is in the same . . . [11]

This disappearance of the centre through repetition happens simply because a sign is originarily in repetition, a sameness of the same only in non-identical repetition. And now here comes the apparently passing reference to *deuil*: for might one not want to say that there *never was* a centre to disappear, that originary difference and repetition entail that there is simply no origin, never was any origin to regret: if the grapheme in its intrinsic repetition thereby has no natural place or centre, why not just affirm that centrelessness or decentring as such:

> As soon as a sign arises, it begins by repeating itself.[12] Without that fact, it would not be a sign, it would not be what it is, namely this non-self-identity that refers regularly to the same. That is to another sign which itself will be born by dividing itself. Thus repeating itself, the grapheme has therefore no natural place or centre. But did it ever lose them? Is its excentricity a decentring? Can one not affirm non-reference to the centre rather than beweeping the absence of the centre? Why mourn the centre? Is not the centre, absence of play and difference, another name for death? The death that reassures, appeases, but from its hole also creates anxiety and puts into play?[13]

Pourquoi ferait-on son deuil du centre? Why mourn for something that was not even lost because it was never there? Why not just celebrate play? (This is probably another way of saying: why not just let it go, get over it – 'take it away, I never had it anyway' – as the song says) and be postmodern?). Derrida's reply (after a quotation from Jabès in which we read that 'Le centre est le seuil [. . .] Le centre est . . . sous la cendre.

[. . .] Le centre est le deuil' [The centre is the threshold . . . The centre is . . . under the ashes . . . The centre is mourning]: this quotation apparently being the impetus for Derrida's 'own' use of the word 'deuil' in these pages) is unusually dense, and arguably all we're going to need to read the rest of Derrida, all the rest of Derrida, his other whole half-life, which would then, in a sense, be written in memory of this:

> Just as there is a negative theology, there is a negative atheology. Complicitously it still bespeaks the absence of the centre when it should already be affirming play. But is not the desire for the centre, as a function of play itself, indestructible? And in the repetition or return of play, how could the ghost of the centre not call on us? This is where, between writing as decentring and writing as affirmation of play, the hesitation is infinite. It belongs to play and links it to death. It is produced in a 'who knows?' without subject and without knowledge.[14]

And this situation is now given an unusually lurid figuration that it scarcely takes psychoanalysis to find at least striking:

> If the centre is indeed 'the displacement of the question', this is because one has always *nicknamed* [overnamed; supernamed] the unnameable bottomless pit whose sign it was, sign of the hole that the book tried to fill. The centre was the name of a hole; and the name of man, like the name of God, bespeaks the force [strength] of what has been erected in order to make a work in the form of a book. The volume, the roll of parchment was to be introduced into the dangerous hole, penetrate furtively into the threatening dwelling, with an animal movement, quick, silent, slick, shiny, slithery, like a snake or a fish. Such is the unquiet desire of the book.[15]

This perhaps surprising reference to animality (and already life, come to that: the animal is 'vif', quick in the sense that the quick is not the dead), long before any obvious thematisation of it in Derrida's work, also shows up in the earlier piece on Jabès from *l'Écriture et la différence*, where this passing reference to life is made explicit, and indeed capitalised:

> There is, then, an animality of the letter that takes the forms of its desire, unease and solitude. [. . .] Of course, the animality of the letter at first appears as *one* metaphor among others . . . But it is above all metaphor *itself*, the origin of language as metaphor, in which Being and Nothing, the conditions beyond metaphor of metaphor, never say themselves. Metaphor, or the animality of the letter, is the primal and infinite equivocality of the signifier as Life. *Psychic* subversion of inert literality, that is of nature or of speech become nature again. This super-power as life of the signifier happens in the unease and errancy of language always richer than knowledge, always with the movement to go further than peaceful and sedentary certainty.[16]

Breaking off here (elliptically) our reading of 'Ellipse', it looks, then, as though simply turning around this passing and unobtrusive reference to *deuil* has brought us, with metaphoricity, animality and life (even Life), to an expanding constellation of terms that set the scene for deconstruction more generally, throwing forward a standing possibility for reading and rereading that can take us up to and back from the very last work too. In this strange, anticipatory but non-teleological structure, that may begin to give a hint of how one day we might be in a position to describe Derrida's *oeuvre* as a whole (if you'll allow me that unsatisfactory formulation), we may find among other things a way of approaching Derrida as constantly 'rereading' himself (perhaps not literally), finding resources in his own textual 'memory' for developments decades later. And this relationship may *itself* need to be formulated in terms of the *deuil* that only barely appears here, but as it turns out appears dramatically and strongly enough to bear the weight of what will be put upon it for years to come. For it transpires that quite a good nickname for this infinite 'hesitation' between a kind of negative relation to the 'lost' centre and a positive affirmation of centreless play, here being aligned with a kind of animal life, is, not of course *simply deuil*, which is only one aspect of the hesitation, but, precisely, *demi-deuil* – and 'demi-deuil', half mourning not half mourning, no end of mourning, would then be a quite good way of thinking about deconstruction in general. If all work is work of mourning, as *Glas* and *Spectres de Marx* argue, and if the crux of that identification of work and mourning is to do with teleological structures, including that of the book itself, with finishing up and finishing off, then we would perhaps be justified in claiming that deconstruction, as always unfinished work, *just is (in) the demi-deuil of metaphysics*, never quite an achieved *deuil* or 'deuil du deuil', that would be the *end* of metaphysics, but the apparently more melancholic situation (affirmed on quasi-ethical grounds in, for example, *Béliers*) that is, however, life or Life itself. But 'life itself' as always life-death, primary survival or living on (as he says in that last interview), living on in the anticipated memory of an inheritance still yet to be read, for this is (half-)life(-death) as *reading*, reading-life only half-life not half life no end

Notes

1. Paper presented to the April 2008 annual meeting of the American Comparative Literature Association, in the context of a seminar organised by Steven Miller under the title 'Jacques Derrida and the Singular Event of Psychoanalysis'.

2. 'To work on mourning is also, indeed, to get into the practical, effective analysis of mourning, to elaborate the psychoanalytical concept or concepts of mourning. But it is first of all – in doing this very thing – the operation consisting in working *on* mourning the way one speaks of running on this or that source of energy, this or that type of fuel, running on high-octane gas, for example. To the point of exhaustion' (*Points de suspension* (Paris: Galilée, 1992), p. 54).
3. *De la grammatologie* (Paris: Minuit, 1972), p. 35.
4. In *L'Écriture et la differénce* (Paris: Seuil, 1967), pp. 293–340.
5. On this status of *Nachträglichkeit*, see *L'Écriture et la différence*, p. 303. For discussion of Derrida's complicated 'declarations' about psychoanalysis at this time, cf. my 'Circanalyse: la chose même', in Patrick Guyomard and René Major (eds), *Depuis Lacan* (Paris: Flammarion, 2000), pp. 270–94; English translation in my *Interrupting Derrida* (London: Routledge, 2000), pp. 93–109.
6. See some brief considerations by Nicholas Royle, in *Jacques Derrida* (London: Routledge, 2003), pp. 16 and 48. See too Jenny Chamarette, 'Flesh, Folds and Texturality: Thinking Visual Ellipsis via Merleau-Ponty, Hélène Cixous and Robert Frank', *Paragraph*, vol. 30, no. 2 (2007), pp. 34–49, which, however, incorrectly identifies *Writing and Difference* as having been translated by Ian McLeod and myself (p. 49, no. 5).
7. *Voyous* (Paris: Galilée, 2000), p. 19.
8. *De la grammatologie*, p. 156. See too *Che cos'è la poesia*, 'a poem must be brief, elliptical by vocation, whatever its objective or apparent extent. Learned ignorance of *Verdichtung* and retreat' (*Psyché, inventions de l'autre*, 1st edn (Paris: Galilée, 1987), p. 304). The affinity of democracy and literature is the object of forthcoming work.
9. *L'Écriture et la différence*, p. 429 – the very opening of 'Ellipse'.
10. Remember already the 'simultanéité théologique du livre' in 'Force et signification' (*L'Écriture et la différence*, p. 41).
11. *L'Écriture et la différence*, p. 431.
12. Cf. the *locus classicus* of this argument in *La Voix et le phénomène*: 'A sign is never an event if event means an irreplaceable and irreversible empirical uniqueness. A sign that took place only "once" would not be a sign. A purely idiomatic sign would not be a sign. A signifier (in general) must be recognizable in its form in spite of, and through, the diversity of empirical characteristics that can modify it. It must remain the same and be repeatable as such in spite of and through the distortions that what is called the empirical event necessarily makes it suffer. A phoneme or grapheme is necessarily always other, to a certain extent, each time it presents itself in an operation or a perception, but it can function as sign and language in general only if a formal identity allows one to repeat and recognize it. This identity is necessarily ideal. It thus necessarily implies a representation: as *Vorstellung*, the place of ideality in general, as *Vergegenwärtigung*, possibility of reproductive repetition in general, as *Repräsentation*, insofar as every signifying event is a substitute (for the signified as much as for the ideal form of the signifier). As this representative structure is signification itself, I cannot begin an "effective" discourse without being originarily

engaged in an indefinite representativity' (*La Voix et le phénomène* (Paris: PUG, 1967), pp. 55–6).

13. *L'Écriture et la différence*, p. 432, my emphasis
14. *L'Écriture et la différence*, p. 433
15. *L'Écriture et la différence*, p. 433.
16. *L'Écriture et la différence*, pp. 108–110.

Write, He Wrote

> 'Pourquoi un faux départ du discours est-il toujours nécessaire? [. . .] pourquoi est-ce toujours à partir du constitué, c'est-à-dire du produit dérivé, que l'on doit toujours remonter vers la source constituante, c'est-à-dire vers le moment originaire?'[1]

This is a false start.[2] And even several false starts. First, the epigraph that is talking about false starts, but which also, like all epigraphs, *is itself* a false start (so this one is a double false start, a false start about the false start). But also, secondly, this paper itself may well turn out to be a false start for our conference, 'Deconstruct, he says . . .', at least in the sense that my title was *dictated* (we'll see in a moment that that's the word for it) by a little moment of bad temper. As though something or someone in me wanted to refuse or at least take some distance from the overall conference title, or wanted at least to react to its Durassian feel[3] (as far as I know, Duras was not an author to whom Jacques felt particularly close), and above all to take a stand against what tended, in this quasi-quotation, to pull the verb 'deconstruct' towards Duras's 'destroy', whereas Jacques's most constant effort, when he did indeed say or write 'deconstruct' or 'deconstruction' (that word that he said one day in Montreal rather unpleasantly surprised him with its worldwide success)[4] was constantly to separate it from that. No, I said to myself, certainly too quickly and reactively, he did not say 'deconstruct' in that way.

Perhaps this can be explained by a mechanical reaction, a *mekhané*, as he calls it in *Papier machine*,[5] which (as part of the work of mourning, or rather the work of half-mourning, as he often calls it, that I have been living with for almost five years now, like survival itself, a work without work that in my case has remained rather massively on the side of melancholia, what I early on christened my 'militant melancholia') – a *mekhané*, then, that has pushed me more and more, in a way that is no doubt rather perverse, and certainly paradoxical, toward the 'origins' of Jacques's thought, as though (as I explain elsewhere) I could hope to find an origin, precisely, get back by dint of reading and rereading to the moment at which Jacques had the (I imagine blinding) intuition, the striking intuition that there is no origin, or that the origin is always already complex, and therefore not really an origin. At the beginning, at the origin, there would have been a moment at which he would have seen a certain impossibility of the origin, an originary complexity or secondarity, an 'originary synthesis', an originary trace, something radically non-simple, the very necessity of the false start. That the origin be complex in this way – and this is the ABC of deconstruction which once again I shall be content to do no more than spell out – complex and therefore non-originary, is, clearly enough, his originary thought.

Approaching this origin, this non-origin at the origin, one does indeed find oneself in the vicinity of his earliest thinking. (For me – and you'll have understood that I'm telling my life-story here, a bit mechanically, that I am confessing, avowing, writing my autobiography, *owning up* – it's as if there were two origins or two beginnings here, or at least two false starts: what I am calling Jacques's first thought is something he had or was had by around the age, no doubt, of 22 or 23, while writing his thesis for the Superior Diploma, on 'The Problem of Genesis in Husserl's Philosophy'; on the other hand, I myself was 22 when I first discovered 'Differance' and *De la grammatologie*.) At the age of 22, then, Jacques was already concerned, in this precocious reading of Husserl, with the complex relations between the transcendental and the historical, between a transcendental genesis and a historical genesis, between *a* (transcendental) origin and *its* (historical) origin, or between *a* (historical) origin and *its* (transcendental) origin.

There, we've started. A true false start.

This originary thought about the non-originary, or about an impossible origin, is something he says much less than he writes, or – more precisely – that he finds already written (if not exactly said), for example in Husserl. And this is the very sense of the irreducible or 'necessary' false start. The false start is what I must always begin by *reading*. He finds this thought written, *sees it in writing*, and rereads it in 1990 when thinking about publishing it. [6] He *reads* it, then, according to the already complex structure that he describes in one of his first published texts, 'Force and signification', in 1963, in which he speaks precisely of a fundamental and anguishing experience of *secondarity* which comes from 'that strange redoubling whereby the already constituted – written – meaning is given as *read*, preliminarily or simultaneously, where the other is present, vigilant, making irreducible the coming and going, the work between writing and reading', [7] or again towards the (so dramatic) ending of 'Freud and the Scene of Writing', where

> . . . pure perception does not exist: we are written only when we write . . . The 'subject' of writing does not exist, if one understands by that some sovereign solitude of the writer. . . [This 'sovereign solitude' is the theme of Derrida's very last seminar, in 2002–3.] . . . the punctual simplicity of the classical subject is nowhere to be found . . . One would search the 'public' in vain for the first reader, i.e. the first author of the work. And the 'sociology of literature' perceives nothing of the warfare and rusing that have as their stakes the origin of the work, *between the author who reads and the first reader who dictates*.[8]

This complex origin, this false start, between 'the author who reads and the first reader who dictates', is what means that deconstruction is written and read before being said, even when it is said, and what means that everything in these now classic texts that has to do with writing in the narrow or 'vulgar' sense remains of the greatest interest for whoever tries to put themselves in this complex position where reading and writing become confused and differentiated *in the same place and time*, as it were. Putting oneself in this position (to try to *read* Derrida in this strong and difficult sense – a little later I'll be claiming that no doubt *nobody* (with the possible exception of Derrida himself) has yet done this kind of reading) consists among other things in letting oneself be taken up by a whole slightly diabolical machinery (every text being a sort of machine that is as such perfectly indifferent to the life or survival of its signatory or its readers) that no doubt still has some surprises in store for the (professional) readers that we are.

(I shall often be invoking here the 'young' Derrida of the 1950s and 1960s, but what is at stake here remains so until the end of his life, and so well beyond. Allow me to quote a few sentences from the very last seminar to show this. This is a passage from the third session of the seminar in which Derrida puts forward a whole rather breathtaking meditation on the possible relation between *on the one hand* the structures of 'auto-' in general (auto-nomy, auto-sufficiency, auto-affection, auto-biography, and so on) and what draws them all, fatally, into auto-immune paradoxes, and *on the other hand* the minimal technical apparatus or minimal machine constituted by a wheel turning and returning upon itself around a fixed axis. According to the seminar, this becoming-machine of the auto-, as it were, has the closest relation to the structures of reading and writing we are, precisely, turning around here:

> One could say that every autobiography, every autobiographical fiction, and even every written confession through which the author calls and names himself, presents himself through this linguistic and prosthetic apparatus – a book – or a piece of writing or a trace in general, for example the book entitled *Robinson Crusoe*, which speaks of him without him, according to a trick

> which constructs and leaves in the world an artefact that speaks all alone and all alone calls the author by his name, renames him in his fame [*le renomme en sa renommée*] without the author himself needing to do anything more, not even be alive.)

This quasi-mechanical configuration of writing and reading most often in these early texts goes via explicit reflections on writing in the most 'mundane' or 'vulgar' sense of the word, 'before' the limitless generalisation of this same term and others close to it such as 'text' or 'trace'. For example, still in 'Force and Signification':

> The thought of the thing as *what it is* already merges with that of pure speech; and that with experience *itself*. Now, does not pure speech require inscription, a little like Leibnizian essence requires existence and pushes toward the world as potential toward act? If the anguish of writing is not and must not be a *determinate* pathos, this is because it is not essentially an empirical modification or affect of the writer, but the responsibility of this *angustia*, this necessarily narrow passage of speech against which the possible meanings push and get in each other's way. Get in each other's way, but also call on each other, provoke each other, unforeseeably and as though in spite of me, in a sort of autonomous super-compossibility of meanings, a potential of pure equivocality compared to which the creativity of the Classical God seems still too poor. Speaking scares me because never saying enough, I also always say too much. And if the necessity of becoming breath or word restricts meaning – and our responsibility for meaning – then writing restricts and constrains still more than speech. Writing is the anguish of the Hebrew *ruah* experienced from the side of human solitude and responsibility; from the side of Jeremiah subject to God's dictation ('Take thee a roll of a book, and write therein all the words that I have spoken unto thee.') or of Baruch transcribing Jeremiah's dictation, etc. (Jeremiah 36, 2–4); or again the properly human agency of *pneumatology*, the science of *pnuema*, *spiritus* or *logos*, which was divided into three parts: divine, angelic and human. This is the moment when we must *decide* if we will engrave what we hear. And whether engraving saves or loses speech. (*L'Écriture et la différence*, p. 19)

Meaning is meaning only in the passage of this passage, then, which is paradoxically both restrictive and liberating, an anguished passage that can be seen or felt more easily in writing than in speech. Why? Because, he goes on to say a little later:

> Paradoxically, inscription alone – although it is far from doing this always –has poetic power, i.e. the power to awaken speech from its sleep as sign. By consigning speech, it has the essential intention and runs the mortal risk of emancipating sense from every current field of perception, from this natural involvement in which everything refers to the affect of a contingent situation. This is why writing will never be simply the 'painting of voice' (Voltaire). It creates meaning by consigning it, confiding it in an engraving, a furrow, a

> relief, a surface that is supposed to be infinitely transmissible. (*L'Écriture et la différence*, p. 24)

Writing constrains meaning (which is, remember, the meaning of experience itself, of 'the thought of the thing as *what it is*') in the anguished passage which both limits and liberates its 'potential of pure equivocality', and does so by leaving a trace that is not exhausted in its immediate context, but emancipates itself and opens itself to the risk and the chance of a pure transmission that never will be pure, but which, through this very impurity, opens the concrete possibility of reading itself. (We'd need to reread here Derrida's Introduction to Husserl's *Origin of Geometry* the better to follow the detail of this logic according to which a certain ideality liberated by writing is then reinscribed in a certain mundane facticity which alone, however, 'delivers the transcendental' (p. 71).) Writing, or so one might imagine, will of course always offer itself (to reading, then) in a given 'current field of perception', but none of these fields will really be 'its' field, it will survive any current field of perception and any current affect, eventually to reappear in another, and again another, indefinitely. Or so he writes, for he writes this so that it can be transmitted and read and reread, to infinity, for example here today, and he writes it again two or three years later, against Levinas (but already for, in view of, or in the name of a certain 'ethics') who thinks writing can only be a *sign* whereas only speech can be *expression*:

> Can one not reverse all of Levinas's propositions on this point? By showing, for example, that writing can help itself out, because it *has time* and freedom, escaping better than speech from empirical urgency? That, neutralising the requests of empirical 'economy', it is in essence more 'metaphysical' (in Levinas's sense) than speech? That the writer absents himself better, i.e. expresses himself better as an other, and addresses himself better to the other than the man of speech? And that, depriving himself of *enjoyments* and the effects of his signs, he better renounces violence? [. . .] The thematic of the *trace* (distinguished by Levinas from the effect, the track or the sign which do not refer to the other as absolute invisibility) ought to lead to a certain rehabilitation of writing. Is not the 'He', whose transcendence and generous absence are announced without return in the trace, more easily the author of writing than the author of speech? (*L'Écriture et la différence*, pp. 150–1)

Write, then, in the name of poetry, of 'pure speech', in the name of liberty and the other, in the name of what liberates meaning for a reading, for the time of reading, and therefore for a history (or at least a historicity). Writing will be generalised (this will be the very movement of deconstruction) on the basis of what is, in spite of everything, first of all *writing*, *inscription* in the most familiar (*heimlich/unheimlich*) sense you like, except that clearly sense and the familiar will be carried or dragged away in the generalisation it makes possible (which is none other than said 'liberation' or 'emancipation'). By taking its time and its liberties with respect to the immediacy of speech, writing also liberates itself, *at the same time*, as it were (or rather time itself, time itself as the distension and differentiation of the same time, its *dislocation*), liberates its originary secondarity and carries off in its passage the domain that speech would have liked to reserve for itself, so that, as he writes a little later, ' . . . if writing is second, nothing takes place before it' (*L'Écriture et la différence*, p. 152).

Write, he writes: and he means *write*. Dictated liberated. Writing thus written is deconstruction in action, de-livering any Book from its fantasised 'theological simultaneity' (*L'Écriture et la différence,* p. 41).

This originary secondarity of writing affects in turn with secondarity any other supposed originarily, and this makes it easier to understand why writing in this sense implies reading. It affects with secondarity, for example, the so-called 'speaking subject', as he will say in 'La parole soufflée', which is also already the purloined letter (I emphasise in passing the moments most relevant to my concerns today):

> Given this, what is called the speaking subject is no longer the very one or the only one who speaks. It discovers itself to be in an irreducible **secondarity**, an always-already stolen away origin on the basis of an organized field of speech in which it seeks in vain a place that is always missing. This organized field is not only the one that might be described by certain theories of the psyche or the linguistic fact. It is first of all – without this meaning anything different – the cultural field from which I must draw my words and my syntax, **a historical field in which I must read by writing.** The structure of theft lodges (itself) already (in) the relation of speech to language. Speech is stolen: stolen from language, and therefore by the same token from itself, i.e. from the thief who has already lost his property and initiative. Because one cannot come before its beforeness, **the act of reading makes a hole in the act of speaking or writing.** Through this hole I escape from myself.
>
> **That speech and writing be always unavowably borrowed from a reading,** that is the originary theft, the more archaic stealing that both hides and *spirits away* my inaugurating power. *Spirit* spirits away. Proffered or inscribed speech, *the letter*, is always stolen. Always stolen because always *open.* It is never proper to its author or its addressee and it is part of its nature that it never follows the trajectory leading from one proper subject to another proper subject. Which comes down to recognizing as its historicity the autonomy of the signifier that before me says on its own more than I think I mean and with respect to which my meaning, undergoing something rather than being active, finds itself in default, or, let's say, inscribes itself *at a loss* [*en passif*]. Even if the reflection of this default determines the urgency of expression as an excess. Autonomy as stratification and historical potentialisation of meaning; **a system that is historical, i.e. somewhere open.** (*L'Écriture et la différence*, pp. 265–6)

Reading, as unavowable theft, thus also implies this 'system that is historical, i.e. somewhere open'. Everything here has to do with history, with the very possibility of history, in this 'somewhere open'. (All the more surprising that Derrida has so often been reproached with a lack of interest for history.) Remember, still within *Writing and Difference*, a remark of Derrida's about Husserl, in his first ever public lecture, 'Genesis and Structure and Phenomenology' – a lapidary remark according to which 'What I can never understand, in a structure, is that whereby it is not closed' (*L'Écriture et la différence*, p. 238). This opening that I cannot understand is not other than what we have seen Derrida call 'liberty' or 'emancipation of meaning', and coincides with the very possibility of reading. I read only (even here, I confess) where I do not understand, in the very opening of my non-comprehension. And, let it be said in passing, my reading (this is what distinguishes and will always distinguish deconstruction from hermeneutics) lives only on and in this opening, which it must not therefore close or fill, even ideally. Reading, in the very strong sense of the term implied by this young thought, this inaugural thinking of reading, takes place on the basis of my non-comprehension (where I read I do not entirely understand). If there is history, this is because this opening (of reading) remains a priori open, and thus will remain open forever, and this is obviously what is at stake in what is sometimes called, in the English-speaking world at least, the 'debate' between Derrida and Foucault around the *cogito* and madness, this opening as madness that for the young Derrida we are especially speaking about here is the very place of philosophy, the place in which I philosophise in 'the *terror*, but the *avowed* terror of being mad' (*L'Écriture et la différence*, p. 96). (This avowal of terror already opens the structure of what much later, after *Spectres de Marx* and *Politiques de l'amitié*, is called 'auto-immunity': here, 'the avowal is, in its present, both forgetting and unveiling, protection and exposure: economy' (*L'Écriture et la différence*, p. 96).) Or, as he says already in 'Genesis and Structure', just before the sentence I just quoted about the opening I can never understand: 'on the basis of the structural description of a *vision of the world*, one can, then, account for everything, except the infinite opening to truth, i.e. philosophy' (*L'Écriture et la différence*, p. 238). There is history (in spite of all the historians in the world, who are professionally occupied in reducing this historicity, in not reading – because the historian as such does not read) – there is history only because there is reading: and if there is reading (which is no doubt what there most indubitably is if we follow the logic of the false start that is ours here) there is no end of history, no last judgement, no arrival that is not a new departure. Still young, and perhaps a bit of an 'idealist' (in the vulgar sense of the term), he calls it 'philosophy', this opening to reading which is also an avowal and a *profession*, but one that the philosophical profession can only want to close down, for what is thus avowed is unavowable. For, let's just come out and say it, the philosopher as such, the professional philosopher, does not read, any more than does the historian.[9]

This historicity, which is a little mad, then, which is the opening of reading or the opening to reading,[10] the thought of which comes to him from writing (in the most current sense of the term), and what in writing 'emancipates meaning from any current field of perception', gives the time of reading as liberty and madness – this historicity is, as he says at the same period about Bataille, 'absolutely adventurous' (*L'Écriture et la différence*, p. 407) or, this time on Nietzsche, '*seminal* adventure of the trace' (*L'Écriture et la différence*, p. 427), to be summed up, elliptically, at the beginning of that strange little text which closes *Writing and Difference*, entitled 'Ellipsis', precisely:

> Here or there we have discerned writing: a division without symmetry sketched out on one side the closure of the book, on the other the opening of the text. On one side the theological encyclopedia and, modeled on it, the book of man. On the other, a tissue of traces marking the disappearance of a God exceeded or a man effaced. The question of writing could only be opened with the book closed. The joyous errancy of the *graphein* was then without return. The opening to the text was adventure, expenditure without reserve. (*L'Écriture et la différence*, p. 429)

Liberty and madness, we were saying, and so, often, 'adventure' and 'risk'. Writing, as in a phrase we have already quoted, takes the 'mortal risk of emancipating meaning from any current field of perception'. This is a risk in the sense that the meaning thus emancipated, thus de-livered, liber-ated from the book, might always dissolve or be lost. He writes of Jabès: 'A poem always runs the risk of having no meaning and it would be nothing without this risk' (*L'Écriture et la différence*, p. 111). In other words, meaning, all meaning, essentially written in the sense we have seen, thus destined in principle to an infinite transmissibility, is nonetheless 'poetic' in that it always runs this risk of being lost, scattered in its dissemination. Already at the end of the Introduction to *The Origin of Geometry*, 'if the light of meaning is only through the Passage, this is because it can also be lost en route' (p. 166). Auto-immunity again or always already, if you will: the writing that emancipates meaning and makes it legible exposes it by the same token to its loss, to unreadability. Which is in fact the same thing: whence the madness. I read only where it is unreadable, whence the fact that this risk is, as he often writes, also *chance*. The risk that meaning be lost is also the only chance for meaning to pass: Bataille's 'absolutely adventurous' writing is then, as he says in the same sentence, 'a chance and not a technique'.

He calls it 'philosophy', we were saying, in an avowal or a *profession* which is, however, not strictly *of the profession*, a profession that is probably not very 'professional'. Although I have hoped for years for a properly philosophical reception of Derrida's work (indeed if I know any philosophy, it's starting from reading his texts), I have also been reading, from the start, in everything we have noted thus far, something that will always remain unacceptable to philosophy as such. Let's be clear on this point. If we affirm that writing according to Derrida, deconstruction if you will, will remain forever unacceptable to philosophy (in spite of this 'idealistic' profession by the young Derrida, according to which the opening itself, and the avowed madness, *just are* philosophy), this is not at all in the name of another recognised or recognisable discipline, especially not literary criticism or 'theory'. Because we must allow for what, in all this work by the 'young' Derrida, is an impassioned defence of philosophy and what he sometimes calls its 'dignity', against the encroachment of the discourse of the 'human sciences' in general, which goes along with an inflation of language (or the sign 'language' or the sign 'sign') that he points out a little ironically at the beginning of the *Grammatology*. [11] This nexus of Derrida's work is quite complex (as I suggested years ago, this is something of the rule that governs the texts gathered in *Margins of Philosophy* in 1972): let me just say rapidly that it is this defence (let's say this *measured* defence) of philosophy against these 'human sciences', all inspired at the time by Saussurean linguistics and its 'scientific' ambitions, that dictates or is dictated by an apparently paradoxical refusal by the young Derrida of all linguisticism. Which is why, extremely vigilant in this respect, he takes his distances from literary criticism in spite of all sorts of at least apparent proximities: for if 'literary criticism is structuralist at every epoch, in essence and destiny' (*L'Écriture et la différence*, p. 11), and if 'the structuralist attitude, and our posture today before or in language, are not merely moments in history. Astonishment, rather, by language as the origin of history. By historicity itself . . .' (*L'Écriture et la différence*, p. 10), one might think there would be an essential proximity between Derrida and that literary criticism or structuralism. But then no, 'in spite of some appearances', as he often says at this time: because if 'philosophy has been determined in its history as reflection on the poetic inauguration' (*L'Écriture et la différence*, p. 47), literary criticism, for its part, 'has already been determined, know it or not, like it or not, as philosophy of literature' (ibid.). Blindly determined, be it understood, following the law of what much later he will call 'transcendental contraband'. Now – this is the crucial point – this contraband, which in this case will prevent criticism from 'explaining itself and exchanging with literary writing' (ibid.), always passes, however paradoxical this may appear, via an inadequate account of language. Just when everybody, or almost everybody at the time thought that they had been liberated by the advances of the human sciences from the age-old illusions of philosophy, so that people thought it possible to reduce philosophy to being no more than the blind and mechanical reflection of linguistic, rhetorical or poetic categories, Derrida with a rare lucidity sees very clearly that (as he will say in the *Grammatology*) even if one might hope that linguistics (with or alongside psychoanalysis) could bring about a 'breakthrough' with respect to the limits of ontology (*De la grammatologie*, p. 35), this breakthrough would have at the same time to shake up the 'theoretical' or 'scientific' bases of that same linguistics, which remains 'enclosed in a classical conceptuality' (ibid.).

This vigilant suspicion with respect to the sciences of language sometimes translates, in *Writing and Difference*, rather mysteriously in fact, into a suspicion about the tendency to cover over all 'thought' with language. For example, in a famous and dense note to 'Cogito and History of Madness' that points out in Foucault the difficulty of doing a *history* of madness 'itself', insofar as any history would inevitably be a history of reason, Derrida goes on to posit the need to dissociate thought and language in a 'non-classical' way. I'm going to quote this note at some length, to show how on the one hand this idea involves his whole relation to the history of philosophy, and on the other how, once again, Derrida still believes in philosophy (note in passing the repeated motif of avowal):

> And if there is history only of rationality and meaning in general, this means that philosophical language, as soon as it speaks, recuperates negativity – or forgets it, which is the same thing – even when it claims to **avow it,** recognize it. Perhaps more securely in that case. The history of truth is, therefore, the history of this *economy* of the negative. So it is necessary, it is perhaps time to return to the ahistorical in a sense that is radically opposed to that of classical philosophy: not in order to misrecognize but this time in order to **avow** – in silence – negativity ['avow in silence' to avoid the trap of the false or dishonest avowal of philosophy that claims to avow out loud a negativity that in fact it recuperates and thus forgets]. It is this negativity and not positive truth which is the non-historical fund of history. We would be dealing in that case with a negativity so negative that it could no longer even be named thus. Negativity has always been determined by dialectics – i.e. by metaphysics – as *labour* in the service of the constitution of meaning. **Avowing** negativity in silence means acceding to a dissociation of a non-classical type between

> thought and language. And perhaps between thought and philosophy as discourse: knowing that this schism can only be said, while effacing itself, in philosophy. (*L'Écriture et la différence*, p. 55: my emphasis on the motif of avowal)

Same gesture, though perhaps still more complicated, in 'Violence and Metaphysics', from which I'd like now to summarise (a little brutally, for lack of time) an argumentative sequence (it's not easy, for one senses in all these texts a slightly mad exuberance, almost an overflowing of thought that is trying to say everything at once, whence a certain irreducible *precipitation* that is also part of the logic of the false start).[12] Here: Levinas tries to 'dismiss' (*L'Écriture et la différence*, p. 165) the current concept of exteriority which, remaining too closely bound to space, tends to lose the radical nature of the alterity that would be absolute exteriority, absolutely non-spatial exteriority. But then, why keep the word ('exteriority') which, through this spatial reference, belongs to the sphere of the same, of totality – why maintain this word to bespeak a 'true' exteriority that would be non-spatial, why must we 'still inhabit metaphor in ruins, dress in the tatters of the tradition and the devil's rags'? Because this metaphor (this spatial metaphor, inside/outside[13]), metaphor itself, the mortal risky emancipation of meaning in writing following the structures we have seen, would be 'the welling-up of language itself', that at best philosophy ('which is only this language') can try to speak as such, and thus to *think* ('in the silent horizon of non-metaphor: Being.' (*L'Écriture et la différence*, p. 166)). Without this originary compromise with a language that is involved in space, and which is therefore metaphorical and *finite*, I would have no chance of saying the infinite. But, speaking the infinity (of the Other) in this way, in the finitude of language (and this would perhaps be the moment to quote again what I once called the 'slogan' from the end of *Speech and Phenomena*, namely 'Infinite differance is finite' (a phrase it would be nice to have printed on a t-shirt) – speaking the infinite in the finite in this way, I make the infinite into no more than an in-finite, I am obliged to say it negatively with respect to the finite, and in so doing I am reduced to 'writing by crossings out and crossings out of crossings out' – and obviously crossing out *writes*, i.e. 'draws in space'. Because this metaphoricity and finitude are originary, they bespeak by the same token the rootedness of all philosophical language in so-called natural language, and thus in natural language*s* in the plural, because there are many of them (whence later a definition of deconstruction as 'more than one language' (or: 'no more of only one language': *plus d'une langue*)). This naturalness, plurality and finitude entail an irreducible equivocality, which the philosopher must therefore *take on*. Taking it on, he must, however, recognise (as Levinas, or Derrida's Levinas here, seems not to want to do) that it affects every positive infinity with an essential negativity which is also the very condition of its alterity: 'The Infinite is heard as Other only in the form of the in-finite' (*L'Écriture et la différence*, p. 68: this is why much later he will say that 'every other (one) is every (bit) other': *tout autre est tout autre*). This moment (at which the properly unspeakable infinite betrays itself as in-finite) is, then, the moment at which 'thought breaks with language'. I quote:

> The fact that the positive plenitude of the classical infinite can only be translated into language by betraying itself in a negative word (in-finite) perhaps situates the point at which thought most deeply breaks with language. A break that will thereafter only resonate throughout language. This is why a modern thinking that no longer wishes to distinguish or hierarchize thought and language is essentially, of course, a thinking of finitude. But it ought then to abandon the word 'finitude', ever a prisoner of the classical schema. Is this possible? And what does it mean to *abandon* a classical notion? (*L'Écriture et la différence*, pp. 168–9)

In any case, after a brief passage via Descartes and Bergson (each of whom, accepting in his own way the separation of language and thought (whereas for Levinas thought *is* language), would be less troubled by this rootedness of language in space insofar as they can oppose it to a thought or an intuition which for their part can claim to be pure of any such rootedness), Derrida shows that this essential finitude of discourse, this irreducible spatiality and therefore this metaphoricity which is also the necessity of the practice of crossing out (and the crossing out of crossing out, thus of 'drawing in space', thus of writing), this naturality (not without relation to everything later to do with animality – he even says, here in *Writing and Difference*, about Jabès, that a certain 'animality of the letter', the metaphor of the animality of the letter, is 'above all metaphor *itself*, the origin of language as Metaphor') – Derrida shows that this finitude, spatiality, metaphoricity and naturality are nothing other than a certain inevitability of violence, or what he will call an *economy of violence*. This irreducible violence, linked in this radical way to spatiality and metaphoricity, to animality and metaphoric naturality, is not fundamentally different from the historicity, madness or adventure that we have already pointed out.

Now this violence, the irreducible 'economy' of this violence, which stems from the fact that meaning is exiled or liberated, 'emancipated' – which we see more clearly in writing because writing, grave, heavy, earthy, as he says in a note about Feuerbach (*L'Écriture et la différence*, p. 19, n. 1), obviously spreads itself out in space, makes us see, as it were, this originary 'metaphoricity' of all language (which is of course not answerable to the philosophical concept of metaphor, as he will explain at length a few years later in 'The White Mythology') – this violence which appears to be *part* of language (to come back at last to the enigma of a 'non-classical' separation of thought and language) entails that everything *not* be language, and that difference, the differences more or less calmly identified as belonging to the supposed 'inside' of the language in Saussure's sense (or even the episteme in Foucault's sense) become *differance*, which bespeaks (or such is my hypothesis today), or writes, rather, not only the dynamism of a process *contained* within the limits of such a system, but the essential opening of this same system (that essential opening that I will never understand, then, the mad opening of history and reading), to events of language, of course, to 'poetic' inventions in which something unprecedented, something really unheard of gets said or written (which is already a good deal, and enough to trouble all the Saussurean-style oppositions between language and speech, synchrony and diachrony) – to events of language, then, but also (and this is where, from being 'a great deal', it gets huge, monstrous as he says, more or less), the possibility of the event *tout court. Of the event as such.* For what comes or advenes (always via 'writing', now emancipated and adventurous), insofar as it comes or advenes, to be, as he says so often later, an event 'worthy of the name' (and therefore, as I shall try to show elsewhere, unworthy of any name, unspeakable, unnameable), that it come or advene always 'traumatically', as he will say in *Papier machine* (p. 114), trace already, is not, or not yet of the order of language. What means that the poem must always run the risk of non-meaning, the risk of the violent irruption of non-sense in sense itself (everything we have seen from the start) also means that we are no longer, at these moments of madness at which the totality is *exceeded* and something maybe gives itself to be read, no longer simply in the order of language. Unlike the 'human sciences' thinkers, then, Derrida never gives in to linguisticism; but unlike many other philosophers, nor does he give in to a referentialism that must always oppose language and world, and then wonder how we are supposed to manage, more or less mysteriously or magically, to cross over the gap between the two. (If we had time here, I would show how these two gestures – enclosing everything in language on the one hand, and positing a ditch or an abyss between language and world on the other – are in perfect solidarity with one another, following a logic that would explain also how the philosophers who wish at any price to exclude literature from philosophy get on so well with certain literary people and can even argue for the excellence or higher importance of the literature thus excluded). According to this properly inaugural thought of Jacques Derrida's, this event, which is traumatic, then, this Derrida-event, comes about in what I have here imagined or fictioned as a moment of blinding insight, a moment that for fifty years he tries to read and reread, grasp and sign – according to this inaugural thought, then, what he still here calls 'meaning' is itself only insofar as it is exposed, by writing (at first, then, in this entirely current sense), spread out in space (and thus exposed too to a certain stupidity, insofar as space and spacing are fundamentally stupid), and by that very fact, because of what we can call 'materiality' only if we take all sorts of precautions, this 'meaning' is meaning only by being also something other than meaning, does not 'make' sense through and through: *sense does not entirely make sense.* This necessary *exposure* of meaning, the very possibility of meaning that means that meaning is impossible as merely meaning, gives as it were the schema of all Derrida's thought, the very signature of Jacques Derrida: that the start always be a false start, that the possible in general be impossible,[14] that infinite differance be finite, that risk also be chance, that promise be a priori inseparable from threat, that in general we find ourselves in a milieu of interminable writing and reading – all that, or so it seems to me, flows from this supposedly original 'insight' or moment of genius.

Closing remark, to begin to pick up on what I said earlier about reading Derrida. Remembering what is said in 'Force and Signification' about the deferred reciprocity of reading and writing, about the first reader who dictates and the author who reads, might one not say that Derrida, obviously a great reader, is also a great reader of himself, that he never stops writing, constantly and continually, a reading of this initial intuition that throws him from the start into this writing-reading, and a rereading of earlier readings of this same 'originary' moment? Which is why, among other things, he is justified in writing sometimes, in avowing or confessing, that everything he writes is autobiographical or confessional, is an avowal, without that structure ever being able to close off anything like a self-sufficiency or an autarchy. For (this would obviously help to motivate his fascination with Rousseau) each written sentence, every event of writing, calls for a reading that must in turn be written and read, and so forth indefinitely. This law, which I have elsewhere called 'autronomy', which allows an 'auto-' effect to appear only by affecting it from the start with the other, exposing as it were its outer surface to a reading – this law (this auto-immunity already) is simply writing itself doing its thing, secreting itself in secret without secret like the silk [*soie*] of the worm that, just because of this secretion, will never quite be a self [*soi*], be itself in or for itself, never quite an ipseity, as he would say in his last texts.

Melancholic and jubilatory, this writing: the thing he has written also bequeaths us melancholy and jubilation in our in-finite reading and rereading. And means that he, wherever he be now, smiling no doubt, after the final false start, is still reading and therefore writing. If, as he said one day, 'Plato's signature is not yet finished'[15] – and that must be true of any signature, which is why every signature signs a sending, an *envoi*, a demand for countersignature whose mourning or melancholic inheritors we are – this would be doubly true of the signature of Jacques Derrida, who also signs (and it is an event, a trauma occurring in the history of writing), let's admit it, the statement of this essential unfinished nature of any signature, including his own, including this one.

There, it's started.

Notes

1. 'Why is a false start in discourse always necessary? [. . .] Why is it always on the basis of the constituted, i.e. the derived product, that one must always move back up toward the originary moment?' (*Le Problème de la genèse dans la philosophie de Husserl* (Paris: PUF, 1990), p. 2, n. 2). See too the false starts at the beginning of 'Limited Inc a b c' (*Limited Inc* (Paris: Galilée, 1990)). Or the first three sections of *Mal d'archive* (Paris: Galilée, 1995), entitled 'Exergue', 'Preamble' and 'Foreword'. See too *Le problème*, pp. 139–40, and the 'Introduction' to Edmund Husserl, *L'origine de la géométrie* (Paris: Presses Universitaires de France, 1961), p. 128: ' . . . the dependency and a certain secondarity of our text. They are those of any point of departure.' And, more famously, in *De la grammatologie* (Paris: Minuit, 1972), p. 233: 'We must begin *somewhere where we are* and the thought of the trace, which cannot not take nose-following [*flair*] into account, has already taught us that it was impossible to justify absolutely a starting point. *Somewhere where we are*: in a text already where we believe ourselves to be.'
2. This paper was written in French for the opening session of the conference 'Déconstruire, dit-il . . . ', Paris, May 2009. In the event I was unable to attend the conference at short notice, and the paper was read on my behalf by Joseph Cohen, preceded by the following note: 'This paper, as you are about to hear, begins with one or more false starts, and among other things puts forward a logic of false starts in general. When writing it, I obviously did not know that between its being written and its being read, in what Jacques Derrida calls the "deferred reciprocity" of reading and writing, which is also my subject today, an even falser false start would intervene and quite simply prevent me from being here to answer for what I am advancing. Allow me, before delivering the letter and the meaning of this little text over to its reader or spokesperson, before exposing it to the risk and chance of reading, to salute the organizers of this wonderful conference, and especially Joseph Cohen who did me the great honour of inviting me to give this opening paper.'
3. Cf. Marguerite Duras, *Détruire, dit-elle* (Paris: Minuit, 1966).
4. *L'oreille de l'autre: otobiographies, transferts, traductions. Textes et débats avec Jacques Derrida* (Montréal: VLB, 1982).
5. *Papier machine*, p. 33.

6. 'This panoramic reading that here ranges across the whole of Husserl's œuvre with the imperturbable impudence of a scanner lays claim to a sort of law the stability of which seems all the more astonishing to me for the fact that, *including its literal formulation*, it will not have ceased, *since then*, commanding everything I've tried to demonstrate, as though a sort of idiosyncrasy were already negotiating in its own way a necessity that would always go beyond it and that would have interminably to be reappropriated. What necessity? Always that of an originary complication of the originary, an initial contamination of the simple, an inaugural gap that no analysis could ever *present*, *render present*, in its phenomenon or reduce to the instantaneous and self-identical punctuality of the element' (*Le Problème* . . . , pp. vi–vii). It will perhaps be objected that the prefatory note from which I quote these sentences starts out with what it calls 'the idiomatic quality of the French expression "*s'écouter*" [to listen to oneself]' (ibid., v): but in fact, far from any 'hearing-oneself-speak', the 'listening-to-oneself' here passes via technical apparatus that make of it a writing, 'like on a magnetic tape or on the screen' (ibid.).
7. *L'Écriture et la différence* (Paris: Seuil, 1967), p. 22. The passage continues: 'Is not what one calls God, who affects all human navigation with secondarity, this passage: the deferred reciprocity between reading and writing? Absolute witness, third party as diaphaneity of meaning in dialogue in which what one begins to say is already a response.'
8. *L'Écriture et la différence*, p. 335, my emphasis.
9. Who reads? A huge question. *Dasein* does not read.
10. In the *Origine* Introduction, he says that 'in all acceptations of the word, historicity is *le sens* [sense, meaning and direction]' (p. 166). Compare with a famous text from the *Grammatology*, which recognises the necessity of the 'moment of redoubling commentary' in 'critical reading' (which otherwise would run the risk of 'going in just about any direction and authorizing itself to say just about anything at all', only to continue immediately: 'But this indispensable guard-rail [*garde-fou*] has only ever *protected* and never *opened* a reading' (*De la grammatologie*, p. 227). It would be interesting to follow this motif of the *garde-fou* in Derrida, which can take on rather different valences depending on context: see, for example, the *Origine* Introduction (p. 97) or *Du droit à la philosophie* (Paris: Galilée, 1990), p. 205, among others.
11. 'This inflation of the sign "language" is the inflation of the sign itself, absolute inflation, inflation itself' (*De la grammatologie*, p. 15).
12. Already in the *Problème*: 'this constant anticipation . . . a certain anticipation is thus faithful to the meaning of every genesis . . . If always some anticipation is necessary, if always the future precedes as it were the present and the past . . . ' (pp. 9 and 14). This motif of anticipation already anticipates on the very opening of *Glas*.
13. Compare with what is said in 'Plato's Pharmacy' on the primacy of the inside/outside opposition as the very force of every opposition in general (*La dissémination* (Paris: Seuil, 1972), pp. 117–8).
14. Cf. *Le Problème de la genèse*, p. 169, n. 89, which also pursues the problem of the internal historicity of Husserl's work with respect to its transcendental ambitions. I shall follow this problem further elsewhere.
15. *L'oreille de l'autre*, p. 119.

Beginnings And Ends

Derrida's early work is often quite plausibly thought to be about origins.[1] Indeed, if we wanted to identify an origin for deconstruction itself, we might say that it comes to Derrida with the thought that the origin is irreducibly complex. 'Originary synthesis', as the work on Husserl was inclined to say, and soon enough 'originary trace'. What Derrida calls 'metaphysics' tries to lead things back to an origin point that would be simple (call it 'presence'): deconstruction involves the claim that in the beginning is a complexity that resists further analysis in the strict sense, and that simple origins are always only retro-jected after the fact in the more or less compelling stories or myths that metaphysics recounts. Derrida wants to account for the (undeniable) *effects* of presence by developing a 'prior' trace- or text-structure which allows for what looks like presence to emerge while never itself being describable in terms of presence.

But if, in the beginning of Derrida's thinking, it was most obviously about beginnings, at the end it was arguably more about ends. Metaphysics, finding itself always in the middle, in complexity ('in a text already', as the *Grammatology* says) tries not only to track back and then derive that complexity from a simple present origin point, but also to put that complexity in the (convergent) perspective of an end point or resolution. Complexity should come from something simple, says metaphysics, and should be headed towards something simple; and that final simplicity often enough involves a kind of recovery of the original simplicity. The deconstruction of the origin, the *arkhè*, entails a concomitant deconstruction of the *telos*, and thereby of the whole 'archeo-teleological' structure that metaphysics is. What has often been perceived as a shift in later Derrida towards more obviously ethico-political concerns might better be described as an often subtle change of emphasis from deconstruction of *arkhè* to deconstruction of *telos*, which was itself there from the beginning.

I think that the 'origin' argument is now reasonably well understood, however difficult some of its implications remain: the 'ends' argument much less so, and that one task Derrida has left us is to think it through a little further, and to show how it is not to be separated from the origins argument itself.

The argument about the *telos* might go something like this: ends, however noble they may appear, and however ideal their status, also *end*, close off, terminate, put to death. In a Derridean perspective, the best chance for ends is that they become interminable or end-less, and that endlessness entails rethinking not just the end itself (an end-less end is no longer quite an end, just as a non-simple origin is not quite an origin), but the implied directionality or 'progress' towards it. Once getting to the end is not clearly just a *good* (because it puts an end to things, including the good itself), and once an even ideal progress towards it thereby becomes problematical, then a number of extraordinarily difficult questions about what we still call 'politics' and 'ethics' open up. In tune with a more familiar deconstructive suspicion of oppositions, this involves nothing less than a rethink of 'good' itself, and must lead to an affirmation of a non-oppositional relationship between good and evil. The least one can say is that this places an unusual weight of responsibility on the ethico-political appreciation of events as they befall us in their essential unpredictability, but in so doing it should also release us from the burdens of dogmatism and moralism that still encumber, in however reassuring a way, most efforts to think about these issues.

The recent emphasis on terms such as 'culture' and 'history' in literary studies seems an unpromising way to respond to this legacy that Derrida has left us. The appeal to history, especially, often provides a reassuring way of avoiding the hard questions that the deconstruction of the *telos* should bring with it. This does not imply that philosophers typically do better with such questions than students of literature. Philosophy will in fact remain unable to respond to the challenge of deconstruction until it can do better with the question of *reading*, which is one place in which Derrida's legacy will inevitably be played out in the years to come. Reading is already an issue when we try to think about legacies in general, and will be the more acute in Derrida's own case: if 'to be is to inherit', as he asserts in *Spectres de Marx*, if there is no inheritance without some effort of reading, and if reading is thought seriously as precisely not to do with restoring the *arkhè* or promoting the *telos*, then it seems probable that reading itself (prior to any hermeneutic determination whatsoever) might become our central problem, just as we struggle to read Derrida's legacy. There seems to be at present no philosophical, theoretical or literary model to account for the complexity of this situation, in which reading is structurally endless. And it seems likely that the current organisation of the university will be ill-adapted to encourage the most fruitful reflection on it. The deconstructive thinking of origins, ends, legacies and readings should also be provoking us to be more inventive in our academic and institutional arrangements than has usually been the case in the past. Attention to the very readability of what we try to read, however unreadable that readability must also remain, does not in principle belong to any particular academic 'discipline', and puts pressure on the very concept of discipline itself. The quite mysterious fact that I can read what I read (however imperfect that reading remains, and whatever difficulties it presents) precedes any particular disciplinary grasp, and indeed is intrinsically quite ill-disciplined and institutionally troublesome, but it is the only reason for doing what I do.

Note

1. This short text was first published (untitled) in the forum 'The Legacy of Jacques Derrida', *PMLA*, vol. 120, no. 2 (March 2005).

Salut à Jacques

Je ne parlerai pas de Jacques Derrida comme du grand philosophe qu'il aura été.[1] Je n'aurai pas l'ambition de dire toute l'importance son œuvre, bien que (comme nous tous) je crois cette importance capitale, inestimable. Je n'aurai pas la prétention, du haut d'un savoir présumé que je n'ai pas, auquel je ne crois pas, de dire la place de Jacques parmi les 'grands philosophes' (palmarès médiatique: catégorie 20e siècle, la première place se joue entre Heidegger, Wittgenstein, Derrida . . .).

Je n'aurai pas non plus la prétention de parler de Jacques comme de mon maître, ce qu'il fut, incontestablement, ce qu'il reste, évidemment. Tout ce que j'ai pu penser, non seulement dans le contexte du travail de Derrida lui-même (sur lequel j'ai écrit sans doute plus qu'un autre, par rapport auquel il m'a lui-même reproché un jour, voyant que j'avais encore critiqué un compte-rendu de sa pensée que je croyais simplificateur malgré ses bonnes intentions,

I will not talk about Jacques Derrida as the great philosopher he will have been. I will not be so ambitious as to try to state all the importance of his work, even though (like all of us), I believe that importance to be capital and inestimable. I will not have the pretension, from the height of a supposed knowledge I do not have and do not believe in, to say what is Jacques's place among the 'great philosophers' (media prize-list: in the twentieth-century category, the first prize is between Heidegger, Wittgenstein, Derrida . . .).

Nor shall I have the pretension of speaking of Jacques as my master, which he was, incontestably, and which he remains, obviously. Everything I've managed to think, not only in the context of Derrida's work itself (about which I've doubtless written more than others, and with respect to which he one day himself reproached me, seeing that I had once again criticised an account of his thought that I thought over-simplifying in spite of its good intentions – reproached

il m'a reproché, gentiment, en riant, d'être un 'puritain rigoriste' par rapport à son travail, plus que lui-même en tout cas) – non seulement ce que j'ai pu dire de lui, donc, mais tout ce que j'ai pu penser, tout, me vient de façon plus ou moins directement de lui.

Je ne parlerai pas non plus de l'amitié qui nous liait fermement depuis vingt-cinq ans, amitié sans doute asymétrique, comme il aurait peut-être dit, marquée par une certaine réserve de part et d'autre, avec des périodes plus ou moins fortes et intenses, mais que je dirai sans faille: une amitié et une fidélité mutuelles qui ont été, pour moi, unique dans ma vie, au centre de ma vie, depuis ce jour ou on s'est serré la main une première fois, à Oxford, en décembre 1979, à travers tant de rencontres un peu partout dans le monde, jusqu'à ce jour en juillet 2004 où nous nous sommes embrassés pour ce qui devait être la dernière fois, ayant marché depuis le British Museum, où on était allés en petit groupe d'amis pour qu'il cherche des cadeaux d'anniversaire pour Marguerite, jusqu'à l'Hotel Russell, d'où il repartait pour l'aéroport. Je ne parlerai donc pas de ces vingt-cinq années pendant lesquelles nous sommes restés d'accord pour ne pas se tutoyer.

Je voudrais plutôt dire ceci, du fond de ma douleur, depuis ce vide que me laisse la disparition de ce très-grand-philosophe-maître-à-penser-qui-fut-aussi-mon-ami-et-

me, in a kind sort of way, laughing, with being a 'rigorist puritan' about his work, more than he was himself, at any rate): not only what I have said about him, then, but everything I've managed to think, everything, comes to me more or less directly from him.

I shall not speak either about the friendship that linked us firmly for twenty-five years, a friendship that was no doubt asymmetrical, as he would perhaps have said, that was marked by a certain reserve on both sides, with more or less strong and intense periods, but which I will venture to say was flawless: a mutual friendship and fidelity that were, for me, unique in my life, at the centre of my life, from the day when we shook hands for the first time in Oxford, in December 1979, through so many encounters all over the world, until that day in July 2004 when we embraced for the last time, having walked from the British Museum, where we had walked as a little group of friends for him to look for birthday presents for Marguerite, back to the Russell Hotel, whence he was leaving for the airport. I will not speak, then, of these twenty-five years throughout which we agreed not to use the 'tu' form to talk to each other.

I would rather say this, from the depth of my grief, from this void that I am left with on the death of this great-philosopher-mentor-who-was-also-my-friend-and-whom-I-loved, from this fear I

que-j'ai-aimé, depuis cette peur que je ressens maintenant qu'il est parti et que je me retrouve un peu seul, même entouré de tant d'autres amis en deuil, même au milieu de tout ce qu'il nous a laissé en héritage: Jacques nous parlait, à nous tous (à nous qui savions l'entendre), et il parlait aussi en quelque sorte pour nous: il parlait à notre intention, mais aussi il parlait *pour* nous, à notre place. Il parlait si bien à notre place. A Londres, c'était l'occasion du voyage que je viens d'invoquer, ayant reçu un doctorat *honoris causa,* il avait dû rester pendant plus d'une heure sur l'estrade, plus magnifique que jamais dans sa toge, à regarder passer peut-être 200 étudiants qui recevaient ce jour-là, un après l'autre, leur licence, leur maîtrise ou leur doctorat. Après la cérémonie, il a exprimé son admiration pour le président de l'université qui, en serrant la main à chacun de ces 200 jeunes personnes, avait dû, disait Jacques en souriant, trouver pour chacun un mot de félicitation *différent*, dire 200 fois une parole inventive. Or, ni lui ni ceux qui l'entendaient n'imaginions que le président l'avait vraiment fait, ni même pensé le faire: 200 fois un mot différent! Mais on sentait tous que Jacques, lui, l'aurait fait: ou du moins se serait senti obligé de le faire, se serait senti tenu d'inventer à chaque fois. Combien de fois ne l'a-t-on pas entendu le faire, d'ailleurs: après toutes ces centaines de communications et de conférences qu'il

feel now that he has gone and I feel alone, even surrounded by other friends in mourning, even with all he bequeathed to us: Jacques spoke to us, to all of us (to those who could hear), and he also spoke as it were for us: he spoke to us, but also he spoke *for* us, in our place. He spoke so well in our place. In London, and this was the reason for the trip I have just mentioned, having received an honorary doctorate, he had had to remain for over an hour on the stage, more magnificent than ever in his gown, as he watched perhaps 200 students pass across the stage to receive their batchelor's, master's or doctoral degree. After the ceremony, he expressed his admiration for the University Vice-Chancellor who, as he shook hands with each one of these 200 young people, must, said Jacques with a smile, must have found for each one a *different* expression of congratulation, must have said 200 times something inventive. Now neither he nor we who heard him imagined that the Vice-Chancellor had really done this, nor even thought of doing it: saying 200 different things! But we felt that Jacques would have done so: or at least felt obliged to do so, obliged to be inventive each time. How many times had we not heard him do this, in fact: after each one of those hundreds of papers and lectures he had to listen to, or even suffer, in several languages, how many times had we not heard him

a dû entendre, voire subir, dans plusieurs langues, combien de fois ne l'a-t-on pas entendu trouver, dans sa réponse, même aux plus médiocres, aux moins invenifs, un mot, une façon d'enchaîner, chaque fois différemment, dans l'invention, sans jamais céder aux formes données de la politesse académique. Au fond, c'est peut-être ce que j'admirais le plus, ce qui me semblait être l'admirable même dans tout ce qu'admirais chez lui.

Ce mot différent, ce mot de politesse, d'accueil, je me dis aujourd'hui qu'il avait à chaque fois un peu aussi le caractère d'un mot d'adieu, de salut, comme il disait naguère. Je l'associe à tout ce qui à été récemment relié dans *Chaque fois unique, la fin du monde*, où, chaque fois, ne croyant pas trouver ses mots, disant le mal qu'il avait à trouver ses mots, Jacques a trouvé les mots, a bien trouvé les mots, chaque fois uniques, pour dire et pleurer la disparition du maître ou de l'ami, pour dire chaque fois uniquement la fin du monde, et le dire uniquement aussi pour nous.

Or pour lui-même il ne le peut pas: malgré tout ce qu'il a pu écrire sur la mort, sur les morts, sur sa propre mort, malgré tout ce qu'il a pu faire pour nous préparer depuis toujours à cette disparition – cela, cet adieu ou ce salut-là, il ne peut pas le dire, et il nous revient maintenant de le faire, pour lui, à sa place, en inventant de notre mieux, au-delà de toute politesse et de tout devoir: et c'est peut-être juste-

find in his response, even to the most mediocre, the least inventive, some different way of responding, inventively, without ever giving in to the usual forms of academic politeness. Deep down, perhaps this is what I admired the most, what seemed most admirable to me in everything I admired in him.

This different word, this word of politeness and welcome – today I tell myself that each time also it had something of the character of a word of farewell, of *salut*, as he was saying lately. I associate it with everything that has recently been bound together as *The Work of Mourning*, in which, each time, fearing he could not find his words, saying how hard it was to find the words, Jacques found the words, and found them so well, each time unique words to say and lament the departure of master or friend, to say each time uniquely the end of the world, and to say it uniquely also for us.

For himself he cannot: in spite of everything he wrote about death, about the dead, about his own death, in spite of everything he did from the start to prepare us for this departure – he cannot say this thing, this adieu or *salut*, and it is up to us to do it for him, in his place, inventing as best we can, beyond all politeness and all duty: and perhaps it is here, in our tears, with all the treasures he has left us, that we miss him most cruelly, here, today, for we know how much better than we he

ment là, au fond de nos larmes, au milieu de toutes les richesses qu'il nous a laissées, qu'il nous manque le plus cruellement, ici, aujourd'hui, car nous savons combien mieux que nous il aurait trouvé ces mots. Il n'y a que Jacques, me dis-je, qui fût digne de dire ces mots pour Jacques.

Et puis il me semble l'entendre dire, ou plutôt murmurer, doucement, comme un encouragement, non pas ces mots pour Jacques que je cherche sans trouver, que je n'aurai pas trouvés, mais autre chose encore, autre chose, encore autre chose, l'autre, même.

would have found those words. Only Jacques, I say to myself, was worthy of saying these words for Jacques.

And then I seem to hear him say, or rather murmur, softly, like an encouragement, not these words for Jacques that I am seeking and not finding, that I have not found, but something other again, something other, again something other, the other, the same.

Note

1. This text was written immediately after Jacques Derrida's death, on the invitation of Bruno Clément, for the memorial event held at the Collège International de Philosophie, Paris, 21 October 2004. As I was unable to attend the event because of visa problems, the text was read on my behalf by Mireille Calle-Gruber, to whom I express my gratitude. Previously published in a special issue of the journal *Rue Descartes*, no. 48 (2005), 'Salut à Jacques Derrida', pp. 51–3.

Jacques Derrida in America

Under this title, 'Jacques Derrida in America', which was assigned to me (or perhaps thrown down like a challenge) by Mustapha Chérif, whom I should like to thank here for his generous invitation, in the name of the National Library of Algeria, to this important and precious event (the more so in that I am – if I can say this – *not even* American, but English, from England, somewhat exiled, it is true, in the USA) – under this title, then, I could for example have offered you a little historical survey of Jacques Derrida's trips to the United States of America.[1] Starting with the first (and by far the longest) trip, by boat, in 1956–7, on the more of less serious pretext ('a bit fictitious', he told me himself[2]) of consulting some Husserl archives the microfilmed copy of which had just become available at Harvard. (A trip during which, far from home and family – and not by chance – he married Marguerite Aucouturier, here present . . .). This type of historical survey might go on to enumerate the very many trips that Jacques Derrida made to the USA during a period of fifty years, his very numerous lectures, but perhaps above all the periods of teaching (his teaching posts) first at Johns Hopkins (Baltimore), no doubt in part a result of his contribution to the famous conference on the Human Sciences in 1966 (to which he gave 'Structure, Sign and Play . . . ' which first made him known in English translation), then his twelve consecutive years of regular visits of several weeks a year to Yale (1975–86, the years of the so-called 'Yale School'), before going to the University of Irvine in California every year from 1987 to the end, not to mention his many visits to New York and to many other great American universities, most often, especially at first, in literature or comparative literature departments, even though one can also subsequently follow the impact of his thought in schools and departments of law, architecture, geography and even sometimes philosophy.

(If one were trying to do a more detailed history of these movements, one would also have to bring out another, slower, movement, with respect to language, and especially the English language: for if at the beginning Derrida's teaching always took place in French, under the aegis of French departments, he grew increasingly comfortable with English (at least in its American version, for I know – and I really do know – that he sometimes had trouble with British English), so that, even though as far as I know he never really wrote any texts in English, he nevertheless had a very refined relation with that language which he used with a definite facility and elegance, just as he on occasion wrote texts in French *with a view* to their English or American translation, already intervening in the translation to come, giving instructions or throwing out explicit challenges to the translator, etc.)

Presented in this way, the chapter 'Derrida in America' would form part of the 'Derrida Abroad' volume of his history or biography. A chapter that would of course be longer than others, because one can say without fear of contradiction that the USA was, both really and symbolically, the very figure of the 'foreign', a very familiar foreign, in Jacques Derrida's intellectual life.

Rather than attempting to be the historian of these many journeys, however, in the time that is given to me here, I should like to draw your attention to a motif that is both vaster and more restricted, having to do with *translation* in all senses of the term. And what I have to say about this could no doubt be organised around the following sentence, obviously unpronounceable [and untranslatable] as such, to be read in all possible senses: 'Jacques Derrida got translated in(to) America(n), and (it) (never) came home (to him) again' [*Jaques Derrida s'est fait traduire aux Etats-Unis, et il (n')en est (pas) revenu*].

1. First, literally, so to speak, in the sense that Jacques Derrida got *translated* in the USA. More, earlier, and obviously with a broader distribution and impact that anywhere else. And when I say anywhere else, I mean anywhere else, *even* France. It would perhaps be worth pondering the fact that, quantitatively at least, Derrida will have been (and plausibly always will be) much more read in English than in any other language, *including French*. (This is already not simple, for one can also reasonably imagine that a non-negligible part of what Derrida does is done in a certain relation to the untranslatable and the idiomatic: if you'll allow me a personal confession here, and even as one of Derrida's translators, I have the greatest difficulty reading him in English, at the very moment I'm trying to make him readable for Anglophones, just as, on the personal level, my friendship with Jacques took place exclusively in French . . .) For one of the paradoxes that must be taken into account

when thinking about this whole history of Jacques Derrida in America is that he was not merely a great-French-thinker who, on the basis of a certain national standing, got translated into other languages, and first among them English or American, but that Jacques Derrida himself *comes back, comes back to France* and has his home there as a 'Great French Thinker' *from* an America that without ever having been an adoptive home for him (he lived there, of course, and lived there quite a bit, but unlike some other French thinkers he never settled there full-time, and after that first long trip never spent more than a few weeks there at a time), an America that is nonetheless the country (and the language) from which he returns to become (at least in terms of recognition, and not merely media recognition) the great thinker he will have been, 'the greatest philosopher in the world', as I heard him presented by Franz-Olivier Giesbert at the beginning of a TV show broadcast not long before his death,[3] a thinker become himself, become Jacques Derrida himself, even in his most intimate relations with the French language and culture, on returning from the USA, returning then from English, in a spectral relationship he also helps us to think through.[4]

This complex relation is part (but not any old part, and no doubt in fact the essential or at least exemplary part) of a movement that can be called, that is often called, 'French Thought', *French Theory* as the French themselves sometimes call it, in English, a little naively astonished to see this image of themselves come back to them from elsewhere, from the USA.

Jacques Derrida himself says something about this in *La contre-allée*, in a little narrative of the history of his relations with the USA that he produced for Catherine Malabou:

> . . . Allied landing in November 1942, no doubt the first astonished encounter with foreigners who came from afar. An other culture. Discovery of America. Before I went to America, America invaded my 'home'. By the way, I do not know if or how you are going to tackle my 'American question'. Of course there is more than one question (first big trip, first long stay abroad, 1956–7, so many universities in which I have taught, so many translations, so many friends and enemies, etc., and I've written a lot, though very unsatisfactorily, about this. But if I were to treat said 'American question' in your place, I would first be tempted by the genre of satire. I have always found deeply comical what is said about this 'American connection', especially in France. There's a lot of incompetence, ignorance or naivety in it, of course, which is not of itself funny, but the posing and the tone make you laugh. The provincial genre ('that little lad of ours is very well-known abroad, you know, you wouldn't believe it, especially over there in America') is nonetheless peremptory, arrogant and anti-American, xenophobic, even, pouting ('it's OK especially for the Americans, but we're not taken in', implying, with sigh and grimace, 'Ah, if only he would stay over there'). The same people

> pretend not to know (for, to talk like them, they are not without knowing) that although I only spend a few weeks a year in the United States, teaching regularly and very full-time in Paris, I am anything but indulgent towards a whole 'American culture' . . . .[5]

2. But there is another relation, perhaps more 'internal' to Derrida's thought, that is in play in 'Jacques Derrida in America'. For Derrida, no doubt in the general optic of a sort of 'definition' of deconstruction as 'what happens', also said one day (even if only to go on to complicate and even take back this sentence that sounds like a provocation): 'but America *is* deconstruction' (*Mémoires pour Paul de Man*). And even if, in what follows this surprising assertion, Derrida goes on to refuse it and even deny it (saying 'In the war raging on the subject of deconstruction, there are no fronts, but if there were, they would all pass through the United States, they would define the lot and the very partition of America. But we have learnt, from "Deconstruction", to suspend these always hasty attributions of proper names . . . No, deconstruction is not a proper name, and America is not its proper name. Let us say, rather: two open sets that partially intersect in an allegorico-metonymic figure. And in this fiction of truth, America would be the title for a new novel for the history of deconstruction and the deconstruction of history' [p. 18]) – so even if he goes on to refuse or even deny this identification, it is henceforth not out of the question to take up this sentence ('America is deconstruction') and repeat it (Derrida does so himself, for example during the TV programme with Giesbert that I have already mentioned, as an at least partial truth.) If America is not, or not simply, the proper name of deconstruction, this is also because deconstruction does not have a proper name (not even 'deconstruction'), and 'America' will then remain, along with a few others, a possible nickname for it. (On the other hand one can imagine that Derrida would no doubt never, but *never ever* have said: 'France is deconstruction'.)

3. Even if nothing is simple in this story, then (but nothing is or ever was simple, and we must, with Derrida, tirelessly affirm this non-simplicity and draw from it the very resources of thought), I would like to conclude these short remarks by insisting on what I believe to be the *unprecedented* status of what is at stake in this syntagma 'Derrida in America'. Not only because Derrida was exemplarily prudent in what he said of the USA, as opposed to many other French intellectuals who have rushed to pronounce on the subject, in a gesture analysed in *Specters of Marx*. But because there has been, and for the moment there is, no other 'philosopher' who could serve as an example of this configuration of foreignness and translation that is, I believe, quite unique. There too, Derrida will

have been unique. He will have been without the slightest doubt the philosopher who travelled the most, throughout the whole world (since the dawn of time no one else 'went abroad' as much, as though this were another aspect of so-called 'globalisation'), and it is the relation with the USA that organises and focuses these journeys, as I have said. So if one would not understand Derrida without taking account of his roots, so tangled and leaving such a mark on him, one would also miss something essential if one did not take seriously Derrida in translation, in displacement, and notably in America. 'Derrida in America' is a new socio-politico-professional figure that we shall no doubt have to meditate for a long time to come. And as we can imagine that the new technologies of the virtual (of which indeed Derrida had a certain experience), still in their infancy today, will tend in the years to come to replace so-called 'real' journeys, then we can wager that this figure, summed up here in this laconic formula 'Derrida in America', will perhaps remain without precedent in the history of thought, a unique case, a unique journey of which I will always be so proud and delighted to have been lucky enough to follow some stages and share some way-stations.

Notes

1. This short paper was written in French and delivered to the conference 'Sur les traces de Jacques Derrida', Bibliothèque Nationale d'Algérie, Algiers, 25 November 2006, the first ever conference devoted to Derrida in Algeria.
2. Cf. G. Bennington and J. Derrida, *Jacques Derrida* (Paris: Le Seuil, 1991), p. 303.
3. 'Culture et dépendances', France 3, June 2004. It is true that during the same broadcast Giesbert also described Derrida as 'the new Bourdieu', which leaves one thinking . . .
4. Especially in *Spectres de Marx* (Paris: Galilée, 1993).
5. Jacques Derrida and Catherine Malabou, *La contre-allée* (Paris: La Quinzaine Littéraire, 1999), pp. 33–5.

Foreign Language (Jacques Derrida and Me)

'I have only one language, and it is not mine', says Jacques Derrida in *The Monolingualism of the Other*, in a formula that has become famous.[1] Meaning at least two things by this: (1) something specific to Derrida himself, as a singular case or example, and (2) something general about the relation anyone at all might have to the language or languages they speak. Derrida speaks French, speaks only French (I will perhaps return in discussion to his real competence in English or more exactly American), but he speaks it from an eccentric place, as it were, a place of foreignness that we can quickly label the place of the 'franco-maghrebian' and more precisely the 'Algerian Jew'. The French that Derrida speaks, a French that aims to be very correct, very pure, that has the ambition of being a French *with no accent*, is nevertheless not 'his' language, in the sense that it is the language of the other, of the metropole, of the colonial power, a language imposed more or less violently on little Jackie Derrida who might, indeed normally speaking should (or so one might think) rather speak another language, for example Arabic.

This *singular* situation, the singularity of which Derrida has fun emphasising (by contrasting his position 'in' the language with that of his friend Khatibi), is also *exemplary*, in the sense that its singularity supposedly reveals a more general truth. Following a logic of the example that has always fascinated Derrida, there is a paradoxical relation between on the one hand the example that is truly exemplary (the very example, and so the best example, a priceless example outside the series, possibly the *only true* example, and so somewhere an *example without example*), and on the other the example which is *only an* example, a sample among others, where *any* example, any old example is as good as any other and stands for any other. The exemplarity of Derrida himself here would also be exemplary of a *general* relation to language, the relation of anybody at all to language as language of the other, and therefore as foreign language, language with respect to which I am *always* a foreigner by definition.

And this would clearly be what is foreign in language, no longer in the sense of the foreign individual, but in the sense of *what is foreign* in language, language itself in its fundamental foreignness which means that I live my relation to this language (I mean this language which is just as much 'my own', my 'mother tongue') as a relation of submission to a law, as Saussure already said, a relation of subjection or alienation, as Lacan says. And we could easily show that this relation to language as relation to the law implies (in a strong sense of implication), entails in the logical sense, the foreignness of anybody at all (me, for example), with respect to language, even with respect to the language I inhabit, or which inhabits me, as familiarly as can be, as familiarity itself. Language *as such* would thus be fundamentally foreign, or else I, as a speaker, would be fundamentally foreign with respect to the language, whatever it be. And, I want to say, a good thing too. Because if the relation of habitation between speaker and language did not have this element of foreignness, non-nativity and non-naturality, if the law that language is did not come to me from elsewhere, from the other, as they say, if the legislator were not a foreigner (as is always the case: Rousseau and Joyce knew this, among others), if I could fully inhabit and integrate its law by speaking it without fault, then I would have not the slightest chance of saying anything, everything I might say would already be said, all the sentences I might come up with would be repetitions, mere *cases* of the law, cases already foreseen by that law. If one understood everything, if we all understood each other, there would in fact be nothing to understand because everything would already be understood. Let's call it a Habermasian utopia which would be an absolute dystopia, a sad consensual eternity in which we would all agree on everything before even speaking, and so in which we would no longer speak. This would be the linguistic equivalent of the perpetual peace dreamed of by Kant (that we still dream of), that he obscurely realised was representable only as a universal cemetery, the peace of eternal rest, *requiem aeternam*.

For only the margin of foreignness that separates me from my language (whatever language it be) allows there to be, however slightly, an effort and a struggle to be waged to say what one has to say, a struggle with the language to produce a sentence that the language had not entirely foreseen, which was, then, not entirely legal, and so not entirely comprehensible (for me first of all, so that I don't always understand what I say, and that's just fine), a sentence that really is a case in the sense that the law is in fact, in spite of itself, necessarily surprised by the cases that come before it to be judged. Which is somewhat the case of what's called literature, that struggle to produce unspoken and quasi-illegal sentences, or that's called more simply writing, to the extent that it is never simply production or realisation in speech of a language given in advance. And this is also clearly a political remark, at a time when it is probably more difficult than ever to say something new in politics, and when one can sincerely feel sorry for politicians constrained to speak almost exclusively the kind of waffle that probably exasperates them as much as the rest of us.

* * *

You will have noticed that up until now I have avoided speaking about myself, my own case, although Christophe Bident politely suggested that I might do so. There are several reasons for this: among others the certainty that you can already hear what there is to hear about this case, even if I say nothing very explicit about it. For, like the very principle of the *schibboleth*, the simple pronunciation of which sufficed, in passing, to separate Ephraimites from Gileadites, you can hear immediately, beyond or before anything I might have said up till now, an accentual trace perhaps first of a simple foreignness, a 'not from here' (where 'here' means the French language in which everyone is foreign, as you will perhaps have granted me, but not in that way), and then of a different origin, but one that can be identified, 'anglo-saxon' certainly, as you say in French, and in the final analysis English. There, I've said it, let's admit it frankly and shamelessly: *yes, I am English.*

English, yes, and not American, nor, as is said rather obscurely, 'bilingual', or at least bilingual only in the sense that is sometimes given to the words 'false bilingual' (ah, the powers of falsity . . .). And even perhaps false-false-bilingual in the sense that not only did I not learn French alongside English in my childhood, like a 'true' bilingual, but I didn't speak a word of French before learning it, badly like everyone else, at school from the age of eleven onwards, and then, without my having any real memory of this process, little by little feeling myself 'inhabited' by this language, especially during the longer and shorter periods when in later life I lived in the country, and within those periods the shorter and longer times when French was my daily language, all day. But the question is not only one of place or personal situation in life, because the false-false-bilingual that I am (in this like many others, and so exemplary if you like, why not) has to this language (that is still less mine than is English) a relationship that is also a *professional* relationship, that of the French professor (or at least of a Professor of French literature and thought, because it is years since I taught the French language as language). I made my profession of French, I profess French, also in the sense that one makes a profession of faith. And if I did this, it is certainly not (even if my motivations for this will remain forever obscure, for me first of all) by reason of necessity, not because of political or colonial force relations, or at least not in the usual sense of those words. If I have become even a little bit French (and the very fact of beginning to speak a language no doubt sets off something of that becoming), and thereby a foreigner in the language even if I sometimes behave in it as though I were at home, this is by virtue of a choice that I would call 'free' in the sense that *nothing* really obliged me to make it. Which, if you follow my drift, makes me still more foreign with respect to this language, because of the supplementary arbitrariness that qualifies my relations with it. It did nothing special to invite me in: it made me feel no obligation with respect to it. At most it allowed me to take refuge in it, without obliging me to do so, without imposing on me anything other than what in it is the law, as we have seen, for anybody at all.

So you see that there is here – it's possible, it's always possible – a certain experience of a certain liberty, or a certain liberation with respect to the old law, be it maternal or paternal, that is the law of one's first language. This is obviously a paradoxical liberty, because the very fact of speaking imperfectly this refuge-language means that one is in a certain sense more constrained, more restricted, that when at home. Which is why it is not in fact the living or dwelling that liberates, but the coming and going, the *passage* from one language to another, without mix or confusion, though, which would lose the passage itself. This passage which I have here tried to describe in French, on the side of French, especially opens for me, as an exemplary foreigner, when I move *into* French, becoming foreign in language once more. But of course, and I'll conclude with this, this experience is not without a reciprocal effect, so that when I go back into English (and this coming and going can take place several times a day, or even, as in translation, several times a sentence), I am now a foreigner 'at home', and so twice foreign (if everyone is already foreign in their language according to the structures we described at the outset), and even more than twice, if you count the fact that my daily language, the language with which I am most often surrounded, has become American rather than British English, American which is a language as foreign for me as is French (but that would be a long story) – and so no longer really at home, henceforth 'at home' nowhere in fact, for better and for worse.

Note

1. This brief talk was written in French at the invitation of Christophe Bident for a round-table discussion also involving Fehti Benslama, Hervé Joubert Laurencin and Pierre Vilar, under the title 'L'Étranger dans la langue', for the Salon international du livre in Tangier, Morocco, March 2007. In the event the participants preferred to improvise rather than read prepared texts.

Wormwords

Friday, 5 October 2007

'Tensile strength' are the first words to hatch out.[1]

Saturday, 6 October 2007

Tensile: capable of being stretched; susceptible of extension; ductile (*OED*). Like writing, obviously enough: indefinitely, if not infinitely, extensible (I promise I won't forget about breaking and cutting, that'll come soon enough). And ductile: see what he says about the *ductus* in *The Truth in Painting*, a kind of artistic signature, but ductile is also not far from duction and even seduction, leading astray, going wrong, getting off the track, errancy.

Sunday, 7 October 2007

Tensile to ductile, ductile to (se)duction: many other words in '-duction' could work for us here too; there's a swarm of them multiplying: induction, deduction, reduction; adduction and abduction . . . An early example has the word 'duction' *mean* multiplication. And multiplication is of course one of our questions here: *un* ver à soie, *a* silkworm (of one's own), one or just a countable few in the shoebox; very many silkworms hatched in your cabinet, multiple worms squirming, or so I imagine it, in my multiple words for worms here, tensile or ductile enough to make it round the globe, destined for your inimitable *ductus litterarum* as you write them up on the wall.

Wednesday, 10 October 2007

Back in my cocoon here in Atlanta (I was in Paris for the first hatchings, around and about the third anniversary of Jacques Derrida's death), just now picking up the thread that seems, more or less incredibly, as always, to have made it across the Atlantic, six hours further away, six hours earlier than it was. I want to start thinking about size and growth (such a strange and difficult concept, growth), the sleepless insatiability that makes them grow to ten thousand times their original size, the molts along the way, what gets left behind.

Thursday, 11 October 2007

That word 'instar': their second instar. Form or figure, instance, maybe. In French, 'à l'instar de . . .' means 'in the same way as . . .', 'after the example of . . .'. *A l'instar d'un ver à soie,* like a silk worm, like one's own worm, following its example here more or less blindly. In English, 'instar' is also a verb: to make a star of, or to set with stars. Here I'm making a star of no one worm, but following the plural, instarring the scatter, the always gathered scatter, the constellation, matter.

Friday, 12 October 2007

A l'instar de Jacques Derrida, following his figure or example, following his star, even, for he is the star here: what's at stake in *A Silkworm of One's Own*? Veils, veiling and unveiling: nothing less than the truth or the Truth. The silkworm and its . . . secretions, let's say (lovely word, 'secretions'), as a tiny but completely relentless challenge to the whole tired Western way with truth and untruth, the hidden and the revealed, concealment and unconcealment, *aletheia* and its veiled secrets, the whole striptease of truth called philosophy. Something's happening here, with the worms, and the words, that really is not philosophy. Let's not rush to assume that that means it's literature.

Monday, 15 October 2007

(Haunted all weekend, in the mental box or cabinet where the silk-worms are constantly eating and growing, by a childhood memory of a drawing (made by my elder brother, I think: the affect is one of slightly jealous admiration rather than pride, at any rate) in a school exercise book, illustrating the circuit of mulberry, silkworm and fish pond in China. Little semi-iconic drawings of trees fertilised by fish manure from the bottom of the pond; worms fed on mulberry leaves; fish fed on shed worm skins; farmers who eat fish and spin silk . . . There were arrows to indicate the cycle. The outsize pencilled silkworm on the stick branch of the tree was, I seem to remember, smiling broadly. This seemed so very satisfying, this circuit, so self-satisfying and self-satisfied, almost smug, like the drawn silkworm itself.)

Childhood memory might have a non-accidental relationship with what's in play here: the form of the 'childhood memory' and its specific temporal quality as a kind of radical memory (by definition I cannot access this, my childhood *in general*, *except* as a memory) might be part of what won't quite work as truth and veil/unveiled, even as the silk will also make the veil . . .

Tuesday, 16 October 2007

Derrida says his childhood memory is 'l'envers d'un rêve', which I translated a little flatly as 'the opposite of a dream'. But *l'envers* is the other side of something, the back or hidden side of a surface: *l'envers du décor* means behind the scenes. There's still some dreaming in here.

Wednesday, 17 October 2007

' . . . secreted its secretion. It secreted it, the secretion. It secreted. Intransitively. [. . .] It secreted absolutely [. . .] Secretion of what was neither a veil, nor a web [*ni un voile, ni une toile*] . . . '. We're not there yet, are we? The secretion to come still held back, still a secret, but we're all waiting for it, that one long long thread turning the worm's inside out, that thread I've already been following, virtually, very virtually, over the Web, what Francophone Canadians call *la Toile*, anticipating already the silk in the worm, ductile tensile textile. Childhood memory still dreaming a little around the absolute future still and always to come of a secret that's not even a secret (not something behind a veil, to be uncovered, ever) but secreting itself, serisecreting.

Friday, 19 October 2007

I'm still tense here on tensile, tensor, tense again: what's the right verb tense here? How to conjugate the specific tense of the childhood (dream-) memory (with at least a touch of the absolute past, something other than 'normal' memory, at least), with the specific futurity of where we are today, waiting for them to grow and molt and secrete what they will always have been going to secrete? And all this in a kind of commemorative and monumentalising re-enactment of what happened in a shoebox in Algeria in the early 1940s? What always will have been going to not happen perhaps here? Across this further bizarre configuration of non-presence that has you fifteen hours 'ahead' of me in the same instant now, already tomorrow: 'Now is night'. Or not.

Monday, 22 October 2007

Still with the wordworms: in JD's French, all those words in 'ver-' that defy translation, but in English a little differently, 'idiomatically' as he would say and love to say, something about that initial 'W' that marks it as a long way from French, in some more anglo-germanic compartment. A whole row of worm-words: worm, word, work, world (those last three that would be the Heidegger version, for another time); worl, worry, worse, worship, worth, there's even wortworm . . . how about 'worg'? Worg? Just 'grow' backwards, I wot, growing slowly, but growth (savour especially that 'wth', nothing less French) is always slow, and growth is always more than growth in the sense of increase; growth brings death with it, there's no growth without dying too, there's no escape, sustainable growth is not sustainable. Life is growth but growth also dies (see Hegel's *Philosophy of Nature*): lifedeath, as JD was saying already in the 1970s. And there's still that crawling multiplicity waiting for us (growth-death is also multiplication): for JD it's related to the virus he also puts in his *ver*-series, along with *vérité* and *vertu*, the virus that 'carries delayed death in its self-multiplication'.

Tuesday, 23 October 2007

Growth, increase, multiplication, death . . . So what am I going to do with the *other* childhood memory that opens 'A Silk Worm . . . ', all about diminution or, as it might have been more accurately translated in the immediate context of the knitting being remembered here, all about *decrease*. But in French it's the same word as, soon to follow, the diminution of the diminished interval in music, or the rhetorical figure of diminution, saying more by saying less, there's an understatement. Here they are, all those wordworms, growing and/or dying, increasing and multiplying, and then here is Derrida talking insistently about his 'interminable diminution', a decrease without breaking or tearing or removing (all still figures of the veil and of truth), about fatigue and extenuation, etiolation, 'diminution *ad infinitum*' that the text itself is supposed to be or supposed to be doing, a writing aiming to *stop writing*, with some kind of petering out, perhaps, some fading away, or maybe just a kind of extreme refinement, an exquisite abstrusion without reconditeness – and here he is returning to it at the very end of 'A Silk Worm . . . ', 'only an interval, almost nothing, the infinite diminution of a musical interval . . . '. What am I going to do with all that, all that little, that abundance of paucity, as time starts running out, running down towards the *verdict* he keeps invoking, verdict without veracity or veridicity, as it gets later and later and the increase diminishes and the diminution grows? Each time growth grows it also slows and dwindles, falls.

Wednesday, 24 October, 2007

Like in the analyses of Freud in *La Carte postale*, 'la mort est au bout', death is at the end, it all ends in death. Growth and multiplication or decrease and diminution: death both ways. But not quite the same way both ways: the veil he's trying to get away from is also a shroud, a winding-sheet, but the silkworm self-worm minutely displaces all that (the tallith is next) maybe here a different way with death and therefore truth and all the rest, of a piece with that last interview protesting against the philosophical view of philosophy as 'learning how to die', and of a much earlier thought, in 'Ja ou le faux-bond' and ever since, about *demi-deuil*, half-mourning, or *faire son deuil du deuil*, doing one's mourning for mourning, *mourning mourning*, doing something other than the 'normal' work or labour of mourning, something that will always look a little like melancholia, a not-getting-over-it, a not-quite-return-to-self, no 'closure', quite, no simple 'getting on with one's life'. Silk not quite self, *soie* not quite *soi*, a silkworm of one's own worms through the own and the self. Which is also what we're doing here, every day or almost, every morning mourning mourning, as the worms worm and the words multiply and diminish, struggling to figure out what just now comes back to me, not a childhood memory quite, but a twenty-five year memory perhaps, in an antiquarian bookstore in Brighton, in gold on the spine of the leather-bound volume three capitalised words stacked one above the other: WORDS, WORTHS, WORKS. So now add: WORMS.

Thursday, 25 October 2007

Just before the tallith enters the *Silkworm* text, we're *right in* this question of mourning, half-mourning, and mourning mourning. Rather not burden the others, says JD, with the weight of inheritance, and more especially the weight of a shrouded corpse, not impose the mourning veil, rather leave without trace, let the other live and be and have no expectation of benefit or profit from this removal of shroud and veil. Not insignificantly for me (otherwise unsuperstitious), page 43 of the original French (42 in the English, but that's a different answer): 'Not even leave them my ashes. Blessing of the one who leaves without leaving an address', *faire son deuil de la vérité*, do one's mourning for truth (and therefore of mourning, if mourning is bound up with truth and its veils), one's mourning for ipseity, for *soi*, have no one mourn me, no veil worn. Blessing, or more literally benediction (but 'blessing' hides a translator's back-reference to the French *blesser*, to wound: a blessing can also leave a *blessure*): and just now blessing and wounding remind me of the last text Jacques wrote just before he died, with a trembling hand, a paragraph in the third person, in quotation marks, to have read out over his grave by his son Pierre, Jacques writes Pierre reads 'he asks me to thank you for coming, to bless you'; and then at the end, new line but now first person, undecidable prosopopeia, indeterminately probably plural address: *Je vous aime et vous souris d'où que je sois*' ['I love you and am smiling at you from wherever I am']. (I wasn't there for the blessing and the *blessure*, not another postcard Plato-Socrates thing, just a visa and green card thing, the kind of thing where even death collides with *bêtise*.) I wasn't there.

Friday, 26 October 2007

Worms' work's worth words' worst woes.

Saturday, 27 October 2007

'Blessing and death', *la bénédiction et la mort*, he says (*Voiles*, p. 45). I was not weaving, still less knitting, when I got the news that Jacques had died, but I was sewing. With a thread made of linen, I think, rather than silk, I was sewing a book made just for him. I knew the chances were slight that he would read on his screen the electronic book I'd just gathered up from scattered essays and articles, already I guess to do with aging and dying and mourning, so I was making a single printed, bound and sewn copy just for him. *Relier de nouveau, c'est un acte d'amour*, he writes in *Mal d'archive*.[2] Some pleasure, just as here, in the mix of high technology and autodidactic manual artisanship. I never finished making the book, its signatures remain unsewn, unbound, unblessed, now scattered. Let me not start in here on all the books, bindings and unbindings in Derrida, all the *reliures*, everywhere that *relier*, *re-lier*, is close to *lire* and *re-lire*. *Je lis, je relis et relie*, I lie and rely (one self-imposed rule of this sequence, apparently: I don't reread it as I go, I'm all in the act and event of secreting the secretion, each morning each mourning, as though each word was written indelibly on the wall as I typed it). Binding is *logos* and re-ligion and the 'theological simultaneity of the Book', all still part of the veiling/unveiling a tallith here undoes or doesn't quite do. Unbound but never entirely unbound, read but never completely read, always (to be) reread/never (completely) reread, still somewhat scattered and scarred, a little scared, regular secretion but no secret, no one secret, nothing sacred, no secret on screen, but perhaps rather in every sense a *screed*.

Sunday, 28 October 2007

Sundayscreed: among others, **Screed**, n., A fragment cut, torn, or broken from a main piece; in later use, a torn strip of some textile material. [. . .] An edging, a bordering strip; the border or frill of a woman's cap. [. . .] A long roll or list; a lengthy discourse or harangue; a gossiping letter or piece of writing. [. . .] A piece, portion (of a literary work). [. . .] A (drinking) bout. [. . .] [From the verb.] A rent, tear. [. . .] A sound as of the tearing of cloth; hence, any loud, shrill sound. **Screed**, v., To shred, tear, rip. [. . .] To produce a sound as of tearing cloth. Hence, of a musical instrument, to make a loud shrill sound. [. . .] ***to screed off, away***: to give audible expression to, to relate or repeat (a matter) readily from memory.

Monday, 29 October 2007

(Surreptitiously, written almost blind, almost literally under the table, during an indescribable meeting about The University Strategic Plan;

I'm squirming and worming): A tallith is not a veil, not simply a veil, because of: touch (not sight); gift (not revelation); law (not Being); event (not truth). Verdict, he keeps saying, without veri-diction.

Tuesday, 30 October 2007

Here, for example: 'If there is a "truth" of this shawl, it depends less on the lifting or the unfolding of a veil, on some unveiling or revelation, than on the unique event, the gift of the law and the "coming together" it calls back to itself. Even if one translates the gift of the Law as Revelation, the figure of the veil, the intuition and the moment of vision count for less than the taking-place of the event, the singular effectivity of the "once only" as history of the unique: the time, the trace of the date, and the date itself as trace' (*Voiles*, pp. 69–70) Unique event, timed dated (my atomically accurate clock has 7:27:46 as I glance still typing) this time only, taking place now: as always caught up in repetition, iterability, transcribability (as your writing on the wall, for example). That's the law: once only always repeated, that's its secret in full view, that's what it still secretes, however clear you make it look or sound, that's why there's never just the law, but also the case, singularity, this time, and thereby multiplicity spinning out again, each time, each date.

Wednesday, 31 October 2007

Repetition, multiplication spinning away out of control of the law. (But even if they are doing their worm-thing with a view to reproduction and multiplication, we're really waiting for them to do that strange thing they do along the way, we'll wait until it's late, until the end or almost the end.) *En attendant*, the thought is that that's an event, perhaps, the event-of-the-law as gift-of-the-law that the law can't understand, the always necessarily possible interruptive undecidable state-of-exception that haunts the law as its always singular this-time case or instance. Law is law insofar as it governs a possible multiplicity of singular cases that it is there to predict and that it can never quite predict, and which it is therefore called upon to decide. That's where decision comes, the crisis-moment of decision that JD likes to recall from Kierkegaard is a moment of madness, the moment of what we're still circling around here, what his text calls the *verdict*. Law requires ver-dict because of failure to pre-dict. Translated slowly, inching its way from French 'verdict' to English 'verdict': *ver*-dict, worm-dict, worm-word. Each and every growing multiplying dying wormword worth a verdict as they spin out the thread of times and dates.

Thursday, 1 November 2007

You will perhaps have been waiting for this, traditionally read, or so I imagine, in the direction of 'man' rather than the direction of 'animal': Lear and Edgar – 'Is man no more than this? Consider him well. Thou ow'st the worm no silk, the beast no hide, the sheep no wool, the cat no perfume. [. . .] Thou art the thing itself; unaccommodated man is no more but such a poor, bare, forked animal as thou art.' (Spin the anagrams: Real Lear, G. read Edgar; lag re-read, a real dreg, this rag dealer in dear Alger). Naked as a worm, as JD says in his fantastic discussion in *Silkworm* . . . of Freud's account of pubic hair weaving, that we may not have finished with yet. And why not, while we're at it, talking of dates and anniversaries, in the middle of this Halloween-All Saints-All Souls sequence, Desdemona's fated handkerchief: 'The worms were hallow'd that did breed the silk'. (The only places I know, among all the silk and all the worms in Shakespeare, where the worms are silkworms, productive, rather than direct agents of death and decay.) Owe the worm no silk.

Friday, 2 November 2007

A little later in *Othello*, follow the handkerchief a little further, a little later and it's already too late: at the end of a famous sequence all about confession and perjury, Othello's last words as he kills Desdemona on the strength of the handkerchief, almost, one might say, with the (tensile) strength of the handkerchief: 'It is too late. [He stifles her]' Too late, *sero*, late is always too late, says JD in *Silkworm*, late is always already absolutely late, already in the first sentence of his text: ' . . . before it's too late . . . '. Too early too late, the absolute *contretemps* that could take us back to his earlier lovely little piece on *Romeo and Juliet*, 'L'aphorisme à contretemps'. Juliet, who's just seen Romeo, and fallen, and found out his name: 'Too early seen unknown, and known too late!' Too early too late the aphorism but 'all writing is aphoristic' he also writes in an 'early' essay on Edmond Jabès, all writing aphoristic like this too early too late now is morning here in New York this weekend, now is morning but in Melbourne now is night here now today already there tomorrow where you are over the other side writing always late so late too late.

Saturday, 3 November 2007

Fall back. Only today, late (or rather tomorrow, early, in the early morning) the USA falls back to the hour of winter, a week later than in Europe (and than in Melbourne, I think, though you must be going the other way). At 2 a.m., officially, it's suddenly 1 a.m. again for a doubled hour, compensating for the spring forward where that hour had disappeared. (I was almost too late, flying back through the time zones the night my mother died, at 2 a.m. to the minute in the early morning of 28 March 2004, time of death undecidably 2 a.m. or 3 a.m. or any time in between: the doctor wrote 3:10 on the certificate to keep it simple. 'She was singing', my father said, having misheard the death rattle in his dream, though it was true she'd somewhat turned into a bird in death. My mother had taught me when I was a child how a silk scarf would spring forward out of a suddenly opened clenched fist into which it had been tightly packed, its elasticity distinguishing it easily from synthetic fibres.) That missing hour (but represented as a time during which the clock stands spookily still for an internally unmeasured hour) is the time for crime in some old movie I vaguely remember. As time goes on and it gets later, time speeds up (just as early time is slow: a few nanoseconds after the Big Bang are like an eternity, time hardly moving, energy all going into spatial expansion instead), we get into what JD often called 'precipitation', suddenly a desperate hurry to get it in as time runs out and we all suddenly get older.

Monday, 5 November 2007

It's getting late, I lost a day to travel yesterday, and now this last week ahead . . . *Sero te amavi*, the epigraph for the whole of JD's text . . . *Sero*, 'late', 'very late', 'so late', 'too late'. But *sero* is also a verb in Latin, not only the future of *esse*, no less, but in its own right as *sero*, *sevi*, *satum*: to sow, to plant, to bring forth, to produce, to scatter . . . to *disseminate* (Lewis and Short). *Sero sero*: late I disseminate, Derrida's motto and at least one signature encrypted here. And signed too by the silkworm itself, *le ver à soie en soi*, seri-culture as sero-culture, I'm quite serious and serene about this series here, for sero-culture just is culture once *sero* means I plant: I plant and watch it grow, watch it bring forth and disseminate in deferral later, always later. The future is late again, a gain again ago.

Tuesday, 6 November 2007

A signature signs too late, after the fact, after the date, *à contretemps*, as JD says in *Silkworm*. I sign and date everything I write, everything I write also escapes that signature and date, first across the ether to Australia, but already, anyway, as a condition that it be at least minimally readable. Like the fringes on the tallith, a signature *ends* the text it signs but is the place (one place) where a text frays out into other texts, more text, for example on your walls. A signature hems the text and times the text, mis-times the text it signs, makes it always early or late, *sero*. Each go ago.

Wednesday, 7 November 2007

Ago again. Late again. 'Ago' not now Latin ('I act' in the sense of 'I take action' but in innumerable idiomatic turns too: 'animam ago', for example, I give up the ghost, it's the final act, the agony), not Latin and not all those '-ago-' words from ancient Greek I could get pedagogical or even demagogical about in the agora, like 'apagogy' and 'agonistics' – not Latin or Greek, then, but English, 'ago' simply enough by contraction from 'agone'. What's long ago is long agone, it's late. But simply add an 'I', there's Iago and we're back to Desdemona's handkerchief, and thence it's only a step to Santiago, where JD writes part of *Silkworm*. Santiago, St Iago, St James: in French, St Jacques, another signature for our protagonist.

Thursday, 8 November 2007

Here I a-go again: today to Chic-ago. ('Chicago', however, seems to come from an Algonquian word meaning either 'skunk' or 'onion'. I learned this morning from the New York Times crossword that an onion can be referred to as a 'skunk egg'.) The thread is reaching its end as the worms finally get ready to spin: as so often with the figure of the guiding thread in Kant, the *leitfaden*, the thread leads only to its own end, and leads back nowhere. The end just is the end, never The End.

Friday, 9 November 2007

JD signs off finally with the silkworm, the childhood memory, the worm that has spun its thread, its double secretion, its single double thread hundreds and even thousands of feet long, spun its thread and waited out its time. And abandons us, cuts us off, late, just at this point of emergence. This is where it starts. That's the verdict. Salut.

Notes

1. These fragments were written at the invitation of the Australian artist Elizabeth Presa to accompany her installation 'A Silk Room of One's Own' at the Linden Centre for Contemporary Arts in Melbourne. The installation, inspired by Jacques Derrida's text 'Un ver à soie', involved cases containing live silkworms which hatched and developed over the five-week period of the installation, during which the artist transcribed onto the gallery walls, alongside other textual materials, these fragments, sent every day or so by e-mail.
2. *Mal d'archive* (Paris: Galilée, 1995), p. 41.

Index